The Church in the Age of Constantine

In the Age of Constantine, Christians experienced for the first time official recognition and support. The Roman Empire used religion not only as cement to unite its different populations, but as a means to win divine favour as well. When this mechanism was threatened by doctrinal dissensions or regional rivalries, the Emperor would intervene, contributing to the supremacy of one persuasion.

In the twentieth century, European Christianity lost its dominant position. Critics, seeing dominance as foreign to the Gospel's nature, blame the Constantinian Age as a time of error and fall. However, African and Asian Christians are fascinated by its successful inculturation. Such discussions demand examination, and in *The Church in the Age of Constantine*, Johannes Roldanus provides a refined theological screening of the doctrinal and ethical thinking during the fourth century.

Roldanus uses the concept of 'contextualisation' to appreciate this process. He makes clear that, however much the winning positions were dependent on the interfering of the State, the theological reflection nevertheless followed its proper course, conditioned as it was by various understandings of Salvation in Christ. There was a natural concern to relate salvation to the most important elements of the existing culture. This study aims to help students and interested lay-people to focus on the essentials and to form an unprejudiced opinion on this crucial period of history.

Johannes Roldanus is Professor Emeritus at the University of Groningen.

The Church in the Age of Constantine

The theological challenges

Johannes Roldanus

Routledge
Taylor & Francis Group

LONDON AND NEW YORK

First published 2006
by Routledge
2 Park Square, Milton Park, Abingdon, Oxfordshire OX14 4RN

Simultaneously published in the USA and Canada
by Routledge
270 Madison Avenue, New York, NY 10016

Routledge is an imprint of the Taylor & Francis Group, an informa business

© 2006 Johannes Roldanus

Typeset in Garamond Three by
RefineCatch Limited, Bungay, Suffolk
Printed and bound in Great Britain by
TJ International Ltd, Padstow, Cornwall

British Library Cataloguing in Publication Data
A catalogue record for this book is available from the British Library

Library of Congress Cataloging in Publication Data
A catalog record for this book has been requested

ISBN10: 0–415–40903–9 (hbk)
ISBN10: 0–415–40904–7 (pbk)
ISBN10: 0–203–96833–6 (ebk)

ISBN13: 978–0–415–40903–2 (hbk)
ISBN13: 978–0–415–40904–9 (pbk)
ISBN13: 978–0–203–96833–8 (ebk)

A Károli Gáspár Református Egyetem Hittudományi Karának, hálám jeléül a 2000-ban adományozott doktori címemért.

Contents

List of abbreviations

Ambr.	Ambrose
	Ep. Epistulae
	Fid. De Fide ad Gratianum
Athan.	Athanasius of Alexandria
	ApolConst. Apologia ad Constantium
	ApolFug. Apologia de Fuga Sua
	EpFest. Epistula Festivalis
	Gent. Oratio contra Gentes
	HistAr. Historia Arianorum ad Monachos
	Inc. Oratio de Incarnatione Verbi
	OrCAr. Orationes tres Contra Arianos
	Ser. Epistulae ad Serapionem
	VitAnt. Vita S. Antonii
ClAl.	Clement of Alexandria
	Paed. Paedagogus
	Protr. Protrepticus
Cypr.	Cyprian
	CathEc. De Catholicae Ecclesiae Unitate
Cyr.	Cyril of Jerusalem
	Cat. Mystagogical Catecheses
Diogn.	*Epistula ad Diognetum*
Eus.	Eusebius of Caesarea
	DE Demonstratio Evangelica
	HE Historia Ecclesiastica
	LausCons. Laus Constantini
	MP De Martyribus Palestiniae
	PE Praeparatio Evangelica
	VitCons. Vita Constantini
GrNaz.	Gregory of Nazianzum
	Ep. Epistulae
	Or. Orationes

GrNyss. Gregory of Nyssa
        Apoll.   Adversus Apollinatem
        Ep.   Epistulae
        OrCatech.   Oratio Catechetica
Just. Justin Martyr
        Apol.   Apologiae
        Dial.   Dialogus cum Tryphone Judaeo
Lact. Lactantius
        IrD.   De Ira Dei
        MortP.   De Mortibus Persecutorum
Or. Origen
        Cels.   Contra Celsum
        Hom. in Nm.   Homiliae in Numeros
        Hom. in Ezk.   Homiliae in Ezechielem
        Orat.   De Oratione
Tat. Tatian of Syria
        OrGr.   Oratio ad Graecos
Tert. Tertullian
        Apol.   Apologeticum
        Iud.   Adversus Iudaeos
        Orat.   De Oratione
        ResCar.   De Resurrectione Carnis
Theod. Theodore of Mopsuestia
        Hom. Cat.   Homiliae Catecheticae

Acknowledgements

The stimulus to write a study of Christianity's turbulent course throughout the fourth century from the viewpoint of 'contextualisation' came to me from Africa. It is the result of lecturing in Cameroon and South Africa and, in a wider sense, of an experience of years as tutor of Church History in the Protestant Theological Seminary of Ndoungué, Cameroon. I observed that when engaged believers, both in Africa and in Europe, reflect on today's position of the Church in society they often refer to the Age of Constantine as a period and a cause of corruption of the values for which Christianity was originally standing. On the other hand, from a modern missiological viewpoint, there is a positive interest in early Christianity's ability to express its message in culturally understandable thought forms and actions, and in its readiness to assume co-responsibility for the public domain. I felt it a challenge to evaluate the crucial and determining 'Age of Constantine' from the angle of 'challenge and response', both terms being involved in the concept of 'contextualisation'. Therefore, my first acknowledgement concerns the colleagues, students and church leaders who had to get along with me in those intensive African years.

By virtue of her own great commitment to African people and to the call for solidarity with the underprivileged, my wife has been an inspiring companion all along my work for church, mission and university. I thank her warmly for encouraging me to undertake and achieve the present study.

Various encouragements and good advice were received from my son Ulric and from colleagues and friends: Dr H.S. Benjamins, Revd A.H. Blom (Cape Town), Prof. Dr G.D.J. Dingemans and Prof. Dr C.J. Labuschagne.

My special and deep thanks go to Dr P.J. Lalleman, Lecturer of New Testament and Academic Dean of Spurgeon's College (London), who once took his doctor's degree under my supervision. In his very kind and efficient way he has been of immense help, both in improving my imperfect English and in making the first contacts with the publisher.

Central Europe's 'Great Turn' of 1989 opened the door for scientific cooperation of the University of Groningen and its Faculty of Theology and Religious Studies with several homogeneous institutions in those countries. It is a great pleasure for me, as one of the inaugurators, that this cooperation is still going on. I dedicate this book to the Theological Faculty of the Reformed Károli Gáspár University, Budapest, in gratitude to the colleagues there for the friendly contacts and for the awarding to me of a honorary doctorate.

In compiling the indexes, I received valuable assistance from Dr Tomáš Novák (Diemen).

Just after the completion of the text for this book, I learnt of the passing away of Prof. Gilles Quispel of Utrecht University, who led my first steps in the field of patristics. He was a great and penetrating scholar, whom I remember with thankfulness.

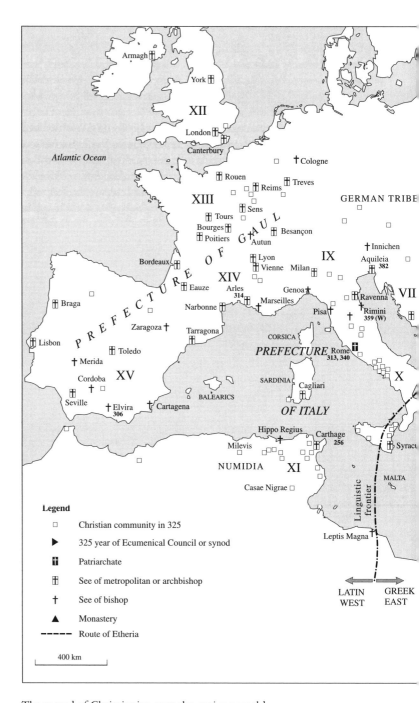

The spread of Christianity over the antique world

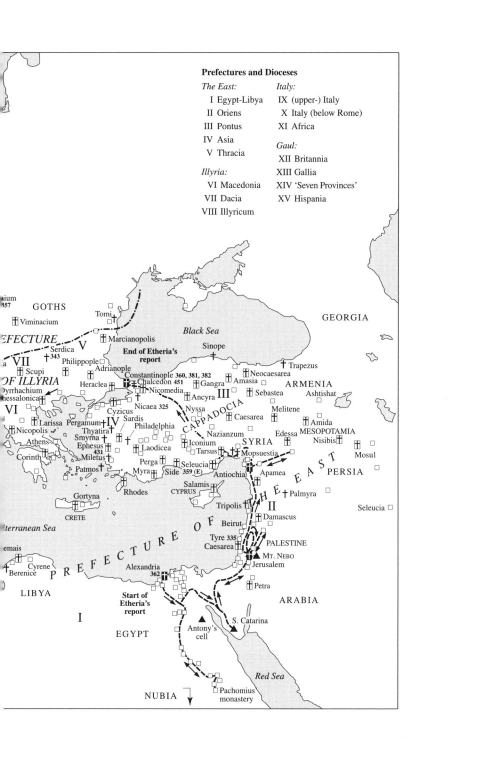

Prefectures and Dioceses

The East:
- I Egypt-Libya
- II Oriens
- III Pontus
- IV Asia
- V Thracia

Illyria:
- VI Macedonia
- VII Dacia
- VIII Illyricum

Italy:
- IX (upper-) Italy
- X Italy (below Rome)
- XI Africa

Gaul:
- XII Britannia
- XIII Gallia
- XIV 'Seven Provinces'
- XV Hispania

GOTHS

Viminacium

Tomi

Black Sea

GEORGIA

EFECTURE

Serdica

Marcianopolis

Sinope

End of Etheria's report

343

VII

Philippople

Scupi

Adrianople

Trapezus

OF ILLYRIA

yrrhachium

hessalonica

Heraclea

Constantinople 360, 381, 382

Chalcedon 451

Nicomedia

Gangra

Amasia

Neocaesarea

ARMENIA

VI

Larissa

Pergamum

Nicaea 325

Nyssa

Ancyra

III

Sebastea

Ashtishat

Nicopolis

Athens

Cyzicus

Sardis

IV

Thyatira

Philadelphia

CAPPADOCIA

Caesarea

Melitene

Edessa

MESOPOTAMIA

Amida

Nisibis

Smyrna

Ephesus

Nazianzum

SYRIA

Mosul

431

Laodicea

Iconium

Corinth

Miletus

Tarsus

Mopsuestia

PERSIA

Patmos

Perga

Seleucia

Apamea

THE EAST

Myra

Side 359 (E)

Antiochia

Gortyna

Rhodes

Salamis

CYPRUS

Palmyra

CRETE

Tripolis

II

Seleucia

iterranean Sea

Beirut

Damascus

emais

Tyre 335

Caesarea

PALESTINE

Cyrene

Berenice

PREFECTURE OF

MT. NEBO

Jerusalem

LIBYA

Alexandria

362

Petra

I

Start of Etheria's report

ARABIA

EGYPT

Antony's cell

S. Catarina

Red Sea

NUBIA

Pachomius monastery

Introduction

The Great Turn

This is a study of the fourth century of the Christian era. It was a century of radical changes and much confusion for the adherents of the Christian faith and for their organisation, the Church. These changes and confusion in the first place affected those who lived in the Roman Empire, and they were the majority of all Christians.[1] The remaining Christians found themselves in eastern neighbour states such as Persia and Armenia, or among the Visigoths, who settled on the northern defence lines (see Chapter 6, pp. 155–7). Shortly after 300, the Christians in the Roman Empire suffered a general persecution, ordered by the emperors, which was not equally severe in every place. But almost immediately after the persecution had been stopped and a limited tolerance been granted (311), an unexpected process started under the leadership of the victorious emperor Constantine I, bringing the Church official recognition, government support and gradual involvement in social life. From now on, the Church had to reckon with interference from the side of the emperors, which at one time consolidated its position and at another enforced obedience to the theological persuasion the Emperor preferred for his own reasons. In the year 380, this policy came to a head when the two emperors of the eastern and the western parts of the empire decreed that all their subjects should adhere to the orthodox Catholic faith. This decree is rightly considered the hour of birth of Christianity as state religion, rather than the so-called 'Constantinian turning point' earlier in the century. But the Christians in the Persian kingdom felt the repercussions of this promotion of their co-religionists under Roman rule, because they were consequently suspected of being the fifth column of Roman imperialism. Armenia preceded the Roman Empire in establishing the Christian faith as the state religion, since this happened at some date before 314.[2] The Goths on the Balkans were hostile to Christian penetration from Constantinople until the conversion of their chief in 376. From then on they became politically and militarily associated with the Roman Empire and its culture. The connections of the Roman state with all these neighbours were so direct that the enormous changes in the political and social position of Christianity not only affected those living under Roman dominion, but also their fellow believers beyond the borders.

The new situation also intensified tendencies and tensions which already existed in the third century, but which now took a more pronounced form. This circumstance makes it necessary to devote the first chapter to the subject of contextualisation before the fourth century. Before defining contextualisation, the keyword of our study, we will delimit the term 'fourth century' in the sense we will use it.

The chronological frame

Historians know only too well that the 'centuries' they are examining never coincide exactly with the 100 years between the turns of the century. What we call the 'fourth century' starts some years before 300 and ends shortly before 400; to be precise, it runs from 293 to 397.

In the year 293 an administrative reform divided the Empire into four *prefectures*: two in the east and two in the west, with on both sides a first (*Augustus*) and an associate emperor (*Caesar*). Constantine's father was one of these Caesars. This imperial college launched a persecution against the Christians in the army and the administration in the year 295, followed by a general persecution of all Christians, which started in 303. The motives behind this persecution – the last and most severe the early Church suffered – as well as the causes and consequences of its failure will be pointed out in Chapter 2. These causes and consequences are stated in the Edict of Tolerance, proclaimed by the dying Augustus of the east, Galerius in 311. Meanwhile, the sudden death of the Augustus of the west had cleared the way for the successful rise to power of his son Constantine. A very decisive moment in his career was the victory he won over a rival in front of the gates of Rome (312). Constantine stopped the persecutions in the west and granted the Christians not only equal rights but also growing support. He urged his co-emperor in the east, Licinius, to follow his religious policy, and in 313 they together promulgated the 'Declaration of Milan', which was the start of a process of privileging the Christian religion. After a period of growing rivalry, Constantine found enough pretext to fight Licinius and eliminate him (324). Through this second victory of Constantine, Christianity rose to the status of fully accepted religion in the whole Roman Empire.

The death of the Emperor Theodosius I (395) brought about a further separation of the Empire into an east-Roman and a west-Roman state, which this time would prove definitive. In 380 Theodosius and his western co-emperor Gratianus had raised Christianity to the rank of state religion. When, as a next step, all pagan cults were outlawed, the still influential old Roman elites gave their support to an insurrection of an army commander against Theodosius. This revolt can be seen as the last significant resistance of the pagan milieu against the close alliance of Church and State. The defeat of the usurper in 394 meant the military as well as religious consolidation of imperial unity on the base of Catholic Christianity. In the same year, the Olympic Games were held for the last time and then abrogated because of their connection with Greek polytheism. Shortly after these events, Theodosius the Great, the last monarch of the unified Roman Empire, died. The funeral oration was held by his close friend, Bishop Ambrose of Milan, who by then was at the height of his influence as church leader and theologian of the west. Both figures, Theodosius, the emperor, and Ambrosius, the bishop, mark the irreversible decline of pagan religiosity and the establishment of the Christian confession that had become the seal of orthodoxy. In the east, this establishment was due to the Bishop of Constantinople, Nectarius. Since he and Ambrosius both died in 397, their disappearance marks the end of a period, which in many respects had been tumultuous and confusing. A new stability had been attained. It is a good moment to close this study of the fourth century.

The frame we have delimited as 'the fourth century' thus gives the term a material rather than a merely chronological sense. We focus on the fundamental transition the Christians were facing when a desperate attempt to exterminate them suddenly changed into an exclusive protection – both supported by all the means of the State. These changes were both radical and gradual: sometimes they surprised the communities and their members, at other times gradual transformations took place, slipping into the relations of the Christians with the authorities and society as a whole. For three centuries they had been familiar with public hostility, physical uncertainty, emotional suspicions, literary polemics and – at best – de-facto tolerance; now they had to interpret the political and social realities in a new way and to adjust their theological concepts and ethical behaviour to this new interpretation. No wonder that different opinions arose and that the confusing newness became the source of controversies. The fourth century is also a century of struggle between divergent theological schools.

These events and developments form the background for the present monograph on the ecclesiastical history of the fourth century. We will focus on the question 'How did the Church assimilate these changes in its context and how did it react to them, either unconsciously or deliberately?' In other words, we present an examination of the new contextuality and of the Christians' response to it, viz., their *contextualisation*.

Contextualisation

We will have to define the meaning of the word 'contextualisation' as applied to the specific history of the fourth century. Contextualisation is a modern word, which originated in the early 1970s as a collective term covering three missiological and ecumenical interests: (1) the translation of the Christian message; (2) the adaptation of expressions of faith and church life to the actual situation; and (3) the liberation from inherited, dominant models that confuse the issue of the community's own questions and challenges. In this threefold sense, contextualisation is working towards plurality and, therefore, also implies (4) the question of the kind of unity that, without being uniformity, may underlie or transcend such decontrolled differentiation.[3]

Is it justifiable to apply such a modern concept to the very different conditions of the Constantinian era and to make it a point of departure for the study of that bygone age? It may be answered that even the New Testament itself can be read as documenting the first patterns of contextualisation.[4] The original *kerygma* about Jesus of Nazareth, viz., of the salvific significance of his ignominious death and of his elevation to universal lordship in communion with God, was first transmitted from Palestinian to Diaspora Jewry, and from the context of the synagogue to the Hellenistic milieu. We find the patterns of this transmission in different writings of the New Testament. This process of transmitting and expressing the message about Jesus as the culmination of God's dealings with Israel and the Gentiles, and of using other languages (Greek, Latin and Syriac) and current religious thought forms for evangelism continued after the New Testament period. This so-called *Hellenisation* of the Christian faith is generally evaluated – either positively or negatively – as a transformation of a number of its original emphases and apprehensions. The third century shows an intensification of this process of adaptation and it is certainly one of the causes of the growing strength of Christianity, which led Constantine to exploit this particular religion for the interests of his empire. During the fourth century, the process went on under the unprecedented impact of the favours and claims of the Emperor. This century may, therefore, be seen as a heyday of contextualisation in the sense of the first two issues of the modern concept, viz., translation and adaptation to a changing situation. This approach fits in with another definition of contextualisation as 'the passionate cry for the acknowledgement of the significance of Time and Space' and as 'a concept of dynamics and topicality in face of actual cultural and social challenges'.[5]

But how about the other two aspects of the modern concept of contextualisation? How far do they fit the historical realities of the fourth century? The third issue, liberation from imposed but irrelevant models of theological expression and church life, is out of order, since we scarcely find any inherited, dominant models that hampered the theological endeavours of such communities that belonged to a different cultural context. It was precisely by the end of our century that the Roman Emperor made Christianity the only admitted religion of the State and suppressed all other beliefs. It is true that there existed other Christian communities, which either had separated from the main Church or had been branded as heretical by the latter. But these groups were either turning away from the world (the Gnostic dualists) or focusing on specific issues (the Montanists on prophetical gifts or the Novatians on the exclusion of deadly sinners) and, therefore, not responding to new situations. The cleavage between them and the main Church had become deep and permanent. The only example of an oppositional group, responding to the new situation of the fourth century in the sense that they struggled for 'liberation' from the increasingly dominant Catholic Church, are the Donatists in North Africa.[6] Beyond the borders of the empire, the Persian Christians were suffering the repercussions of the alliance of their Roman brothers with the state that was the hereditary enemy of the one they lived in. Thus, with regard to the fourth century, the modern equation of contextualisation with a liberation from dominant models is only applicable to some communities on the fringes of the Roman world. It was the contextualising church itself (in the sense of the first and second aspect) that was in need of liberation and only gradually involved in a process of becoming a dominant model.

The fourth aspect, however, the tension between plurality and unity, was much more at stake. True enough, the fourth century only shows strong tendencies towards unification. In this respect, too, the third century had bequeathed to the next a strongly unified Church, and this well-organised religion was highly attractive to an emperor whose great concern was the unity of his disintegrating empire. Constantine's political programme led to heavy pressures upon the Church to unify its administration (in accordance with that of the Empire), its doctrine and its liturgical life. He tried to suppress the Donatist schism in Africa right from the beginning; and, taking advantage of his action, western church leaders achieved the standardisation of baptismal practice. These are examples to show that a search for unity was 'in the air' on both sides. Religious unity was mainly thought of as uniformity, which in turn was seen as an instrument to achieve political unity.

On the other hand, it must be said that there were local particularities and that these could not easily be suppressed. We referred to the 'Hellenisation' of Christianity in the Graeco-Roman world of the first centuries. Hellenism was a unifying culture, spread over the entire Mediterranean world as a result of the campaigns of Alexander the Great (333–323 BCE), followed by the conquests of the Romans (third–first centuries BCE). However, this culture, to which ancient Greece contributed most, did certainly not penetrate everywhere to the same degree. Whereas at the beginning of the Christian era, genuine Greek culture found its way to Egypt and its capital Alexandria received the main philosophical traditions and developed them, Greek culture did not wholly supplant the cultural substratum of the Semitic east and the Latin west. The respective centres of these Semitic and Latin subcultures were Antioch and Rome. Under the superstratum of the common Hellenistic civilisation, Syrian and Latin cultural patterns persisted and contributed to shape Christian beliefs. These persisting patterns lie at the root of the differences in theological opinion, which collided once the circumstances asked for a greater unification.[7] We have, therefore, to keep in mind that there were three distinct cultural spheres that influenced the theological and social developments of fourth-century Christianity. Without being acknowledged as a necessity or programme, plurality was, nevertheless, a reality.

Donatism is a case apart. This schismatic church came into being immediately after the end of the last persecution (312) and dominated the North African scene till the end of the century (and beyond). By embodying some traditional North African features and nationalist tendencies, Donatist Christians resisted all efforts by the Roman State and the Catholic Church to reintegrate them.[8] But in this case, the specific cultural background did not manifest itself in a debate on theological issues, but in a dissident view of the nature of the communion of the faithful.

In a fundamental article on the theme of contextualisation, Shoki Coe, by then director of the Theological Education Fund, argued that true contextualisation is always connected to the relation between the particular and the universal; in other words, with catholicity as both space and unity. Coe distinguished between *contextuality* and *contextualisation*. The first is 'the missiological discernment of the signs of the times, seeing where God is at work and calling us to participate in it.'[9] Contextualisation is the response that springs from it. The discerning of what makes a context significant for God's plan should be matched by an active and ongoing contextualising theology. Contextuality, according to Coe, does not mean 'taking all contexts equally seriously', but a 'conscientization of the contexts in the particular, historical moment, assessing the peculiarity of the context in the light of the mission of the Church as it is called to participate in the *Missio Dei*'.[10] We may summarise his distinction by speaking of *interpretation* and *response*.

In a study of the early Christian mission, Norbert Brox has pointed to the fact that mission was an interpretation of contemporary history in relation to God's ongoing work of salvation in the world, rather than an organised activity. This conclusion does not, of course, undervalue the many spontaneous testimonies and practical examples given by individual Christians through which the new faith was propagated. But on the theoretical side, the Christians did not so much consider the world a yet-pagan missionfield, but rather a space fundamentally changed by the coming of Christ and the apostles' preaching.[11] This view confirms Shoki Coe's definition of contextuality as missiological discernment of the signs of the times and of mission as the Church's participation in God's work. There have been efforts of interpreting particular historical contexts and moments from *c.* 200.[12] We may, therefore, suppose that this tradition of selectively interpreting contemporary events continued afresh in the time when Christianity underwent such obvious changes as took place in the multi-ethnic Roman Commonwealth![13]

Therefore, we can apply the modern concept of contextualisation to the fourth century in a twofold manner:

1 In the sense of Shoki Coe's 'contextuality': as a key to describe those historical events which the Church and its theologians could not avoid to interpret in order to discern God's hand in them and to define the stand they had to take.

2 In the sense of Shoki Coe's 'contextualising': as a criterion for the

distinction between the evidence of stealthy annexation and transformation of cultural heritage and a clear and critical awareness of what was
happening to the Church and its mission in this process.

The distinctive fields on which contextualisation was at stake are:

1   the relation between Church and State. Here we have to ask in which
    respects the religious policy of the State acted upon

    • the appreciation of the Christian Emperor and of the legal framework
      of the Empire as a missiological factor;
    • the settlement of doctrinal and personal conflicts in the Church;
    • the experience of being victorious over internal and external
      adversaries.

2   The pagan legacy: under this angle, we have to consider how far
    Christianity absorbed the functions of the old religions and philosophical
    themes

    • in civil life;
    • in assuming or correcting the current cosmological, anthropological
      and ethical conceptions of the pagan world with Christ as their
      modelling centre;
    • in the development and enrichment of a cultic life that could supplant
      any gripping pagan cult.

3   The critical reaction to some of these developments: we also have to look
    for signs of uneasiness with the growing docility and dependence of the
    Church vis-à-vis the State and with the growing worldliness of the
    Christians

    • in those theologians and leaders who experienced the burden of
      imperial interference;
    • in the interest in monastic life and radical commitment.

In formulating these questions, we depart from a particular view on the task
of Church history: we study our object as a field of interaction between the
living traditions of an already shaped Christianity and a series of hitherto
unprecedented events in the surrounding world. This implies that we refuse
to see the developments of that particularly moulding period as an organic
evolution of intrinsic germs of divine Truth or of a doctrinal deposit which
waited to be unfolded in an internal process of understanding under clerical
guidance. Our leading supposition is that those developments were, rather,
attempts to find appropriate answers, made by a faith community and leaders
who were just as surprised and confused by new challenges as they were
supported and inspired by living traditions.

The agents of contextualisation

What is the subject of contextualisation? Who contextualises? The presupposition in the modern concept is that it is a conscious act and process. Manas Buthelezi, in opposing his 'anthropological' to an 'ethnographic' approach, speaks of an 'initiative of (the African) man in the context of his actual existential situation', and of 'method or technique of theologising'.[14] With regard to the fourth century we must ask, was there a discernment of the missionary *kairos* in the events that brought recognition and patronage for Christianity? And was this discernment followed by active responses to the new situation and to the public role the contextual change imparted to the Church? To whom do we have to look in order to discover if this is what happened? Where can we expect to find the 'contextual eyes' of that time?

Most church historians will admit that before the fourth century, 'self-made' thinkers, who dispensed their doctrines as freelance teachers, had taken some highly influential initiatives in theology. The important apologist of the second century, Justin (*c.* 100–*c.* 165), stayed with several philosophical masters of reputation before, as a convinced Christian, he went to Rome and founded his own school of 'Christian philosophy'. North African Tertullian (*c.* 160–*c.* 225) was a lawyer, who took up the defence of the Christian community and way of life, but never became a bishop or presbyter. In Alexandria, Clement (*c.* 150–*c.* 215) and Origen (*c.* 185–254) were heads of the 'Catechetical School', an open academy where philosophical traditions were discussed and confronted with the apostolic teachings, but they never attained a rank in the local hierarchy. In the third century, other influential theologians, however, held ecclesiastical ranks. Cyprian of Carthage (d. 258), formerly a pagan rhetorician, was elected bishop of his city only two years after his conversion. And in the fourth century all important theologians were clerics. More and more they sprang from prosperous families; this is understandable since bishops were no longer pastors of their own flocks but called to fulfil important social roles. They were, to a large extent, the agents of contextualisation, either in political or in theological respect.

Those bishops acted as individuals, mainly through their publications, which often were occasional writings (letters, treatises), but also as spokesmen and interveners at synods. The synod became the principal instrument for the regulation of doctrine and discipline, which often had to decide conflicts in these fields. It had already developed in that way during the third century. The first synod was held in the year 195 and, after some occasional meetings during the first half of the third century, regular local and provincial synods became common practice from *c.* 250 onward. In the fourth century, the ecumenical synod was introduced by the Emperor as a means for the unification of the Church's doctrines and practices. Notwithstanding this external pressure on its decisions, the Church's representatives were the persons who took them. Synod meetings, too, may give us evidence of the search for a new obedience under modified circumstances. At the beginning of the fourth century we meet a largely *ministerial* church. The period of wandering charismatic teachers and of individual investigators of the revealed Truth was over.

However, the rise of monasticism represented a kind of countermovement against the growing worldliness of the Church's ministry and against its way of Christian life which was gradually becoming a comfortable existence in a society in which they could rejoice in so many privileges. Therefore, the monks are just as well to be reviewed as possible agents of the fourth-century contextualisation.

1   Earlier contextualisation

Our first question is how Christianity had developed to take the shape it had on the threshold to the fourth century. Of the areas we identified as fields of our investigation of contextualisation, we will concentrate on the first two: the relation between Church and State and the legacy of paganism. Both recommend subdivision into two aspects, the latter being the logical consequence of the first. Thus we will treat four issues:

1   the relations between the Christians and the Roman Empire and its social and religious life;
2   the repercussions of Church growth and of the persecutions on the traditional group morality;
3   the selective association with philosophical school traditions on themes of ethics and anthropology;
4   the Salvation in Christ as response to the various needs for salvation of the epoch.

The Christians and the Roman Empire and society

Exposed to the arbitrariness of the emperors and their political motives, as well as to the contemptuous masses, third-century Christians had to reflect on their position. On the one hand, they assented to the allegation of being different and keeping aloof from common ceremonies and amusement, accounting for this attitude. On the other, they emphasised their positive contribution to society in the fields of true worship and of morality. Most Christian leaders appreciated the Roman Empire as a peace-assuring world order, and the Emperor as God's mighty servant, but not without attacking his claim on religious veneration by his subjects.

The third century began with persecutions, provoked by Emperor Severus' prohibition of conversions to Judaism and Christianity (202). These persecutions also struck those who were already Christians, and they were particularly felt in Egypt and North Africa. Beginning with Severus – himself of African origin – the emperorship came into the hands of army commanders who had been successful on the battlefield and – often as well – in eliminating one or more rivals. After their victory, the Senate in Rome would entrust such 'saviours of the State' with the imperial dignity. These 'military emperors' were more and more natives of the eastern provinces. They introduced their religions from at home and during the period up to 249 the imperial court sometimes showed an interest in the Christian religion. But the general climate was one of syncretism.

A page was turned in the attitude of the Roman State towards the Christians in the year 249. Emperor Decius gave the unusual command of a general sacrifice to the Roman gods in order to satisfy more effectively the military and economic needs of the time. These public sacrifices, to which the entire population was summoned under strict police control, were meant to secure the favour of the gods who once had made Roman dominion so glorious. A cultic act of this tenor had no relation with personal religious needs; it only aimed at public welfare and did not preclude anybody from participating. Only the Christians, who held to the exclusive worship of the God who had revealed himself in Jesus, rejected all other religious allegiance. The Emperor's edict put heavy pressure on the Christians to betray their faith and commit apostasy. The Christian standards forbade not only the veneration of other gods but also all bloody sacrifices, since the sacrifice of Christ on Calvary had made them obsolete.

The Roman authorities knew well that Christians were not allowed to sacrifice. Therefore, the pressure to sacrifice was used as a shibboleth either to make those accused of being Christians renounce, or to ascertain their tenacity, regarded as a foolish and punishable obstinacy.[1] New is that from Decius onwards the sacrificial act was no longer a means of detection, but a purpose in itself. This has to do with an increasing intertwining of religion and politics, a trend we shall meet again as background of the last persecution and of Constantine's preference for the Christian religion. Decius' aim was not primarily to exterminate the Christian population but to align them with the Roman conception of civic duty and allegiance to the Commonwealth. Another new aspect was that the authorities were now taking the initiative and, consequently, had to keep their eyes on the Christians and their leaders, lest a part of the population would dissociate from placating the gods (who would not fail to notice this hiatus).

According to Decius' aims, the first wave of coercion brought more cases of imprisonment, torture and banishment than of death penalties. There were some martyrs, but many more so-called 'confessors', i.e., those who did not deny their faithfulness in spite of the torments they had to undergo. Their perseverance was seen as sign of an indwelling divine force. They gained high esteem in comparison to the many others who cracked under the pressure, or even tried to escape from it by rushing to the ceremony and obtaining a certificate. Confessors gained even more authority than leaders of the community who withdrew themselves for a while, as Bishop Cyprian of Carthage did. Nevertheless, the Emperor's action did not bring the result he had expected. The communities did not dissolve.

The action fizzled out and stopped abruptly at the sudden death of Decius in 251.

After a pause, Valerian renewed the general persecution in 257. Because of the previous experience of the authorities with the admonition and support given by the church leaders, the Emperor aimed at an elimination of the leadership in order to break down the organisation of the Church. This time, Bishop Cyprian neither could nor would escape and he suffered martyrdom in 258. During the first wave and immediately afterwards the leaders had succeeded in keeping together and in encouraging their flocks, as we will see in the next section. Now the clerics were the first to be forced to sacrifice and, in case of refusal, to be put to death immediately. Christians of high status suffered loss of their social rank and their goods and were, in many cases, condemned to imprisonment or forced labour. Church attendance was threatened with capital punishment. But again, the persecution did not cause a complete apostasy, and in 261 a new emperor, Gallienus, recalled all the edicts against the Christians.

This was the beginning of a period of peace and de-facto tolerance, which lasted forty years until a new general persecution was launched by the edicts of Diocletian of 303 (see Chapter 2, pp. 29–30). During this period of calm, the Christians increased in number and influence and counted among their members many soldiers and court officials. This poses the question of how far the Christians, in spite of their illegal status, were loyal to the Roman Empire and its institutions.

There is evidence that from *c.* 200 Christians were accused of withdrawing from normal social life, from religious solidarity and from active support of the Empire. We start with social life and will soon touch religious attitude since, as a matter of fact, social life was linked up with religion.[2]

The unknown author of the *Letter to Diognetus* and Tertullian in his *Apologeticum* both emphasise that Christians do not differ much from their fellow human beings: they do not have different languages or habits; they have the same professions and contribute to economic life. They do not live in separate territories nor intend to become a nation or political group. All they do is to exhibit a different and remarkable morality, but in spite of that they are treated as outcasts, accused of hatred of mankind and of being the cause of disasters.[3]

Tertullian particularly stressed that his fellow believers were no political agitators and were not after any glory or power: 'we just have in mind one commonwealth for all, the world'.[4]

Most apologists of the period between 125 and 250 point at the inoffensive, gentle and moderate character of the Christians, which results from the fact that they follow Christ's teachings: Roman society and state do not have to fear any revolutionary action from them. At the same time, they also mention the kind of feasts in which no Christian would ever take part.[5] Tertullian cites the *Saturnalia*, an effusive midwinter carnival, theatre performances, gladiatorial fights, incense burning before the idols and *ex voto* offerings in the temples. 'Even though I do not attend your ceremonies, am I not a human being at those days?' he ironically asks.[6] But, in their opinion, the refusal to take part in licentious pleasures and erroneous ceremonies was not just a negative attitude: by their example of true worship and their high morality, the communities are an agent of education. Origen points to the prayers which, when combined with just behaviour and abstinence from pleasures, are a contribution to public welfare. Christians exceed others in usefulness for their fatherland, because they teach their fellow citizens piety towards God, who is not only guarding the earthly city, but also preparing for the heavenly city those who lead a good life.[7]

Some early Christian writers defined their group as a 'new people' or the 'third race'.[8] This led some of them to emphasise the sharp difference between their way of life and that of others.[9] Clement of Alexandria says that each of the three races is characterised by a particular way of life.[10] Origen contrasts two types of communities: Christians are the 'political opponents to the communities of superstitious, licentious and unjust men'; in every city they form a countergroup, over against the normal, civic community.[11] By stressing their specific Christian rules and conduct, they tended to present themselves as a people in their own right, and as a political entity. This emphasis on contrast, however, did not exclude declarations of loyalty to the Roman world dominion and legal system.

By stressing both aspects, viz., turning from idolatry, debauchery and violence, and the service of the only true God by self-control and neighbourly love, the apologists often presented the Christians as the Emperor's most devoted subjects. They argued that if the others behave correctly it would be because they dreaded punitive measures, whereas Christians would obey the laws because of their obedience to Christ's admonitions. Their motivation to behave correctly was the consequence of an inner conviction: 'They obey the laws, and by their way of life are even exceeding them'.[12] This type of argument implies that most of these writers indeed appreciated the Roman Empire as a state based on justice and thought that they could obey its laws without coming into conflict with their loyalty to Christ.

Responding to Celsus' criticism, Origen admits that pagans are capable of having well-ordered states, but he thinks it impossible that 'according to the laws which are in force in the worldly state, one could practise genuine devotion to God'.[13] This line of argument means a kind of partition of specific, God-given competences between the State and the Church and a demand for their mutual recognition. In the concrete case of the Roman Empire, Origen is still more positive.[14]

One of the achievements the Romans were proud of was the peace they had imposed on the Mediterranean world, the *Pax Romana*. Origen and others welcomed the *Pax Romana* as convenient for the spread of the Gospel. They saw the foundation of one commonwealth of peoples by Augustus as an act of divine providence, since under this reign Christ was born. His coming into the world brought justice and peace of a higher level. God prepared the nations to receive this grace by first reconciling them under Roman rule. If he had not done so, they would have remained alien and hostile to one another. And 'how could the doctrine of peace, which does not even permit to repay your enemy, have penetrated, if at Jesus' coming the political relations had not been set at rest everywhere?'[15] Thus, the Roman order was appreciated as a favourable frame for the spread of Christianity, and the universal peace as referring to the still better realm of Christ. Tertullian and Origen knew well that Christianity was not stopping at the Roman borders.[16] Yet both concentrated on the implications of being Christians within the Roman Empire.

In the same line of thought, Tertullian had interpreted the Roman Empire as the 'restraining force' alluded to in Paul's Second Letter to the Thessalonians.[17] Explaining why Christians say prayers for the Emperor and the safety of the Roman Empire, he suggests that, apart from the scriptural order to do so,[18] there is another, more urgent reason for intercession: as long as the Empire stands in force, it is restraining the universal catastrophe of the End, 'with all the horrible disasters which we don't want to see'; so that 'by praying for its delay, we contribute to the continuation of Rome'.[19] Obedience to the established authorities (Rom. 13:1–7 and 1 Pet. 2:13–17) was the general guideline. But not without the distinction the second text makes between *fear* and *honour*.[20]

The importance of this instruction was that it recognised the supreme position of the Emperor and, at the same time, drew a clear dividing line between him and God. Together with the other apostolic recommendation, to pray 'for kings and all who are in high positions',[21] this meant a desacralisa-tion of the emperorship. Whatever proleptic veneration of his posthumous divinisation was practised, what kind of miraculous blessings were expected from his 'genius' (superhuman spirit), or which relationship with a particular pagan god he claimed, for Christian consciences this was just arrogance and blasphemy. 'Fear' was due to the only God; the Emperor could only claim to receive 'honour', which was no more than a respectful acknowledgement of his unique office. They were fully prepared to invoke God's favour for its prosperous fulfilment.

We hear Tertullian assure that 'we invoke the eternal, true and living God for the good of the emperors', suggesting that they themselves know to whom they owe their life and power. The emperors, he is willing to admit, hold the second rank immediately after God, because 'they are over all men, like the living over the dead'. But any emperor is inferior to Heaven, inas-much as it is the same God who first made him a human being and then appointed him emperor.[22] Wholeheartedly we 'always pray in favour of every emperor that he may enjoy a long life, a government without troubles, the security of his house, brave armies, a faithful senate, an honest people, world peace – in short, for everything that a human and emperor wishes.' These things have to be implored from the only One who grants them; rites and sacrifices never can assure them![23] Origen compares the Christians with an army, fighting for the Emperor 'by the supplications we address to the divinity'. By the way, he makes the reservation that this intercession only concerns 'those who fight a just fight, and him who governs righteously, so that victory may be won over all those forces, which oppose those who act righteously'.[24]

We may call this an attitude of critical solidarity with the Roman State and its supreme chief. The office of the emperor is considered as God-given; critical alertness concentrates on his divine claims and on the 'just' character of his government and wars.[25] The increasing emperor cult of the third century, particularly practised in the army, was the cause of many conflicts between Christians and the State. Among all religious people, the Christians were the only to be aware of the fact that their faith meant a choice. The others could combine the devotion of their preference with the cults the State required; the Christians could not because of the strict monotheism that was a central element in their religion.

To summarise: leading figures of third-century Christianity actually interpreted the given context of the Roman Empire, trying to find a positive relationship between its institutions and God's plans in history. They focused mainly on three realities of the Empire:

1   legislation and administration of justice;
2   the peaceful commonwealth of nations, though the dangerous 'barbarians' had not yet been pacified;
3   the monarchical system of rule, which went together with the attribution of divine qualities to the Emperor and with his cult.

Facing this context, Christians propagated the following active responses:

1   they presented their members as inoffensive, loyal citizens, who were even giving a good moral example to others;
2   they welcomed the order of the Empire as a positive framework for the spread of the Gospel, under the reserve that the authorities would not obstruct that spread;
3   they respected the Emperor because of his God-given office, but refused to accept his divinisation.

Ethical standards and group morality

Christians had a set of ethical standards, which had to prevent notably three 'mortal sins': adultery, apostasy and manslaughter. The general and severe persecutions of the 250s brought many cases of apostasy. Since mortal sin implied lifelong excommunication, this would have decimated the Church. The debate arose whether the Church should indeed be pure in all its members, and consequently small, or whether it should tolerate different degrees of religious zeal, assume a pedagogical vocation and be a popular religion. The second option prevailed.

When Tertullian was defending the Christians and their behaviour, he explained why they were so determined to refrain from religious ceremonies and popular feasts. As soon as he addressed his fellow believers, he often criticised their laxity. There was indeed a gap between standards and practice, and this became a big problem in the Church of the third century, when systematic persecutions caused a lot of apostasies and put the strict discipline in respect of mortal sin under heavy pressure.

Community leaders tried to keep up the moral standards in order that the Christian identity would be safeguarded. This objective is visible in the conditions and requirements for admission to the *catechumenate*, which was the preparation for *baptism*.[26] These were a correct matrimonial situation and (for a slave) obedience to the master. The future Christian should have no earnings from brothel-keeping, manufacturing idols and amulets, magic and astrological practices or fortune-telling. He should not be an actor or teacher (because plays and general education were impregnated with pagan mythology), nor incur the risk of bloodshed (as soldier or city magistrate charged with administering justice).[27] All these occupations were forbidden because they would contaminate the neophyte with either polytheism or immorality. The uneducated (they were the great majority in Roman society) had to be imbued with the awareness that becoming a Christian implied choice and determination in things they had thus far been practising and combining with religion without any problem. In the same way, it was a task for an educated Christian such as Clement of Alexandria to show the well-to-do city-dwellers how a Christian lifestyle could be practised on their familiar social level.[28]

As a result of this, the Christian communities showed a somewhat closed character. Their group morality was a kind of shell, which kept them together and marked some obvious contrasts to the way of life of the majority. This situation underwent a fundamental change by the middle of the third century as a direct result of the persecutions by Decius and Valerian mentioned above. Christians were put under pressure to sacrifice (or to perform some substitute act that would leave them alone as well) and many of them succumbed. The question arose, what to do with them after the persecution? Traditionally, there was no pardon for the mortal sin of apostasy.[29] These standards were certainly known to the authorities and they may have expected that those Christians who joined the sacrifices would never be taken back into the communities so that these would be decimated. But, once the persecution had ceased, a high number of repentants asked for pardon. In North Africa the 'confessors' appealed to their steadfastness as a God-given charisma and, by virtue of that, propagated a general amnesty and reconciliation. Others, in North Africa as well as in Rome, categorically held to the old view that no apostate could ever be readmitted into the eucharistic community. A heated debate arose on the question whether the 'lapsed' could be reintegrated or not, and if so, on whose authority.[30] In this debate three parties were opposing each other: the rigorists, the advocates of complete and immediate pardon and the bishops. The first based their argument on the old conception that baptism had to be the door to a new and holy life, the second invoked the spiritual authority they had proved to possess, and the bishops advanced their prerogative to control admission and, consequently, readmission as well. The first two viewpoints were traditional, the third was new and was going to prevail. What did it imply?

The leading bishops in this debate, Cyprian at Carthage and Cornelius in Rome, held on to their authority in this matter. They were prepared to make distinctions between degrees of apostasy. Against an easy reconciliation of the lapsed via a general amnesty, as advocated by the confessors, they defended a serious inquiry into each case. But at the same time, they mitigated the traditional rigorism by opening the possibility for less guilty apostates to be reconciled after proofs of earnest repentance. Cyprian appealed to God's mercy and showed confidence that such reconciled repentants would stand firm in a next trial.[31] Bishops of his kind saw the danger of discouraging believers who probably would benefit from penitential exercises.

The prevalence of this new approach in matters of Church discipline meant no less than a fundamental change in ecclesiology. Instead of a small flock of faithful and mature believers, the Church gradually became a religious assembly for many, because it now accepted those who were still in need of spiritual consolation and clerical control. The closed community became an open one; the community of saints became an educational institution, a 'mother church', embracing both mature and weak members. Because of this turn, Christianity not only retained the apostates, even pagans felt attracted to a religion which promised them both salvation and indulgence with their weaknesses! It was a parting of the ways that deeply modified the nature of the Church.

Another result of this change was the increase of episcopal authority. As heads of the local community and decision-makers in local and regional meetings (synods), bishops became more and more the leaders and representatives of 'their' church (or church district). Cyprian developed the theory that the unity of the Church is resting upon the consensus of all the bishops, because all are partakers in the one ministry that Christ entrusted to the apostles as one college, when he gave them the authority either to forgive or to retain sins (John 20:23).[32] The Church was existing more and more in its bishops: they not only maintained religious discipline but also sat in judgement over the quarrels between members of their flock. In the eyes of the Roman authorities, the Church began to look like a state within the State.

The fact that bishops found a fresh answer to the crisis of the large number of apostates showed that Christianity was capable of being a religion for the majority as well as a social and pedagogical force backed by strong internal organisation and coherence. This creative answer pushed the Church on the way to take to the masses. It had not crumbled under the first general attempt by the Roman State to break its influence and to bring the entire population back to the common religious duties. In spite of the large number of victims and lapsed, the Church was unbroken and even more respected, when after Valerian's death (260) a series of emperors awarded her a time of peace, which was to last forty years.

The fact that the Christian religion found more and more acceptance was not only due to the differentiation of the ecclesiastical discipline or to the de-facto tolerance: the Church attained the cultural elites and the illiterate masses by relating its message to the religious aspirations and needs.

Connecting with philosophical themes

As part of the Hellenisation of the Mediterranean world, Greek philosophies had spread everywhere. The centre where the main schools of thought continued and developed was the city of Alexandria. Philosophy was more than a theory about cosmos and man: it also pretended to teach how human conduct could be in best harmony with the structure of all being, including the self. This climate of scholarly discussion stimulated some outstanding Christian thinkers to present the Bible and the Christian message as the ultimate Truth that could satisfy the best philosophical searchings. As the common ground was a mix of cosmology, anthropology and ethics, those thinkers advanced doctrinal theology.

Since Socrates (470–399 BCE),[33] classical philosophy had been dealing with ethics. Philosophers of different schools were raising questions on 'virtue', i.e., acting correctly, and on the natural principles that should give direction and goal to human actions. This approach implied a fundamental role for reflection and resolution, that is to say, for an activity of reason, and for knowledge as well. 'Care for yourself' was, so to say, the watchword, which meant doing justice to the better and more valuable element of yourself, the immortal soul. Such a watchword implied restraining one's impulses and emotions, which were seen as irrational and carrying away from the very goal of life.

Christian thinkers appreciated this philosophy because of its earnest character and its appeal to the responsibility of the individual. This ethical philosophy stood out from the Roman civil religion which only required partaking in public cult ceremonies, without any demand for personal convictions. On the whole, philosophers did not see any conflict between their doctrines and the public cults. But the Christians did so because of their monotheistic faith. They also saw their ethical conduct in direct connection with the vocation and mandates given by God. Christians also knew the action of evil forces upon humans. Satan and his demons were constantly leading into temptations and errors. They were looking for points of entry and found them in man's longings for lust. On this point, Christians showed affinity with the anthropology of several philosophical schools, recognising the importance of reason and will, and of instruction and intelligence. But they understood that man's own faculties are insufficient because of the demonical attempts and of the inner inclination to sin. Christ gained victory over both and the believers in the moment of their baptism appropriate his forces. These forces, however, are not magical: continuing struggle against demons and sinful inclinations remains a necessary commission. The anointment following the act of immersion is supposed to impart the gift of the Holy Spirit who stimulates human reason by enlightenment and strengthens the will by his force. The best contribution of the Christians themselves is to be moderate and in control of their affections.

To Justin Martyr (d. 155), Stoa and Platonism seemed to hold some congeniality with Christian convictions: the first in ethics, the latter in systematic respects. In Alexandria, Clement (*c.* 150–*c.* 215) regarded philosophy as a divine gift to man and used it in order to explain the faith of the Christian community and to supplement this with some philosophical ideas. His effort to contextualise the Christian message is apparent in his application of the Greek ideal of *paideia*, i.e., education to good morality and civic behaviour. In accordance with this ideal, Clement developed a detailed 'Christian lifestyle' for educated and well-to-do city-dwellers, presenting the role of the incarnate Word as that of a divine pedagogue.[34] He assimilated Christian ethics to self-control and moderation, and made Stoic *apathy*, i.e., freedom from passions, the essential virtue of the advanced Christian.

The Alexandrian doctrine of God showed influence of the Stoic ideal: God's highness was defined by denying him passions, because these were seen as emotions and as signs of unsteadiness. According to Origen, 'Divine nature is totally free from any affection of passion and change, remaining always without emotion and undisturbed on its blessed height.'[35] Yet Origen assigned to God compassion with the humans: as our Father he suffers from the sinful ways of his children and because of his love for them he descended to their level in his revelation.[36] What these theologians tried to avoid was an idea that God was subject to inner conflict. His unalterable nature had to be safeguarded. The tension lies in the combination of the elevation of God beyond human emotions with the concept of God being personal and caring for humankind, as he has shown through the mission and passion of his Son and Image. Consequently, Origen did not propagate a total absence of passions, but restriction to the higher and pure, esteeming the positive Christian virtues of humility and neighbourly love of greater value than indisturbedness.

However, Origen's greatest achievement in contextuality lies not so much in the field of ethics as in that of doctrine. His esteem for philosophy was more limited than Clement's. Among all the philosophical traditions, he most appreciated the Platonic School. There was more 'theology' in Platonism than in Stoicism, which saw God as the Spirit of the Universe but not as a real creator. Though human philosophy could render good services, it could never produce good theology, viz., true knowledge of God and his mysteries. But philosophy is useful in order to win intellectuals for the Christian faith and to develop good arguments against Gnosticism, which Origen considered a falsification of the apostolic message, because even in its Christian form it denied people free will and their own responsibility for their salvation.[37] The help philosophy was deemed in a position to offer is founded in the fact that human reason is an image of the *Logos*, who is the universal and creative Reason. The idea that an image permanently participates in its original model was part of the Platonic explanation of everything's existence. Greek thinking mainly concentrated on being: its presupposition was that all beings, including gods, humans and nature, were part of one great cosmological order and subject to fate and providence. This raised the problem of the space left to human free will and decision.

However, philosophy is not sufficient to attain the best possible human knowledge of God and of the right conduct in life; for this one needs a thorough study of the Scriptures, combined with prayers, ascetism and crowned with the gift of the Holy Spirit, which will follow these efforts. Philosophy could supply arguments against Gnostic determinism, but only the Bible gives insights into the interactive relation between freedom of the rational beings and God's pedagogical providence. These corrections, however important, did not impede the formal structure of Greek thinking, to which Origen linked. At a young age,[38] he composed four books *On Principles*, which took a typically Greek approach, but the elaboration was on the basis of the apostolic preaching and of the Bible as a whole. Confronted with the questions philosophers used to raise about cosmos and fate, and about unity and diversity of phenomena, Origen came to the conclusion that the apostles had preached all that is necessary for salvation, whilst remaining silent on questions which engage inquisitive minds. Such questions are subject to discussion; answers may be deduced from examining Scripture texts and from logical comparison of them. In the Preface, he proposes to discuss the following items:

1   the relation of the Holy Spirit to God;
2   the origin of the soul: generated together with the body or added to it from elsewhere?
3   The nature of the devil and the wicked 'angels';
4   what did exist before the genesis of our world, and what will happen after its end?
5   The creation and attributes of good angels; the power of the heavenly bodies upon the earth-dwellers.

In the theological reflection of the early Church these were new themes and Origen is rightly called 'an experimental theologian', because he ventured opinions on them which he was prepared to give up for better ones.[39] It is clear that he not only tackled problems that were preoccupying his intellectual audience, but also thought of theology as including anthropological and cosmological insights, necessary to stimulate man's striving upward to God and his spiritual realm.

In our days, the contextual Latin American church historian Hoornaert blames both Alexandrian theologians for having brought about a fundamental change in early Church theology. In his eyes they have 'marginalised the theology of marginality', which was the characteristic of the first two centuries. During this time Christian theology was a theology of self-understanding of the poor and marginalised. But influenced by the hierarchical structure of the Egyptian society Clement and Origen bartered this authentic theology of the poor for the doctrinal satisfaction of the intellectual elites.[40] By drawing a sharp dividing line between the first two and the third centuries, and between Egypt and the rest of the world, Hoornaert misjudges earlier attempts to build bridges between philosophical doctrines and the Christian message and to situate the latter on the line of divine revelation and human search as the most true and complete 'philosophy'.[41] Clement and Origen continued this development when they approved of the ethics of Stoics and Platonists, but just as well they filled the idea of 'knowledge' as saving condition with the experience of a personal and caring God and with the love we owe him in return. Hoornaert's fundamental partiality in favour of Latin American 'base communities' seems responsible for his scanty appreciation of our Alexandrian theologians. It should be appreciated that the Alexandrians did not avoid meeting the search for truth and the attraction of the Gnostic redemption myth, so prominent in the religious climate of Alexandria and the Egyptian countryside.[42] The experimental theology of the two Alexandrians was highly 'contextual' in the sense of our definition. The attempt to show a way towards 'higher' knowledge and spiritual progress did not just reflect a specifically Egyptian hierarchical society. Had that been the case, why would Origen's theology have obtained such broad and deep a response in all the eastern provinces and have taken root in Palestine and Asia Minor?

Responding to religious feelings and needs

Third-century society suffered from economic decline and cultural weariness. Whereas intellectuals sought after freedom and an uplifting inner life, common people badly felt their subjection to the shortage of goods and to the restrictions of earthly life in general. They longed for immortal happiness after death. A flow of eastern cults and religions promised incorruptible life through initiation into the power circle of a victorious hero or life-spending god(-dess). Christianity met with these needs and adapted its central message of salvation through Christ to the distinct religious contexts of the Greek, Syriac and Latin subcultures of the Hellenistic world. In this adaptation, Christianity upheld two principles: God as transcendent creator and his loving care for everyone's personal redemption and renewal.

What were ordinary people longing for? Since they left but few written documents, we know little about their aspirations and needs. But there are indirect sources for their hopes and the ways they were coping with the problems of daily life. People of the third century were searching for contact with the sphere of the gods. They experienced everyday life as subject to limitations of corporeal existence, with its needs and passions pressing heavily on the innate qualities of the soul – limitations of illness, mortality, subjection to fate and demons, of economic insecurity, poverty and slavery. People were, thus, longing for all that promised to overcome these limitations of existence by means of communion with higher and everlasting being, such as was proper to the divine world. The cultivated people were striving after this promise in a rational and intellectual manner; the common people did so through irrational and magical means. Anything that could establish a helpful contact with the divine world was popular: on the one hand, instructions for a pious and disciplined life; on the other, magic practices, incantations, exorcism or visiting a 'holy man', who obviously disposed of better forces to lighten the burdens of life.

The existence of invisible forces was an essential part of the world-view. They were called 'demons' and a distinction was made between good and wicked ones. Christianity also met this belief. We have seen that Origen included into his theological research programme an explanation of the origin and action of both good spirits ('angels') and demons. Whereas 'angels' (literally: 'messengers') were God's good servants, demons were declared evil, since deceiving humans by sowing errors about God's will and immoral life conduct was their steady business.[43]

The official state religion did by no means satisfy existential needs. It was only meant to ensure public welfare and prosperity of the State. For their personal needs, people looked for help in cults of eastern origin, which spread over the Mediterranean after the eastern territories had come under Roman rule. These cults and religions mediated to their adherents an initiation into the mysterious fate of a hero or god, who suffered death but came to life again. The myths that told such fates were mostly linked with the cycle of nature and not with any event in history. People who partook in these cults expected to become participants of the mysterious forces that would guarantee life after death. Since Christianity did not want to become a ghetto religion, but to address the whole society, it had to give its particular answer to the widespread longing for immortality. As we said, one answer was to present Jesus as the nations' teacher whose teachings unmasked the tricks of the demons. Third-century Christian thinkers developed this issue, which originated in the apologists of the second century. It was part of the claim that Christ is the unique and universal mediator of salvation.

For ordinary humans there were other ways to experience the impact of Christ's victory in everyday life. The canonical Acts of Apostles inspired the composition of similar stories in which apostles such as Paul, Peter and John played a central missionary role, and much cogency was expected from miracles and conversions of prominent citizens to a different, sober lifestyle. Those Acts were obviously meant to attract middle- and lower-class people to come to a more spiritual understanding of Christ. The bond with his

victorious person was most impressively demonstrated by martyrs and confessors, who scorned death in order to 'be with the Lord in his glory'. The
communities used to commemorate the anniversary of the martyrs' 'glorification' (execution) by gathering at their tombs, where a cult enabled them to
partake in the same power that made the martyrs so victorious. The sign of
the cross was used to avert demonic attacks, since Christ's crucifixion had,
once and for all, deprived them of their power.

The common means to preserve and improve life were reshaped, with
elements springing from the apostolic preaching. Christianity set out to meet
the needs and strivings of its contemporaries. However, it was led by two
fundamental insights: whereas pagans thought of the gods as being more
powerful and therefore inspiring of fear, but nevertheless part of one and the
same order of being as the humans, Christians held to a transcendent God,
spending grace because he is moved by his love for the world. The second
characteristic the Christians held on to was that life was not determined by a
hidden fate to which people could better submit, but a field for imitation of
Christ, the unique Saviour. For these reasons, the Christian answers were at
the same time assimilative and contradictory.

The third century shows not only a social stratification but also a geographic
differentiation. Three main cultural areas can be distinguished. The conquest
of large territories with different cultural traditions had paved the way for the
spread of Greek civilisation (language, basic conceptions). However, under
the upper crust of this Hellenisation, original cultural patterns subsisted and
they mixed with Hellenism without losing their proper characteristics.[44]
The cultural 'landscape' to which this acculturation process had led was just
as much a given context for the missionary religion as was Christianity. For
the ongoing interpretation of Christ's person and work it meant that different
cultural and religious backgrounds resulted in hopes of salvation with specific
accents. During the third century, three distinctive hopes show their influence upon the development of theological thought. As we said above with
regard to Clement and Origen (see p. 19), Alexandria had preserved Greek
culture in its purest form: here the classic philosophical views of humankind
and cosmos were not only passed on, but also developed further. The longing
to overcome the limitations of human existence was commonly satisfied by
the concept of an *ontological* union with the Divine, to be attained by setting
free (from the bonds of the body) the divine image. Correct discernment of the
composite human structure, especially of the nature of the higher, spiritual
part which is akin to the divine, was considered an indispensable condition
for one's salvation. In this context, Christian theology thought of Christ as
the divine *Logos*, who had assumed a human existence in order to make his
brothers and sisters participants in godly, incorruptible life.

In Syriac Christianity, which had Antioch as its centre, Semitic culture and
religious views were operative. Here the ultimate union with God was seen as
a goal that would be attained along a *historical* rather than a physical line, viz.,
as a natural recompense for an earthly existence during which man has proved

a true, obedient ally of God. In this context, Christian salvation was not seen as the fruit of the ontological assumption of human nature by the *Logos* of God, but rather of humankind's accordance with God's instructions. In his human existence, Christ had gone this way and had so become 'the first-born among many brethren, to whom they are predestined to be conformed' (Rom. 8:29), 'the beginning, the first-born from the dead' (Col. 1:18).

Latin theology, having Africa and its capital city Carthage as its centre, bore a more *juridical* stamp. Man's duty was to conform to the ever-valid rules the gods once had established. Disturbance, rebelliousness and modernism were seen as dangerous infractions of that divine order; piety, faithfulness and respect as the way to beneficial harmony with the Divine. Piety was not an inner feeling but the actualisation of a kind of mutual contract, because the gods would not fail to reward the performance of people's duties. When put into Christian terms, sin was, above all, an infringement of God's lawful order. The primary need was for the restoration of the relation between humankind and God, and for a juridical and practical redemption through Christ's mediation. Words such as 'grace' and 'sacrament' originated in North Africa. As we saw above (pp. 17–18) the Latin west produced the first reflections on the genuine conduct of the faith community.

In all these contextual translations of the apostolic message of God's love in Christ, the central idea was that of an exchange: Christ assuming our situation in order to let us partake in his. For such a soteriology of exchange, both his godliness and his humanity were of crucial importance. But the accents differed in accordance with the basic conceptions in pre-Christian religiosity.

At the beginning of the fourth century, Christianity had shown a remarkable ability to find answers to many contemporary questions and needs. It had shown its universality, not being restricted to any region or local cult, or to a particular social class. It had proved to possess a strong coherence and organisation. The Church was no longer a small group of firm believers, but had accepted a differentiation between members of some maturity in knowledge and sanctification and members still in need of a disciplinary and educational framework. The 'catholic' conception of the Church as a patient mother, having children of different character and holiness, had prevailed and had prepared the Church to assume the role of majority religion.

2 Crisis and recognition

Introduction

A completely new and inexperienced context for the Christians within the Roman Empire (and on the rebound even for those outside) came into being through the rise to power of Constantine, Emperor from 306 till his death in 337. Thanks to his two decisive victories on the battleground – 312 in the west and 324 in the east – the Christian religion obtained full recognition and even a position of privilege. Shortly before, the Church had been exposed to the most systematic and cruel persecution of its first centuries, which ranged over ten years (303–13), though with remarkable local differences in duration and toughness. The execution of the measures against the Christians depended on the interests of regional rulers, who often were each other's rivals. Religious considerations were also at stake.

It is, therefore, our first task to depict the political events that led from one administrative reform to another, viz., from a government by four rulers, the *tetrarchy*, installed in 293, to a renewed government by one single emperor, the *monarchy*, achieved by Constantine in 324. Our aim is to show the intertwining of politics with religious concepts and motives. These motives had their impact on Constantine's preference for the Christian religion, a choice which, in its turn, acted so profoundly upon Christian life and thought.

The immediate political context was determined by the administrative, economic and military dangers that made the Empire crack both on its borders and internally. The majority of the emperors were army commanders, who saw themselves proclaimed *Augustus* by their troops after a victory, to be thrown over before long by the next one.[1] The administrative instability was aggravated by the attacks of Germans and Persians on the northern and eastern borders and by local insurrections. It was against this background that two energetic leaders tried to consolidate and unify the extended territory of their empire by introducing vigorous *reforms*. These two personalities were the pagan Diocletian and the Christian Constantine. In spite of their contrasting religious preferences, they had quite identical political aims and religious presuppositions.

The difference between them was that Diocletian built his measures, progressive as they were, on a religious conservatism: he turned to the old Roman gods for help and legitimisation. Constantine looked to the future and took a chance on a new religion. This was revolutionary, since traditional Roman thought considered any new religion as *superstition* and stigmatised it as dangerous, because it would dissuade the people from the old religious and moral duties and, consequently, irritate the gods. It is incorrect to think that for both emperors religion was just a means to bind the population to their government: they were convinced that the Empire would only be saved if the entire population venerated the right, i.e., most powerful god(s). Both emperors also showed a strong conviction of being 'called' to a mission in the name of their god. There was both continuity and discontinuity in the way both emperors enforced religious duties upon their subjects in order to please the godhead for the State's welfare. This background must be kept in mind with respect to the radical change the Christians experienced when they passed from Diocletian's to Constantine's reign.

This chapter deals with the period from 293 to 324. Diocletian held the supreme power over the Empire from 284, but he introduced the system of the tetrarchy only in 293, the year we have chosen as our starting point for this study. The year 324 was not the end of Constantine's reign, but the moment he eliminated his last rival and so became sole *monarch*. The next year he would introduce a new instrument to control the internal unity of the Church, the imperial synod or *ecumenical council*. This establishment of new, reciprocal relations between Church and State will be dealt with in Chapter 4.

The present chapter is divided into three sections:

1   The reform by the last pagan emperors and its failure (293–312).
2   Politics and religion in Constantine.
3   The Christianisation of public life (312–24).

The reform by the last pagan emperors and its failure

The division of the Empire into four administrative units, each placed under a ruler of imperial rank, was meant to assure a more effective defence and tax levy. After twelve years, the system broke down as a result of rivalry among the second shift of rulers. It was the beginning of a return to the monarchy, which eventually came into the hands of Constantine. Before his seizing of power in the western part, each ruler had invoked the patronage of a trad-itional Roman god. The logical consequence of this move was the elimination of those who refused to join in the veneration of these gods. In spite of the rigour and cruelty of the persecution, the Christian communion as a whole did not submit. Having first obtained tolerance from the last pagan emperor, the Christians received equal rights and even a beginning of privileges, from the newly converted Constantine, who established this radical change all over the Empire as soon as he became its sole monarch.

The tetrarchy

In order to cope with the military and financial problems, Diocletian invented a system that would replace the weakness of the administration by a greater stability and a stronger control over the provinces. For that reason, he introduced a government of four rulers, united in one imperial college, the tetrarchy. Diocletian was its genius and for twelve years he would be the head of the team. The others were successful army commanders whose eventual ambitions for the supreme power were now channelled by giving them control over a large part of the Empire and a prospect of promotion to the highest rank.

Diocletian had already installed an army comrade in the west, Maximian, who like himself bore the title of *Augustus*. But in 293 each half of the Empire was again subdivided into two parts, one of which was placed under a *Caesar*. The first two Caesars were obliged to divorce from their wives in order to marry a daughter of their respective Augustus and so to become his committed son-in-law. At the end of the twelve years, both Augusti would retire and have their Caesar promoted to this rank; two new Caesars would be installed. By this construction Diocletian hoped to commit qualified rulers to a system of mutual obligation, to prevent excessive personal ambitions and to guarantee a better administration and defence of the provinces.

According to this experimental system of rule, the east was divided as follows:

> Egypt, Libya, Palestine, Syria and Asia Minor: Diocletian, *Augustus*
> Greece and the Balkans: Galerius, *Caesar*

The west:

> Italy, Africa and Spain: Maximian, *Augustus*
> Gaul and Britain: Constantius, *Caesar*

Initially, the concept proved to be successful and about the year 300 peace and unity were restored, though at the expense of a considerable tax increase.

Divine patronage

Although the system of tetrarchy looked progressive and appropriate to the circumstances, in the religious respect, the imperial college of Diocletian was conservative and restorative. Diocletian did not only believe in the salutary effects of a correct observance of the old state religion, he and his college opted for the traditional Roman gods and their cult. The crisis of the Empire required a reactivation of the favours of the gods that in the past had made the Romans so victorious and capable of imposing their peaceful and lawful order upon many different peoples. Irrespective of whatever religious practice the subjects adhered to for their own needs, there was need of a common civil religion: that of the old Roman cults and sacrifices. The objective was *one Empire, one Emperor* (or college), *one Religion*.

The tetrarchy connected the reforms with a state ideology. Each of its members placed himself publicly under the patronage of a god of the traditional pantheon, selected for symbolic reasons:

* Diocletian presented himself as 'son of *Iuppiter*'; Iuppiter was the 'monarch' of the pantheon and seen as the founder and tutelary genius of the Empire.
* Maximian was proclaimed 'son of *Hercules*', Iuppiter's powerful executive on earth.
* Galerius, the eastern Caesar, stood under the patronage of *Mars*, the war god.
* Constantius, the western Caesar, stood under the patronage of *Apollo*, the main god of the Greeks, also associated with the sun god, the universal benefactor.

By these specific affiliations, the emperors did not pretend that they were of divine nature. They were 'sons', i.e., elected instruments of the most indispensable deities, acting under their mandate. All military emperors were in need of a legitimisation 'from above', since their rise to power was not based on a dynastic descent but on a coup. Moreover, the tetrarchs wanted a clear legitimisation for their reform measures. The numerous statues of the emperors, erected everywhere on public squares, were meant to inculcate respect for their divine office. They were a means of state propaganda, as were the effigies on the coins. The veneration of the emperors also fulfilled the people's want for a supernatural saviour on Earth.

The persecutions

The logical consequence of this policy was an effort to prevent the spread of new religions. Diocletian condemned as 'a very great crime to oppose the institutions and prescriptions that once have been established by the forefathers and are, and should remain, immutable.'[2] To be sure, traditional thinking would allow adherence to strange beliefs as long as these did not keep the citizens away from the public cults or pushed them to infringe the traditional manners and customs good Romans wanted to keep up in the interest of their world order. They were disgusted with *superstitions*, which they neatly distinguished from correct *religion*; especially with those superstitions which introduced new manners and different moral standards.

In 297, Manicheism was interdicted, because it originated from Persian soil and also because its theories were new and unprecedented. The equally popular veneration of the sun god was not anathematised, since earlier emperors had promoted it and since it was serving so well the ideology of unity. We shall return to this cult when dealing with Constantine's religious career. But after Manicheism, it was Christianity's turn to suffer proscription.

Meanwhile, Christians had profited from a forty-year period of de-facto tolerance. Their numbers had increased, which was also due to its decision to be a hospitable and pedagogical faith community, rather than an exclusive group of rigorists (see Chapter 1, p. 18). The tolerance of the State went so far that Christians were accepted in the administration and in the army, and in these services they were usually dispensed from sacrificial ceremonies that were incompatible with the obligations of their faith. These ceremonies were taboo for them, because they were devoted to gods that were not real and because sanguinary offerings could not please the true God.[3] But in the year 299, Diocletian started a purge of the army and the civil service,[4] and this was only the beginning. On 23 February 303, the day of the Roman feast for the god of the *limits*, Diocletian and Galerius decided to limit the Christian expansion, which was such an obvious hindrance to the state cult and to other religions as well. Their measures may be seen as the final step in their policy of religious restoration and alignment.

Galerius hated the Christians and wanted to exterminate them; Diocletian rather aimed at their marginalisation, saving as many lives as possible. Diocletian seems to have asserted his will, since the persecution was carried out gradually, by the following succession of decrees:

1   destruction of Christian buildings and books; deprivation of prominent Christians of all their rights and liability to expropriation, slavery and torture;
2   apprehension of members of the clergy;
3   coercion of clergy to sacrifice, in order to set an example of subjection;
4   extension of the order of sacrificing to all Christians (issued only in 304).

As in the persecution of Decius (see Chapter 1, page 12), the principal aim was to involve all subjects in the indispensable 'piety' towards the gods of the Empire, the second purpose being to break the backbone of the Christian community, the church organisation. The mass of church people was only to be attacked after the leaders in doctrine and discipline had been eliminated.

The rigour of the application of these decrees varied from area to area. The persecutions were the hardest in North Africa and in the east, where they only ceased in 313 (and, thus, covered a ten-year period). In Britain and Gaul, the territories of Constantius, their execution remained restricted to the first measure.[5] Although three of the four tetrarchs were willing to execute the decrees, the application mainly depended on the zeal of the provincial governors. It is certain that, in spite of Diocletian's intention to avoid many death penalties, there was much resistance and faithfulness on the side of the Christians, so that the persecution caused a great number of victims and was characterised by abhorrent cruelties.

A twofold failure

Diocletian's policy of restoration ended in a double failure, both on the administrative and on the religious level. The second of these failures implied radical consequences for the position of the Christian community as a whole. The first paved the way for a renewed centralisation of power, which also prepared a uniform settlement of religious interests.

The system of tetrarchy broke down at the first promotion of the *Caesares* to the rank of *Augusti* and the appointment of two new Caesars (305). Galerius, the new head of the imperial college, appointed two creatures of his own, bypassing the natural choices of Maximian's son Maxentius and Constantius' son Constantine. From then on, both frustrated pretenders eagerly looked for a chance to obtain imperial power and dignity; finally, it was between them that the decisive battle for the dominion over the west would be fought on 28 October 312 in front of the gates of Rome. Constantine soon got his first chance: at the sudden death of his father in 306, the troops proclaimed him *Augustus* straightaway, passing over the *Caesar* rank.

A period of complicated political chaos began, caused by a variety of claimants to the available thrones, fighting against each other.[6] The mutual cohesion and equilibrium that Diocletian had tried to install were totally lost; the absolute power of monarchy was tempting. In the decisive years 312/13, there were still four rulers on the political scene. But they were no longer a tetrarchy in the sense of a coherent college: each of them tried to eliminate his neighbouring colleague.[7] Contemporary writers compared those years with the period of civil war, ended by Octavianus in the year 37 BCE, who remained as sole monarch, surnamed *Augustus*.[8]

By the end of 313, the Empire was again in the hands of two emperors: Constantine in the west and Licinius in the east. Each of them had succeeded in eliminating his rival: Constantine by beating Maxentius at the *Milvian Bridge*, Licinius by getting rid of Maximinus Daia in July 313. Both rivals had provoked the war in which they went down.[9] Before engaging in battle with Maximinus, Licinius made an alliance with victorious Constantine, marrying his sister at Milan. It was at that occasion that both emperors, surely at Constantine's instigation, promulgated the famous 'Declaration of Milan' on the religious rights and duties in the Empire (see below). Their concord was not for long. After a few years, their rivalry led to a series of military confrontations, ending with a total triumph of Constantine in 324, who then became the sole monarch of the Empire. The system of tetrarchy had completely collapsed.[10]

Still more obvious was the failure of the religious restoration. The great persecution did not bring about the dissolution of the organisation of the Church, nor did it achieve a mass desertion from the Christian faith. Galerius, who had so hated the Christians, finally had to admit this failure of the tetrarchy policy. From his deathbed on 30 April 311 he promulgated an *Edict of Tolerance*, which reveals the typical Roman conception of the function of religion and even draws the permission of Christian worship into this traditional, contextual view. The text is, therefore, very interesting, especially when it is compared with the Declaration of Milan of two years later.

Galerius first recalls the objective of his religious policy, 'to arrange it all according to the ancient laws and the public discipline of the Romans, and to see that the Christians, too, who had abandoned the way of life of the forefathers, come to their senses.' He then explains that Christians are to be seen as stubborn and foolish people, who 'do not follow anymore the institutions, which their forefathers have established, and have made their own laws, bringing here and there members of different nations together into a community (of their own).' To stop this, was the aim of the persecution.

The Emperor, however, had to accept the fact that 'most of them were determined to keep their intentions with the result that they *did not discharge to the gods the cult and veneration which is due to these, nor practised the cult of the Christian god*' (viz., because of the persecution). For this reason Galerius states that 'regarding Our endless generosity and grace', he thinks it essential 'to immediately extend equally to those people Our indulgence and to allow them to be Christians again and to restore their meeting houses.'[11]

We hear the Emperor reasoning as follows: because of the tenacity of so many Christians on the one hand, and of the impediment of their assemblies by the Government on the other, a substantial part of the Empire's subjects does in fact abstain from worshipping gods at all. This causes, so to say, a 'cult vacuum', and this is not profitable to the public welfare of the Empire. It is, therefore, better to allow the Christians to worship their god in their own way. But the motivation behind Galerius' tolerance clearly meant an – at least temporary – abandoning of the ideal of *one common religion that would unify the whole population and bind all subjects to the intermediary of divine favours, the Emperor*. Unity was now seen as less important than divine favours and, therefore, less essential than actual devotion and the risk of so many people remaining 'impious'. But it only was for the time being; the ideal of one, common religion was not to be abandoned.

For the moment, the decree of tolerance was circumvented by Maximinus Daia. Waiting for his chance to take over the whole east, he dedicated himself to Iuppiter, Diocletian's patron, and continued the persecution of the Christians, until he was defeated by Licinius. Again there were Christian martyrs, especially in Palestine and Egypt, among whom was Alexandria's bishop Peter.

If we look next to the Declaration of Milan of Constantine and his fresh brother-in-law Licinius, we are struck by some similarities in arguing, but should note the differences as well.

Concerned – as they say – with

> public welfare and security in the broadest sense, we thought that of all

questions related to the benefit of the majority, that of the veneration of the godhead most urgently needs a new arrangement. We should grant all, the Christians as well as all the others, the freedom and possibility to adhere to the religion of their choice, in order that *whatever godhead there may be on the heavenly throne may be placated and act propitiously towards Us and all who belong to the empire.*

Therefore:

it should not be made impossible for anyone to commit himself to observe the religion of the Christians or the one that rather appeals to him, so that the *Supreme Godhead, to which we perform religious cult with freedom of mind, will show us in every respect Her usual favour and grace.*[12]

In parallel with the Edict of Tolerance, the Declaration is based on the presumption that for the safety and welfare of the emperors and their subjects a widespread veneration of 'god' is indispensable. The basic Roman conception of piety, *do ut des* (I give so that you may give), is being maintained. The performance of religious duties is by no means a side issue, but a main political concern of any emperor.

A second similarity is the abandonment of religious unity: plural worship may even be better, since it will address and oblige 'whatever godhead there may be'. This is a renewed utterance of the idea that religious plurality is less dangerous than the existence of a cult vacuum.

A difference is the more generous granting of freedom: instead of tolerance for the Christians, the observation of their religion – we shall see later what this meant in Constantine's opinion – 'should in no way be made impossible for anyone'. Freedom of devotion even seems to become an important condition, of equal value to the old ritual correctness.

Another difference is the use of the term (Supreme) Godhead (*divinitas*) instead of the traditional word 'gods'. This term will appear to have had the clear preference of Constantine. It may have been an expression of political wisdom at a moment of transition. It is probably also an indication that he shared the 'enlightened', philosophical notion of one divine essence behind and above the various deities of the pantheon.

Returning from Milan to his territories, Licinius entered his battle with Maximinus also as a religious contest, dedicating his fight to 'the Great Holy God', over against the adversary who pretended to be Iuppiter's servant. After his victory, the persecutors were pursued and often suffered similar punishment as they had been inflicting on Christians just a moment ago. But Licinius' dedication to the sake of the Christian religion was not firm and was rather ambivalent. Gradually he put impediments to the Christian communities, tried to paralyse Church life and gave way to his subalterns to commit acts of persecution. Constantine welcomed this change of mind as pretext to liberate the Christian east from its last oppressor.[13]

Politics and religion in Constantine

Constantine shared the enlightened idea of one Supreme God, but it took some time before he identified him with the God of the Christians. He obviously adhered to the contemporary veneration of the sun as highest god. But impressed by the Christians' resistance against the most systematic and cruel persecution they ever had to suffer, he devoted his way to Christ when he had to give battle against his rival in the western part of the Empire. His victory confirmed him in his conviction to have engaged the 'right' god. From now on there should be no hindrance to the Christian worship to be practised everywhere for the welfare of the Empire and of himself. Divisions threatened the role Constantine assigned to the Church and he set out to suppress them: first in North Africa, where they were of canonistic nature, and after a second victory in the east, where they were doctrinal and ingrained.

Preliminary remarks

Constantine inaugurated a new approach to public worship and freedom for the Christians, and he did so with consistence. 'After 28 October 312 the emperor thought of himself as God's servant, entrusted with a divine mission to convert the Roman Empire to Christianity'.[14] What can we know about the background of this remarkable choice for Christianity by a pagan Roman emperor?

Dealing with Constantine's religion, a distinction must be made between his personal religious evolution and his public gestures, measures and propaganda. The latter aspect is easier to demonstrate than the first, but there is no good evidence for the theory that the first aspect is not relevant at all. The link between the two aspects is the conviction of being entrusted with a divine mission. We saw that such a conscience already was in Diocletian. The difference between him and Constantine lies in the god who entrusts. We shall see that, from the beginning of his public appearance, Constantine, abandoning the gods of the old Graeco-Roman mythology, turned to the conception of a universal divine being. On this universalistic line he identified the supreme divine being (the *summa divinitas* of the Declaration of Milan, see above, p. 33) more and more openly with the God the Christians worshipped. Does this religious evolution leave room for a *conversion*?

Before we look at these questions, two explanations of Constantine's religious policy and personal attitude must be rejected as implausible. The first is that Constantine had been a Christian all the time. This explanation undervalues the pagan gestures, which are unmistakable; no doubt it springs from the wish to overestimate the person of the first Christian emperor. The second explanation denies him religious feelings and motivations at all and sees him as only a very clever politician, who was using religion for purely political ambitions. But this explanation does not fit the evident intertwining of religion and political aims we found in Constantine's predecessors. As young 'prince', Constantine had grown up at Diocletian's court.[15] It is natural to imagine that the dominant ideas about the link of political success to correct 'piety' influenced him. This was fully part of his context!

The education at Diocletian's court at Nicomedia also provided Constantine with contemporary philosophical insights. Constantine was not the rude soldier he has often been taken for. By that time, North African Lactantius was teaching Latin rhetoric and literature at Nicomedia, having been appointed by Diocletian himself (see Chapter 3, pp. 45–6). When persecutions started, Lactantius held to his Christian conviction and lost his job. As a teacher of rhetorics he was acquainted with philosophical trends and from these, or through these, he came to the Christian faith. Such a gradual transition, without a sudden 'conversion', was quite possible in the context of the late third century. Constantine may very well have known him: in 317 he ordered him to his own court at Treves to become his son's tutor. With great interest Lactantius followed Constantine's rise to power and *c.* 315 he wrote a history of the attitude of the Roman emperors towards the Christian religion. It is in this work that we read the first Christian report about the events at the Milvian Bridge, which reveal Constantine as a Christian. These remarks serve to point to a widespread climate of enlightened, philosophical thinking about the divine, from which transition to the Christian religion could gradually take place.[16] But Constantine's turn to Christianity was nevertheless a great surprise and was not self-evident.

Public manifestations of Constantine's turn to Christianity

Immediately after having been raised to the rank of *Augustus* at his father's death, Constantine released the Christians in his territories from all persecution, granting them full freedom of worship. After his victory in 312, restoration of the Christian worship was one of his priorities. However, in a campaign against one of his rivals in Gaul, he is reported to have deviated from the highway in order to visit a famous sanctuary of Apollo, where he offered laurel crowns to this god and to the goddess Victoria. Moreover, it is suggested that, receiving a visionary sensation, Constantine was granted a direct contact with Apollo, 'who rules the world'.[17] We have already mentioned that, during the first tetrarchy, Apollo was the divine patron of Constantius, and also that Apollo was identified with the sun god. This act of worship took place in 310 and from then onwards, the 'Invincible Sun' (*Sol Invictus*) appears on the coins, together with Victoria.[18] The representation of the sun as god, notably as the highest god, was appealing to many educated persons, emperors as well. The symbolic value of the sun is that it is visible and beneficent to all without distinction, and therefore venerable as the one origin of life and welfare. Such an idea of one supreme godhead could satisfy the monotheistic tendencies of the epoch.

If Constantine can hardly be seen as being a convinced Christian as early as 310, by October 312, just before the battle at the Milvian Bridge, his attitude had changed. He went to war against Maxentius in spite of the objections, advanced by his pagan oracle interpreters and cool-headed strategists. He ordered his soldiers to fix the so-called *Staurogram* (a cross with the sun on top) on their shields. And when he entered the city of Rome victoriously in order to be welcomed as Emperor by the Senate (as was customary), he refused the usual offering of thanks to Iuppiter on Capitol Hill. On the triumphal arch, which the Senate and people of Rome erected to his honour, it was marked that Constantine owed his victory to the 'Supreme Divinity'. Ever since that moment, the pagan gods were disappearing from public life – albeit gradually.[19] Constantine extended freedom of worship to North Africa, where the persecution had done much damage to lives and properties: churches were to be handed back or to be rebuilt at the expense of the State.[20]

His personal convictions

Is the change between 310 and 312 due to a sudden *conversion?* We now have to look at another *visionary experience* Constantine is recorded to have had on the eve of his battle against Maxentius.

There are two records of this event: one by Lactantius, the other by Eusebius of Caesarea.[21]

The story told by Lactantius is the oldest (314 or 315) and most sober report, and this pleads for a higher degree of authenticity. Nevertheless, Eusebius' version is often considered as more trustworthy, since the Bishop of Caesarea reports that Constantine personally told him about the event, confirming his words 'with oaths'. The moment of their conversation, however, is very late: 335. It contains the story that Constantine's soldiers were witnessing a luminous cross in the sky and that this miracle was followed by a dream in which Christ explained the sign to Constantine himself. Now the question arises: how could a record of an event with so many witnesses have remained secret for a man like Eusebius, who was the most learned and scrutinising historian of his days, so that he needed to be informed and convinced more than twenty years later? We hold to Lactantius' version.[22]

This version implies two facts:

1 There was only a *dream* of Constantine himself.
2 There is no mention of a *conversion* as the immediate result of what Constantine experienced.

What remains is the following: on the eve of the battle, during his sleep 'Constantine was summoned to fix on the shields [of his soldiers] the heavenly sign of God and so engage the enemy. He did as he was told and [. . .] thus painted [the sign of] Christ on the shields.'

Constantine was prepared to receive an instruction through a dream, and he acted in compliance with it. For people in Antiquity, a dream was a normal way of being illuminated 'from above', and many a prominent person took his decisions on the basis of dreams. Constantine must also have been prepared to entrust his career, at this very critical moment, to the God the Christians pretended to know and to worship in the only adequate way. Being already a monotheist, he made the next step by identifying the supreme godhead, thus far equated with the sun, with the Christian God.[23] We may suppose that he did so because the conviction had ripened that the Christians obviously had a better relationship with the Supreme Godhead than others. The events that followed seemed to confirm his conviction and choice.

There is no reason to imagine a sudden, abrupt moment of 'conversion' to the Christian faith and, still less, to the Church. Constantine received baptism only on his deathbed. As a convinced monotheist he was the Christians' friend and protector. For the next years he kept to the new, general appellations of God. He also maintained the ex-officio title of *Pontifex Maximus*, High Priest of the State,[24] but expressed his new piety by presenting himself as 'Worshipper of God' and through his legislation (see below, p. 42).

Through his efforts, the worship of the true God should now become general. Soon after his victory and investiture in Rome, and in conformity with his orders for Britain and Gaul in 306, Constantine gave orders to remove all impediments to Christian liturgical assemblies. We have letters in which he ordered the Proconsul of Africa (who had been very active in the persecution) to render to the Christian communities all their confiscated property. Moreover, he wished a substantial sum to be paid out of the public funds to the 'ministers of the legitimate and most saint catholic religion for their expenses'.[25] Clergymen would soon be freed of the orderly duties to which all citizens were submitted, a privilege the priests of the old state religion were also enjoying. The idea behind this measure was that, in the interest of state and society, nothing should hinder the priests from their most specific duty, viz., placating the gods. This traditional conception was, henceforth, transferred to the Church, which Constantine saw primarily as a cult institution.[26] With regard to the army, Constantine ordered that the Christian soldiers should go to church on Sunday, whereas the non-Christians should address a prayer in more general terms to the Supreme Godhead.

Constantine apparently was as abhorrent of the cult vacuum as were his predecessors. He also shared their conviction of being divinely called to fulfil a historical mission. A strong sense of vocation marks his religiosity. *His ultimate objective was that all the subjects of his empire would be Christians on the basis of free choice*. It would soon force him to intervene in the affairs of the Church and to appreciate it as a faith community and not only as a cult institution.

Constantine discovers the Church and its divisions

In the Roman administration, the 'Diocese Africa' was subdivided into five provinces: Africa Proconsularis in the centre, Numidia and Mauritania to the

west and Byzacene and Tripolitane to the east.[27] The penetration of Roman
civilisation was greatest in the centre and decreased the further one moved
from there. Roman presence and influence were most perceptible in the cities.
Carthage, the former capital of the Punic state, became a 100-per cent Roman
town when it had been rebuilt after its capture. But there were also great
numbers of Roman colonists, since the State remunerated its veterans with
landownership in Africa and in the larger provinces of Numidia and Mauritania. These colonists employed seasonal workers, thus creating a proletariat of
agricultural labourers who remained unemployed during most of the year.
The Punic invaders, who had settled many centuries earlier, had been reduced
to a second-class population. Christianity spread among the Romans, expressing itself in their language,[28] and, to a lesser extent, among the Punians (see
Chapter 6, pp. 174–5).

We have seen above (Chapter 1, pp. 17–18) that the third-century opposition between the conception of a large, patiently educating 'mother church'
and the ideal of a small but convinced 'community of saints' was most visible
in Africa. In the words of Kraft, the African Church was always marked by
'the contrast between the active, enthusiastic piety that urged to martyrdom
on the one hand, and the efforts to regulate this piety by tying it down to the
Church-institution on the other.'[29] We also saw that Diocletian's persecution,
although of short duration, was severe in the territories of his western
Augustus, Maximian – that is to say, in Italy, Spain and Africa. As early as
305, the Numidian episcopate undertook a purge to eliminate those members
who had contaminated themselves in some way during the period of trial.

When the Bishop of Carthage underwent a house search by the police, he
had handed over some books, heretical books, as he later said. Since Cyprian's
pastoral classification of the lapsed, this was considered a minor betrayal of
the faith and such a person was called a *traditor*. The Numidian purifiers
suspected the Bishop. But things got worse when, after the Bishop's death,
the Carthaginian clergy consecrated a certain Caecilian as his successor,
without waiting for the arrival of the Numidians. These provincial bishops
felt slighted once more by those of the capital: they made common cause
with some local malcontents and chose a house priest of their group to be
Bishop of Carthage and, automatically, the Primate of the Diocese Africa.
They declared void Caecilian's consecration on the argument that one of the
consecrating bishops had been a *traditor*.[30] The counterbishop was soon
replaced by Donatus of Casae Nigrae, a small town in the deep south of
Numidia. He became the real leader of what gradually expanded to an ardent
religious movement and, before long, to a full organisation, the *Donatist
Church*.[31] It is clear that Donatus' followers did not expect the really devoted
and true Christians to be found in the Romanised Carthaginian area and that
the small towns and villages of the Numidian hinterland would become their
stronghold.

As soon as Constantine had taken possession of the whole west and set out
to restore freedom for the Christian cult, he found himself confronted with

the unpleasant fact of African Christianity being divided into two hot-headed camps. When he gave orders to distribute public funds to the Church, there were two bodies claiming to be the rightful beneficiaries of the subventions. Constantine had to investigate which of the two was the genuine Church of religious zeal and martyrdom. His concern was not only to give public money to the right heir, but also to reunite the two factions as soon as possible. Now that he had opted for the Christian God, an internally divided Christian community was most inconvenient, since a schism would diminish the number of the worshippers of the one and true God; it also would scandalise the pagans and strengthen their position.

Thus, Constantine had enough reasons for a drastic attempt to reconcile the parties. On the other hand, according to traditional Roman thought, the cultic domain was sacred and the Emperor's responsibility was rather to guarantee unimpeded worship than to intervene in questions concerning the legitimacy of priests. He therefore decided that the Church itself should settle this discord and that he should only offer the facilities. The Donatists asked for arbitration by Gaulish bishops and Constantine called three of them to Rome, where Bishop Miltiades took the lead.[32] The Emperor hoped that his own role could be limited to the application of an impartial sentence, pronounced by this small arbitration committee, and that it would become clear which head of the African Church he had to do with, Caecilian or Donatus. The Donatists hoped that a better-informed state would grant them the exemption of taxes, which initially had been given to Caecilian's party.

The Roman Bishop thwarted Constantine's plan. He invited fifteen Italian bishops, thus arranging a meeting which had the character of a synod, rather than of an arbitration committee. Since the days of Cyprian, there had been a disagreement between the Church of Rome and that of Africa about the necessity to rebaptise heretics and the lapsed who turned back to the Catholic Church: the Africans used to rebaptise, the Romans only laid on hands. An agreement had never been reached. But now Miltiades used the occasion of a new controversy in Africa to settle the old one in his sense. The Donatists held to the African tradition: in their view no ordination or sacrament could be valid when it was administered by someone who was not pure (because he belonged to a false church community, or was a lapsed, or even ordained by a lapsed). Such a cleric had first to be rebaptised and readmitted to his ministry by a new imposition of hands. By making the Roman practice the criterion of the cause, Miltiades succeeded both in confirming the legitimacy of Caecilian and in persuading the Africans who held communion with him to adopt the Roman practice.

Donatus incurred a formal condemnation. The Donatists rightly felt that they had not got justice and called anew upon Constantine. This time the Emperor reached out for a more energetic step in order to restore harmony in the Church: he summoned the bishops from all the provinces over which he ruled to a council, to be held at a neutral place, Arles, in the summer of 314. Arles was the capital of southern Gaul and it had good road-connections in all directions. The bishops were allowed to travel on the imperial mail coaches and they were lodged at public cost, which was quite an experience for them so soon after the persecutions.[33] But once again the ecclesiastical company did not comply with Constantine's wish of negotiations with the Donatist party for a settlement. The Catholics already possessed a style of dealing with heretics and schismatics: they simply had to submit! The bishops at Arles proved not willing to revise the previous sentence on the Donatists; they even confirmed the Roman practice of readmission, rejecting the African custom.[34]

Constantine had not obtained what he wanted, viz., unity of the Church through its own wheels. Reluctantly he took the affair in his own hands. He ordered an investigation by state officials and when they came to the same conclusion as the Arles synod, it was up to himself to pacify the African diocese by forcing the Donatists back to restore communion with Caecilian. This they fiercely refused. Constantine wrote to his governor in Africa: 'I will show those people which and what kind of worship should be offered to the Godhead.'[35] A new kind of persecution was the consequence: that of a separated Christian group by a Christian emperor. For the first time, the State made use of the weapon of removing a bishop from his see. The army was deployed. The State started to be a factor in a dispute between Christians and Christians, who both regarded themselves as the true Church. As the measures against the Donatists also made victims, they considered their community all the more as the true and faithful Church, remaining in the typical African tradition of Christian radicalism and willingness to suffer martyrdom. Constantine faced the fact that he could not succeed in suppressing the Donatist opposition. In 321 he gave up his efforts, turning his attention to the east, where the increasing tensions with Licinius demanded greater alertness (see above, p. 33).

The results are the following:

- Constantine had to tolerate two Church communions in the African diocese; he probably accepted this inconvenience seeing that Donatism did not spread outside the area.
- Constantine had involved himself in the internal questions of the Church: he threw his weight into the scale in order to reconcile opposing parties; if one or both were stubborn, he was obliged to put one of them in the right.[36]
- The instrument of reconciliation was the council, which would bring together representatives from all over his territories and would meet at the Emperor's initiative and costs.

We will see how Constantine continued on this way as soon as the newly conquered east confronted him again with a church splitting up because of controversies, this time of doctrinal nature and even more serious (see Chapter 4).

The Christianisation of public life

Constantine never proceeded to an active persecution of the pagan religions: he allowed them to endure, but they were deprived of their traditional function of assuring the Empire's welfare. This vital function was from now on assigned to the Christian religion. The God of the Christians had proved to be the real ally and patron of the successful Constantine, who therefore committed himself to spread Christian worship all over his realm. Soon after the decisive victory at Milvian Bridge, he started to translate his faith into concrete measures for the promotion of the Christian religion and its liturgical life, as well as of its moral standards, which should from then on determine the conduct and conscience of all. Part of these measures was the promulgation of new laws. They can be divided into two groups:

1 laws to repel paganism and to promote Christianity;
2 laws turning ethical Christian principles into 'rules of right conduct'.

Privileges for the Christian religion

It was above all in the area of public legislation that Constantine felt himself God's instrument for promoting the true religion. His ultimate goal was to bring all his subjects to this religion, however, not by constraint but on a voluntary basis. Thus, as we saw, as soon as he had brought the west under his authority, he ordered to render and restore church property. He dispensed clerics from orderly duties to which civilians could normally be constrained. The Church was allowed to have untaxed property and to receive donations, even from the State. We also mentioned the fact that on Sundays Christian soldiers were obliged to attend church services and that their still-pagan colleagues had to pronounce a monotheistic prayer. In 321 the Sunday was declared a day of rest for everybody.

In the army, helmets and standards were fitted with the *Christogram*, an emblem that gradually replaced the earlier *Staurogram* (see above, p. 36).[37]

Some pagan temples were closed down, notably when their obscene cult practices were hurting Christian moral principles. Public funds were no longer available for the construction of new temples.[38] Private fortune-telling by means of examining the intestines of a sacrificed animal was forbidden. Since private gatherings practising this kind of oracle-finding could be hotbeds of plotting against the Government, this prohibition might have had political rather than purely religious grounds, for public oracles in relation to the interests of the State were admitted.

With regard to the Jews, conversion of Christians to Judaism became liable to punishment; conversion in the opposite direction, however, was stimulated.

Bishops received the authorisation to administer justice in civil lawsuits between Christian laymen; cases among the clergy had to be dealt with by a synod. Internal hearing of cases was usual, since up to then Christians had every reason to be afraid of the official administration of justice in their respect. The sanctioning of this custom imparted further prestige to the bishops, notably since their verdicts were declared indisputable.[39]

Another Christian custom received legal validity: the release of meritorious slaves, provided that it happened by a formal act and in presence of the congregation.

Legislation in conformity with Christian ethics

His conviction of having the mission to bring his subjects to the cult of the one, Supreme Godhead, and to help the Church to be the leading religious community in this respect, also motivated Constantine to promulgate new laws. He wanted public life to reflect some of the sacred ethical principles of the Christian religion. We point at the most significant ones.

Crucifixion as death penalty was abolished, as well as the disfigurement of faces by branding. The motivation may well have been of Christian inspiration, since the cross was 'sanctified' by the execution of Christ and the human face was a particular sign of man's being created in the image of God.[40] Ten years later the gladiator fights were officially prohibited. From Tertullian onwards Christians had manifested their aversion to this kind of popular amusement because of its bloody character. It is certain that, in spite of this interdiction, these popular fights continued to be held. If the measures had no immediate effect, the result, nevertheless, was a gradual humanisation of society.

The laws that were promulgated in order to protect marriage and children had a more positive effect on morality. The old inequality before the law of the unmarried and the childless was abolished. This was also a recognition of the Church's high esteem for the voluntary celibate. Other new laws were introduced in order to counter easy divorce,[41] concubinage of married men and the high number of children born out of wedlock. In order to protect these children, the killing, selling and exposure of children, so current in the Roman world, were made liable to punishment. The State not only inflicted punishment but also gave social help in order to prevent parents in need from disposing of their children. All those measures reflect the Christian conception of the holiness of marriage as a God-given institution and the belief that children, just like adults, were endowed with a soul created by God.[42]

Constantine started as soon as he could with the adaptation of Roman state laws to some principles of Christian ethics, which were obviously known to him. A certain humanisation was introduced, though not across the board. Without being on his guard not to antagonise pagan circles and public officers – his sense of having a divine mission was too strong for such timidity! – he did not transform the State all at once. There was contradiction in his own character: mild and respectful on the one hand, cruel and ruthless on the other. He probably had to find out, both in state affairs and in himself, how a Christian emperor should be and how he had to rule.

The Christian monarch

Constantine's victory over Licinius enabled him to extend this religious policy to the eastern territory. Here too, he maintained tolerance for non-Christians but recommended the Christian faith.[43] The idea of piety in itself presupposed freedom of choice in religious affairs. But he increasingly made use of his means to spur his subjects on to recognise the same truth as he had done. He considered it an obligation to 'persuade his subjects to worship God [and to] reform the wicked and unbelieving.'[44] In a letter to Alexandrian church leaders from 324, Constantine declared to have deduced two main charges from his office as emperor: for one thing to 'uniform the religious strivings of all peoples', for another 'to heal and bind up the so to say wounded body of the earth.' He was convinced that 'the State would achieve happiness, if he would succeed in bringing about concord among all God's servants.' He was confident to find in the church leaders 'conductors for the peoples' salvation.'[45]

We may say that in the beginning of the fourth century a religious emperor took the lead in Christian 'contextualisation'. Constantine gave evidence of an open eye for changing contexts. At the same time he created a new context for Christianity. We summarise the main aspects.

First, Constantine adhered to the traditional conception of religion as 'state-sustaining' ideology. He was also dependent on the basic Latin thought of religion as a system of duties to be fulfilled for promoting public welfare. But, contrary to his predecessors in the tetrarchy, he turned away from any attempt to revive the old Roman religion, holding instead great hopes of the Christian religion. This faith had proved its capacity to be a religion for everyone and its ineradicable strength was proof that it was pleasing to the highest and mightiest god of all. Moreover, it seemed to converge very well with the philosophical and popular monotheism of the epoch. In his view, the attempt of the tetrarchs to destroy the Christian community and its worship was a religious and (consequently) political miscalculation.

Second, Constantine shared with his predecessors the idea of having a divine mission to save the Empire. This was another main feature of his religious conviction. The success of the past years had corroborated his assurance of being the elect instrument of the Supreme Godhead, and both convictions shaped his personal theology. When he connected it with the Christian God, this 'mission' became charged with two new elements:

1   He had the mission to combat religious errors and to propagate the truth about God and the way he must be obeyed. Constantine did so through prudent legislation; but he also presented himself as 'pious'. He saw God's action not only in the cosmic order, but even more in concrete historical events. He believed in retribution within the field of history – God punishing wicked rulers with a miserable fate and blessing the pious emperors.[46]

2   When against all expectation 'error' manifested itself within the Church, he felt called upon to combat it there as well. This happened when the African Church split into two communities. His actions, however prudent at first, pushed him to impose authority and decision-making. He also came to learn the persistence of the ideal of a pure church of saints (see Chapter 1, pp. 17–18). The Church as communion, covering up internal diversities and sensitivities, was a new context for an emperor, who had committed himself to its harmonious spread. This situation obliged him to decide which of two opposing groups represented true Christianity.[47]

The first opposition against this intervention of the State in the affairs of the Church came from the Donatists. It was not a very fundamental resistance, since they had first tried to win Constantine's support and obtain his funds. But when the bishops outside Africa had spoken out against them, both in Rome and at Arles, old and typical African traditions of a pure community of faith, surrounded by a hostile world, surged up again and led them to criticise the Catholics who made an alliance with the State.[48] Before long, the Church would gain another experience with the interventions of an emperor who had committed himself to promoting its strength and unity.

3   The Church Fathers assess the change

Introduction: three voices

We now turn to the Christian side in order to examine the first reactions to the victory of an emperor willing to favour and promote the Christian religion. In this chapter we will pay attention to three authors who represent the generation of those who witnessed the unexpected turn from persecution to privilege.[1] Though succeeding each other in age they experienced the radical changes of the epoch in overlapping periods and they reacted to these in their publications. By their writings they join the ranks of early Christian apologists, i.e., of those authors who set out to prove the fundamental truth of the Christian faith. Their argument often contained a strong plea with the authorities to acknowledge the positive contribution Christians were making to Roman society, in spite of their being marginalised, arguing that they could do even more if they would be given a free hand. It is therefore logical to assess the first reactions on the Christian side to the changing religious policy by paying attention to writers who belonged to this specific tradition.

Lactantius was born in Africa before 250. The Emperor Diocletian called him to his residence in Nicomedia as Professor of Latin Literature and Rhetoric. He lost his job when the persecution broke out in 303 and for several years he disappeared from public life. Back in the capital c. 310, he witnessed the tolerance granted to the Christians in 311 by Galerius and the full freedom laid down in the Declaration of Milan of 313 (see Chapter 2, pp. 32–3).

Eusebius, born c. 263 in Palestine, became bishop of the important see of Caesarea soon after the persecutions.[2] He spent nearly all his lifetime in Palestine, with the exception of a short period of refuge in Egypt and of imprisonment there when the last persecution, launched by Maximinus Daia, was raging (311–13).

Athanasius, an Egyptian, was born in 293, but was already an adolescent when he witnessed this final attempt to oppress Christianity. The Bishop of Alexandria, Peter, lost his life. Athanasius became a deacon under Peter's successor Alexander and succeeded him as bishop in 328. From that year till his own death in 373, he was the head of the Egyptian Church and played a crucial role in the doctrinal controversies which are the subject of the next chapter.

What these three authors had in common was not only that they were witnesses to the most violent and systematic persecution of early Christianity and the struggle for political power that brought an end to it, it was also the fact that, during some time in their life, they were in direct contact with Constantine himself. It seems very likely that Lactantius and Constantine already knew each other when, as son of the Caesar of the far west, the latter was kept at the Nicomedian court as a hostage (until he found the means to escape and flee to his sick father in 305/6). In 317 Constantine summoned Lactantius to Treves as a teacher for his son Crispus.

Eusebius came into contact with Constantine in the preliminaries to the Nicene Council. Admiring Constantine, he won the Emperor's esteem as a great Christian scholar, to such an extent that on several occasions he was marked out to address Constantine in public on behalf of the Church.

As a deacon and personal secretary to his bishop, Alexander, Athanasius attended to the Council mentioned above and he may have met Constantine there. Soon after his consecration as Bishop of Alexandria, he became the target of two ecclesiastical parties that used every available means to get him removed from his see. Eusebius was prominent in the group which proved most successful in winning Constantine's support against Athanasius. Just like his adversaries, Athanasius sought to obtain the Emperor's sympathy and to convince him of the falseness of the charges against him. At first it was he who was successful. But finally Constantine confirmed the dismissal of Athanasius, decided by a synod in 335 and sent him into exile at Treves.

In all three contemporaries of the Constantinian turn we see an attempt to find a theological interpretation of the events that seemed to confirm the successful spread of the Christian message in the Roman world. They evaluated the unexpected events and tried to explain what they meant in relation to God's dealings with humankind and how the great changes were to be seen as demonstration of God's victory over his adversaries.

Lactantius merits our attention as the last apologist to have written during the years of the great persecution, without knowing how this trial would end for the Church. His principal work, the *Divine Institutes* (seven books), is a response to pagan literary charges: Lactantius counter-attacks the pagan religions and philosophy and then expounds Christ and his teachings as true wisdom and justice. He shared current conceptions on the connection of true insight and just action to such an extent that he actually Christianised paganism. After the year of freedom and peace, 313, Lactantius wrote *On God's Anger* and then *On the Deaths of the Persecutors*.[3] Dealing mainly with the period from Diocletian to Constantine, the work on the wretched end of the persecuting emperors is the first Christian 'theology of history' written in Latin. *On God's Anger* laid down the basis for the view that God's hand can be seen in historical events by presenting God as zealous defender of justice.

Eusebius of Caesarea became a true apologist under the weight of the circumstances. He wrote his first apologetical work after Diocletian had started the purge of the army and the public service. A second, voluminous work appeared when imperial legislation had almost paralysed the cult of the Christian assemblies.[4] Most important is the double treatise, the *Preparation for the Gospel* and the *Proof of the Gospel* (respectively in fifteen and twenty books), written between 312 and 322. Tolerance had now been granted, but the situation of the Christians in the east was still far from secure. Moreover, the intellectual world was being presented with the most learned and fundamental pagan attack on the Christian beliefs, launched by the philosopher Porphyry. Pillorying Christianity as incompatible with civilisation, this well-informed literary work was offering a dangerous ideological incitement to persecution. Eusebius felt obliged to write an elaborate reaction. In the *Preparation*, he defined the position of the Christian faith and community in relation to Greek religion and philosophy, in the *Proof*, its relation to Judaism.[5] The *Theophany*, a popularised defence of the Incarnation, shows Eusebius' mature views; for this work he made use of his earlier apologies, giving them a more theological setting.[6]

However, Eusebius was not an apologist in the traditional style. Basically he was an exegete and a biblical theologian who used the results of this discipline as the basis of a comprehensive framework of world history.[7] Eusebius became the very first church historian. Before the outbreak of the persecution in 303, he had written the first seven books of his *Ecclesiastical History*: starting with Jesus, the work originally ended with the peaceful and promising period of tolerance that began in 260. Afterwards he added three more books: Book VIII deals with the persecutions until the Edict of Tolerance in 311.[8] Books IX and X finally describe the rise of Constantine until his victory over Licinius in 324.[9]

Eusebius should be understood as living in three highly distinct periods: a time of tolerance, the great persecution, and after the Constantinian turn. He was in his forties when the trial fell upon the Church and he kept a memory of the peace it had known during four decades. Bewildered by this sudden hostility from the State, then by Constantine's conversion, his victories and support of the Church, Eusebius saw his earlier optimistic view of history confirmed. His *Panegyric to Constantine*, a laudatory speech delivered at the *Tricennalia* in 335, the thirtieth anniversary of Constantine's accession to the rank of *Augustus*, was an occasion to applaud the blessings of Constantinian reign. He embroidered this speech with long parts taken from the *Theophany*. After the Emperor's death, Eusebius set himself to write a *Life of Constantine*, and this work may be considered as the final book of the *Ecclesiastical History*.

In several respects, Eusebius' production is comparable with that of Lactantius, but it has a much wider scope and reflects a greater theological erudition. This was not in the last place due to his great indebtedness to the Origenistic tradition in which he had been brought up.

The events of the time may have pushed Athanasius to write the double treatise *Against the Gentiles/On the Incarnation of the Word*. It is generally classified in the category of apologetic writings, though its catechetical tone should not be overlooked. In this work, the triumph of Christianity is already presupposed, but it shows a fresh memory of the courageous attitude of the last martyrs. The refutation of Greek polytheism and moral depravity as well as of Jewish religion is rather traditional and does not show much 'contextuality'. Some scholars hold that Athanasius deliberately composed the treatise as a counterpiece to the *Theophany* of Eusebius, because in the first half of *On the Incarnation of the Word* he develops a theology of the Incarnation and its healing effects that is neatly different from Eusebius' views on the matter. For that reason it has been supposed that he worked on his treatise in his exile years at Treves (335–7), when he had been evicted, whereas Eusebius rejoiced in the Emperor's high esteem. Others have found reasons to think that it was composed in Alexandria in the 320s. Recent research points to a date between 330 and 335 as the most likely moment.[10]

We shall present these three theologians in the above-given order and limit ourselves to the titles that have been mentioned. In a final section we shall draw some comparative conclusions.

Lactantius

Lactantius is the oldest of the three witnesses to the events that changed the position of the Christians in the Roman Empire. Imbued with the philosophical spirit of the age as well as with the Latin conception of justice, he adapted current ideas to biblical thought. By attributing the functions of the Roman 'family father' to God he made room for the emotions of anger and compassion in the conception of God that had been so heavily coloured by the axiom of impassivity. This move paved the way to present God as interfering in recent and contemporary events: the fall of the tetrarchy, led by ferocious persecutors of the Church, and the rise of a protector in their place. Exposing how the persecutors came to a bad end, Lactantius intended to demonstrate the execution of God's judgements on the wicked and the pious through revolutionary changes.

Congeniality with Constantine

Like many other intellectuals of his milieu, Lactantius had known no sudden conversion but rather a gradual transition to Christianity. In the second half of the third century the Church effectively met the religious longings of pious and philosophically trained people of education. Here they found a doctrine based on Revelation and a communion 'which was both obliging and assisting'.[11] These minds had often been prepared by the edifying philosophy of Platonism, which taught that true knowledge and veneration of God are the goal of human life. Lactantius shared the conviction that a correct insight into the truth of one supreme and perfect Godhead was important, since such a knowledge would bring forth a serious lifestyle; it would also prove a shield against the demons, who were always out to confuse the mind and to cause moral depravity. This linking of knowledge and insight with virtue proves that Lactantius' conception of religion was essentially Roman. He was indeed a native of Africa, but a Romanised African and indebted to the ethical ideals of Cicero. His 'Platonism' was practice-oriented. He also shared the optimistic conception of Divine Providence: since God was one and perfect, he was supposed to lead human history and to prove himself by observably recompensing of both the pious and the wicked.

The fact that they shared these basic outlooks shows that Lactantius and Constantine were spiritually congenial. They both shared the climate of philosophico-religious enlightenment, being at the same time indebted to the typical Latin conception of religion as a set of duties which will be recompensed. To some extent, these conceptions belonged to the sphere of the epoch, notably the enlightened monotheism. Lactantius, being his senior by thirty years and, as we have said, official Latin professor at the eastern capital Nicomedia, some direct influence upon Constantine may be assumed for the years preceding the persecution and his escape to his father's headquarters. Once Constantine had seized full control over the west, this influence became manifest as 'the decrees and speeches of Constantine showed such a principal conformity with Lactantius, that this can hardly be coincidental.' Even 'the strictly theological basic thought of Lactantius largely fell in with his [Constantine's] own aims in religious policy.'[12]

However, Lactantius was a philosophically trained theologian and not a politician with only popular monotheistic ideas. We must therefore ask how he introduced genuine Christian doctrines and values into this contextual way of thinking.

Lactantius as an apologist

The *Divine Institutes*, this last voluminous apology of the Christian religion before the Constantinian turn, was written at the time when Lactantius refused to comply with the decrees of Diocletian, his employer, and consequently lost his job as professor.[13] The motivation he gave for this sacrifice is a mixture of philosophical asceticism and Christian hope: one ought to manifest a low opinion of wealth and accept to suffer, looking to the heavenly treasure that awaits the faithful.

In this work, the central notions are those of truth and righteousness, which both unite the humankind with God. From a structural point of view, this point of departure joins the pagan connection of true insight with pious worship and good actions. The Christian element is found in his emphasis upon divine revelation as an absolute condition for attaining knowledge. The human mind is not, by itself, able to attain the ultimate truth, which is so close to God and which only comes from him through his words and actions. Although the relation with the Divine is inherent to our being, it is God himself who must pave the way to authentic knowledge of him and of our own nature. Christ, therefore, is the unique teacher of true religion and virtue. The kind of righteousness, produced by this revealed knowledge, also receives a biblical substance, which replaces the traditional Roman and Stoic virtues. Instead of man's own correctness and imperturbability, social virtues, such as mercifulness, are in front.

God's revelation is attainable to all men without distinction. The apology is at the same time a canvassing of all those who are prepared to acknowledge the evidence of this message and to embrace the prospect of inheriting the highest goods as recompense for a life according to the God-given instructions. True wisdom manifests itself in this way. This surely is self-evident for everybody.

Such are the transitions between late-antique and Christian elements of thought. Although Lactantius confessed to be in need of the Spirit of God in order to acknowledge and to expose the Truth, a great deal of his material is from pagan origin.[14] The phenomenon is described by Haendler in these words: 'Once more it becomes visible, to which extent Christian and Roman thought were converging, notwithstanding the heavy conflicts just in those years!'[15]

Lactantius' view of history

Another heritage of classical, especially Greek, thought was the belief that God is above all emotions and passions to which human beings are subject and which disturb their faculty of level-headed action. God was considered as the opposite of human nature and his character could only be described by attributes put in the negative. God must be impassive, free from all passions. Such a conception, however much it expressed respect for God's 'otherness', was difficult to combine with the biblical representation of a God who loves his creation, goes in search of his creatures rebelling against him, and takes the risk that his Holy Servant or Beloved Son be rejected. How could a merciful God be represented as impassive? Origen had already wrestled with this problem.[16] Lactantius, too, felt the need to correct the current pagan image of a god without emotions and to defend the scandalising biblical anthropomorphisms such as anger. The God of the Bible apparently shows affections and, therefore, had to be 'defended' for that. To argue his case, Lactantius took another element from the cultural pattern of his time, viz., the generally accepted role of the *pater familias*. A good father will make himself respected as the head of his household; he has the obligation to be righteous, i.e., to be severe and eventually to punish. Anger is part of that. Pagans should not be astonished to hear about this attribute, since it is inherent to the true lordship of God and not incompatible with his goodness.

In this way, Lactantius attempted to make acceptable biblical expressions that could scandalise pagan mentality. This effort converges with one aspect of contextualisation: translating the Gospel into ideas familiar in the socio-cultural context. However, a further step in contextualisation is made when contemporary history is interpreted and 'claimed' in order to corroborate the sake of the true Faith. Lactantius' treatise *On God's Anger* paved the way for the view that God had also played a role in the events of the persecution and the struggle for power won by Constantine.

The work *On the Deaths of the Persecutors* was written between 313 and 315. In these years the west was ruled by Constantine who protected and promoted the Church, whereas in the east Licinius' stance did not inspire the same confidence. In this work Lactantius did not strive for philosophical persuasion, as he did in the *Institutes*, it is rather 'a triumphant demonstration of the way in which recent events have illuminated the operation of divine judgement in human history.'[17] Lactantius wrote as a passionately participating observer, full of prejudices and resentment, particularly with regard to the tetrarchies led by Diocletian and by Galerius. He 'describes with a wealth of lurid detail the horrible deaths of the persecutors of the Church'.[18] The atrocious deaths of the persecutors by slaughter or disease are presented as the outcome of the vengeance of God, who conversely has protected his pious and righteous servants, Constantine above all. Through the punishment of the enemies of his community on Earth God reveals his greatness. It is a kind of application of the Deuteronomistic view of history, theme and form being rather Jewish and Christian than classical.[19]

On this view, the way of the Church is getting intimately connected with the fate of the Roman Empire which improved the position of the Christians. It also implies the assumption that correct theology can coincide with political success. There was a strong tendency to read off divine guidance from the 'conversion' of the mighty and the change for the better of God's worshippers. Von Campenhausen called the book a 'document of the growing political conscience of a Church called to dominate'.[20]

Two striking implications of this way of interpreting the historical context

The speed at which the Christian self-consciousness turned over is quite surprising: instead of feeling like strangers in the world, called to stand and suffer for a Truth which is totally different from what the world is aspiring after, they hastened to embrace the perspective of reciprocal support and to link their mission with the fortunes of the Empire. Distance gave way to alliance, suspicion to confidence. Two main hindrances to accepting the Roman State appeared to have been removed definitely: the cult of the Emperor and the persecutions. The transition to an alliance with the State even seems to have taken place so rapidly that one could ask if there had been a kind of mental preparation. At the end of this chapter, we shall return to this question.[21]

In the second place, we observe a confluence of two conceptions of Justice, viz., the Christian and the Roman, the one ethical, the other political. The idea of Justice becomes the common base for Church and State. Since the One and sovereign God rules justly, he will protect both ethical and political justice, which have now come together in the person of the pious emperor. From this confluence originates the transference of the Roman representation of legal lordship to the Christian God. God's way of ruling is explained by means of the figure of the Roman *pater familias*, who cannot do without anger and compassion. Consequently it is as a universal family father that God exercises his authority over the world. Contextualisation has the effect that conceptions and images that are chosen to translate a biblical truth, viz., emotions in God, also transform this truth by the weight of their own specific connotations, in this case those of legal and severe authority over subordinates.

Eusebius of Caesarea

Being an involved eyewitness to three deeply contrasting fortunes of Christianity, Eusebius set himself to find assurance of and evidence for God's powerful lead. He interpreted the abrupt transitions of his days by looking for biblical models and for as-yet-unfulfilled perspectives. Trying to prove the rightness of the Christian religion he extended the argument to the field of historical events and evolutions. His underlying theological vision was that of a progressive restoration by the *Logos* of the relation between humankind and God, which had been corrupted by sin. Within this preconceived pattern of thought Eusebius could smoothly characterise the role of Constantine as a decisive step forward. The same theological presuppositions made him uncritical towards the precarious aspects of interference by the Emperor in Church affairs. This attitude became a legacy that disarmed the Church for the subsequent decades.

The shock of the Great Persecution

Palestine was the theatre of cruelties and courageous martyrdom during the decade of persecution raging under Diocletian and, after 305, under Maximinus Daia who, disregarding the tolerance ordered by his superior Galerius, continued the oppression of Christians till Licinius defeated him in July 313. Eusebius was not only an eyewitness to the tribulations the Church had to endure, he himself was also a victim: during the last upswing (311–13) he fled to Egypt where he was arrested. He knew many of the Palestinian martyrs, among whom, in the first place, his own teacher and benefactor Pamphilius (d. 309 or 310), who once had recruited him as his assistant for the maintenance of Origen's library and for research into his scholarly legacy. On all his writings, Eusebius would add to his own name 'Son of Pamphilius'. The promulgation of imperial decrees against the Christians was a personal blow for Eusebius, who until then had rejoiced in seeing the Church prosper, increase and become socially accepted, even if it did not enjoy legal recognition. In that time of tolerance Eusebius had planned a cycle of seven books for the *Ecclesiastical History*, the last of which presented the peaceful period after the Decian persecution as a 'normal' situation, in which the world was making room for the Christian message. At that time Eusebius neither foresaw a Christian emperorship that would protect the Church, nor did he consider hostility as 'natural' concomitants of the elements of subversion the Gospel contains. Far from that: he presented his materials in such a way that Christianity has always met a positive response in the form of recognition and widespread adherence. 'Eusebius believed that God intended his Church to prosper on earth.'[22] In his view, it was not the acceptance of the Message that had to be explained, but the amazing fact of opposition to it. After the terrible decade had come to an end, Eusebius decided to continue the *Ecclesiastical History* by an account and an interpretation of this recent trial.[23] Before we look at this, we must dwell a bit longer on the philosophy of history that underlies the original plan of the *History*.

Eusebius' philosophy of history

Eusebius was not a disciple of Origen in a proper sense, since he was born nine years after the death of the master. Pamphilius was the intermediary, administrating Origen's library in Caesarea,[24] but he did not write anything himself. Through this channel Eusebius adopted three typical elements of Origenistic thought: (1) the method of biblical exegesis; (2) the positive but selective use of Greek philosophy; and (3) an ascetic attitude to life. But Eusebius did not merely repeat Origen, because he can never have inherited from him the stimulus to develop a theology of history, which must be seen as Eusebius' own significant contribution. Origen, indeed, had not really been interested in earthly history. In his view the creation of the material world was a punitive, pedagogical and consequently transitional measure of God, which intervened after the Fall of the spiritual beings. Salvation consisted in the restoration of the spiritual world and not in achieving a redeemed and purified material world. It is true that, in response to Celsus' charge of Christians keeping aloof from the interests of the Roman State and civilisation, Origen developed arguments concerning a proper Christian contribution to the welfare of the State and its emperor. He even said in that context that, thanks to the Christian mission, the enemies of the Roman Empire would become less barbarous and, therefore, cease to be a threat to the Roman order.[25] The idea of a progressive improvement of earthly society was not quite absent from his perspectives, but it appeared only in a late stadium and on the margin of his thought. For Eusebius, on the contrary, the Fall did not call forth creation but history. On the other hand, he rejected the perspective of chiliasm, i.e., the hope for an earthly millennium that would bring material compensations for what the faithful had been suffering or lacking during this life. We see Eusebius on the one hand distancing himself from a cyclic conception of salvation, according to which the temporarily embodied souls will return to God, and on the other from the apocalyptic idea of a sudden coming of God's kingdom which would interrupt the steady deterioration of history by Satan's actions.

Between these two orientations he held to an optimistic view of history. I do not suggest that Origen's theory of salvation was not optimistic, but – as Rebecca Lyman rightly says – Eusebius 'translated Origen's optimistic cosmology into universal history.'[26] Since Origen considered the material world and the soul's confinement to it as a preparation for the ultimate restoration of the spiritual world, his soteriological interest was indeed far more cosmological than historical. In his exegetical work he would always try to reveal the action of God in 'the slow transformation of the individual', and not so much in 'the public growth of the Church'.[27] Eusebius, likewise, nourished a fundamentally optimistic and pedagogical conception of God's salutary action in humans,[28] only the field of action is different! The real difference with Origen – we may say – lies in Eusebius' view of a continuous action of the *Logos* who shapes and reforms the world and through historical processes will establish his lordship on Earth. Rebecca Lyman presents Eusebius' way of thinking under the remarkable title 'Power and Progress'. The first term indicates God's action, the second the human one.[29] Origen's model of Divine Providence shaped Eusebius' view of a concomitance of God's guidance and human free will.[30] The *Logos* is the central agent of this divine action in man. Eusebius 'celebrated the miraculous will of God in history, which, through the teaching and incarnation of the *Logos*, altered human society and life for ever [. . .] not only at the individual, but also at the communal and social level.'[31] This means – and it is important to note it already – that his attention forcibly had to go out to 'demonstrations', to visible and convincing acts of God on the level of history.

Therefore, notwithstanding periods of backslide and crisis, history is progressing towards a higher and more adequate level of religion, viz., towards total communion with God. Historical events possess a meaning and purpose, and it is up to humans to investigate them in order to grasp their theological sense.[32] Kraft correctly formulates:

> In Eusebius, it is the *Logos*, acting in Christ and in the Church, who is shaping and spiritualising the world and so brings it to its completion [. . .] This formation of the world is the sense of history, which stretches from the first actions of the *Logos* to his final Kingship.[33]

Interpretation of contemporary events

In the philosophy of history which we described above, the Church must logically play a decisive and convincing role, since it is the foundation and instrument of the *Logos*. We have pointed out above that Eusebius started to present Church history as a success story, assuming that 'Christian churches had always been numerous, prosperous and respectable.'[34] It is important to note that this idea of success was not dependent on the privileging of the Church by Constantine: propagation and acceptance existed long before the great turn and this assumption of Eusebius coheres with his conception of history as I summarised it above. In the opening words of Book VIII, Eusebius speaks of 'the great honour and liberty which the message of piety towards the universal God, proclaimed to the world through Christ, was enjoying among all men, both Greeks and Barbarians, *before* the persecution of our days.'[35] The same image of 'honour and liberty' helped Eusebius to situate the victories of 313 and 324 in his overall conception of the activity of the *Logos*.

But then it was all the more necessary to explain the last persecution: why did God permit it to happen, now that Christianity had already made such a progress in becoming accepted by the Roman world? Eusebius put it down to dissensions within the Church. The ever-sharper decrees of Diocletian were God's successive warnings, but the Church appeared insensible to these signals. Eusebius drew a parallel between those dissensions and the Fall: in both cases the abuse of the free will had led to enslavement to the demons.[36] God had to permit a new castigation, but that could not discharge the perpetrators: they, too, deserved to be punished for their religious aberrations. But, when dissensions in the Church are so condemnable, the person who restores consensus is to be welcomed as God's servant. We will see how much indeed Eusebius applauded Constantine's actions aimed at unity in matters of doctrine, liturgical practice and Church discipline, to which end he convoked the Council of Nicaea. But at the moment when Eusebius took up the thread of the *Ecclesiastical History*, Constantine's victory in the west had just come about. At this time Eusebius could not yet think of a Roman Empire that would become a full ally of the Church, but only of a tolerant, yet still-pagan state.[37] That was the situation in which Eusebius had grown up and which he had made the guiding thought for the first version of the *Ecclesiastical History*.

The main polemical aim of Eusebius was to demonstrate the existence of 'an essential harmony or identity between Christianity and all that is best in Greco-Roman civilisation'.[38] This harmony had been the aim of most apologetic writers since the days of Justin Martyr. As such the issues of the *Preparation for the Gospel* and the *Proof of the Gospel*, viz., to present the Gospel as the complementation, correction and fulfilment of Greek and Jewish heritage and to mark Christianity's central position in relation to both, were not original themes. The originality and significance of Eusebius lie, however, in the following:

1   Never before had these arguments been exposed so broadly, attested with so much evidence and amplified by an explanation of roots and character of pagan, philosophical and Jewish religiosity. Eusebius constructed an overall view of history as a story of decline and rise of true piety, and in connection herewith of human civilisation.

2   His apology was not an abstract piece of scholarship but, in spite of its weight of demonstration, an appropriate reply to Porphyry, who had attacked Christianity with great knowledge of its written sources. It was 'contextual theology' in the sense that it met an urgent actual need.

3   The way in which he used biblical models to explain contemporary events was responsible for a theology in which direct lines were drawn from revelation to actual situations.

Eusebius put the whole range of actions of the *Logos* as well as the human answer in a comprehensive scheme of the historical course of 'religion'. After the Fall, a process of gradual deterioration had started leading to a widespread obscuration, manifest in primitive religiosity. Only a few particular persons responded faithfully to the revelation of the *Logos*: the Patriarchs of the Old Testament. They almost lived as Christians, even if they did not know Christ, i.e., the incarnate *Logos*. Moses was the last of them and he transmitted the Law, in order that the faith model of the Patriarchs should be preserved in the midst of the Gentile world and gradually spread among them, preparing them for the coming of Christ. But then the Jews rejected the *Logos* and kept to the Law in a spirit of exclusiveness. Eusebius states that they seclude themselves from the right understanding of the Scriptures, and he interprets the loss of Jerusalem and its temple as God's punishment.

On the other hand, the coming of Christ coincided with the establishment of Roman world rule. The Church, which then appeared on the historical scene, was called to Christianise the inner mentality and structures of Roman dominion and order. These two factors in world history, Christianity and the Empire, were, so to say, shaped for mutual harmony. Of course, not every aspect of Roman civilisation and achievement was fit for Christianity: paganism was still of vigour. But in the best elements of Graeco-Roman civilisation an essential harmony with the Christian revelation was latent and so the two were not at all incompatible, unlike what Porphyry had tried to prove.

However positive Eusebius was about the contribution of classical culture as preparation for the Gospel, he emphasised that the human mind can never do without divine revelation and enlightenment. Therefore, God has sent messengers in order to confer on humankind the illumination needed for true participation in the divine nature.[39] The *Logos* of God is the true agent behind those messengers and finally the greatest messenger, who leads the progressive restoration of humanity to its climax. This means that the pinnacle of all revelation, the Incarnation of the *Logos* himself, must naturally be followed by a progressive impregnation of all peoples and their social and cultural spheres. In a speech in the year 315, Eusebius said: 'The *Logos* elected for himself the souls of the supreme men in power and with their help purified the whole earth from godless and pernicious men as well as from the atrocious tyrants who were hated by God.'[40]

The role of Constantine in Eusebius' scheme of history

The figure of Constantine and most of his acts seemed to Eusebius to fit in with the aim and progress of God's dealings with the world as he saw it. We may distinguish four aspects:

1   Convergence of missions.
2   Evidence of Truth through historical successes.
3   A special mandate and relationship with God.
4   Constantine analogous to the *Logos*.

Convergence of missions

Like Origen, Eusebius held that the Church, as the universal community founded by Christ, essentially has a missionary and pedagogical vocation. For this universal vocation and shape the Roman Empire offered a beneficial framework. In his *Panegyric to Constantine* in 335 he says: 'The Roman rule and the "Doctrine of piety" sprang up together for the benefit of men.'[41] But the Empire's attachment to false religion had been an impediment to the propagation of this doctrine of salvation. Victory over the demons and over religious error had, in principle and reality, been accomplished since the incarnated *Logos* had accomplished his mission. Biblical promises with regard to the Church were on the way to realisation, but they still were not fully accomplished. But now the orbit of peoples, united in one empire under a single monarch, was conducted to embrace true religion, just as the Emperor himself declared in his speeches and by his decrees. Consequently, now must be the time of fulfilment, since the religious policy of this emperor so evidently converges with the mission of the Church. The Emperor has essentially taken on the same pedagogical and civilising task as God has imparted to the Church. Constantine gives fine examples of piety and self-command and is therefore suited to be the most effective world missionary.

Evidence of truth through historical successes

According to Barnes, 'the observable success of Christianity provided a theme which permeates all Eusebius' writings.'[42] In this success, Eusebius saw the evidence of the superiority of Christianity over both the pagan and the Jewish religions. The events of his time were his main argument for the cogency of the Christian faith. In a speech at the dedication of a newly built church at Tyre (315), Eusebius praised the cheering effects of the great turn in the following words:

> We now do know the 'strong hand and outstretched arm' [Ps. 136:12] of our all-good God and King of Kings no longer by hearing and telling words; but it is by deeds and with our own eyes that we see the credibility

and the truth of what has been handed down from old times, and this
allows us to raise a new song of victory.[43]

It is understandable that the successive victories of an emperor who supported
the sake of Christianity were regarded as the great turn in world history,
unfolding the salutary purposes for which the Incarnation of the *Logos* had
happened. Since the true aim of world history was no other than the establishment of the kingship of the *Logos* on Earth, it is no wonder that Eusebius
sometimes gives the impression that he considers his days as those of the final
rejoicing.[44]

Several scholars state that in Eusebius' view Constantine is no less than a
messianic figure, but others contest that he saw the first Christian emperor
in that light. Ruhbach strongly stresses that Eusebius assigned to the
emperors a merely instrumental role in God's designs, and that he did not
change this view with regard to Constantine. He states that 'Eusebius did not
assimilate the proper objectives of Constantine's religious policy, but only
interpreted the first Christian emperor from his own viewpoint, which was
that of salvation history, and thus remained true to his basic theological
conception.'[45] It was the epoch of salvation that Eusebius applauded, and
not the Emperor, because in his eyes the true actor is not a human person but
the *Logos*.

In my opinion, this is a forced separation which seems quite alien to
Eusebius' thought. Other scholars admit that Eusebius never taught an identity between Constantine and Christ but, because of the many parallels he
wanted to see between them, do not hesitate to say that Eusebius assigned to
the Emperor a messianic significance. Berkhof wrote: 'Constantine's victory
did not bring anything new, but it brings to light the victory of Christ [. . .]
Therefore one may say that for Eusebius Constantine has a messianic significance in so far that he was God's elect to actualise what in potentiality was
already achieved in the Theophany.'[46] The dominion of the *Logos*, promised
for a long time, rapidly approaches thanks to the piety of the Emperor. The
facts prove that his piety and obedience are pleasing to God and that this
explains the blessings he enjoys in every respect.

A special mandate and relationship with God

Eusebius fully approved of Constantine's conviction to stand in a special
relationship with God. He was not baptised until on his deathbed and, therefore, was no regular member of the Church, probably because it was admitted
that in his function he could never keep the ethical obligations that baptism
imposed on neophytes.[47] Another reason to postpone baptism may have been
that the Church had not yet defined a proper place for a Christian emperor as
a member of the community and that Constantine would not have accepted
the rank of an ordinary member of the Church, which meant to be under
episcopal control. But this evidently did not bother anyone, and certainly

not Eusebius. On the contrary, he concurred with the view that an emperor enjoyed a direct line of inspiration with God, who elected him to be his special instrument. Such a direct relationship had already been assumed for Constantine's pagan predecessors and there was no reason to think that it would be different in the case of an emperor who served the supreme Deity and, in Eusebius' words, was 'drawing his good qualities from God'.[48]

Another striking proof of the assumption of this special relation is given by Eusebius in the *Life of Constantine*, in which Eusebius reports that Constantine compared himself with the bishops, saying to a group of them: 'You are the bishops of those inside the Church, I should be regarded as appointed by God to be bishop for those outside'.[49] As the Greek words can also be translated 'inspector of the things outside', which could refer to the political realm, the significance of what he meant is under discussion. If he meant the political realm, i.e., the Emperor's authority in civil matters, this would include the Christians. What kind of control over them would then be left to the bishops? The competence to take disciplinary action against sinners or to administer justice?[50] It is unlikely that either Constantine or Eusebius conceived of splitting up the life of a Christian into a political existence under the supervision of the emperor and a religious existence under the authority of the bishops.[51] But the first interpretation is hindered by the fact that Constantine had gradually abandoned his earlier hesitations to interfere in typical Church affairs. He thought it his task to stimulate the commitment of the Christians and to reestablish unity when this was being undermined. To be sure, only bishops had competence to watch over the admission of new members to their community and to exercise church discipline. We saw in Chapter 2 that Constantine refrained from intervening in the sacral sphere of religion, leaving it to bishops to take decisions in matters of ministerial legitimacy. He acted that way in the Donatist quarrel. But at the Council of Nicaea he would no longer be so reticent. In the next chapter we will see him taking part in the theological debate, proposing solutions as if he were an expert, seeking for the common denominator and steering the discussion in that direction, but leaving the elaboration of a doctrinal formula to a conciliar commission. Once the decision had been taken, he put his force to its application. Eusebius proved grateful for this kind of imperial watching-over of the Church. According to his conviction, the Emperor bore full responsibility to see to it that all his subjects would live in the spirit of Christianity,whether they were Christians or non-Christians. Eusebius makes it clear that he, too, understood 'those outside' as 'all who are governed by the Emperor'. In this respect, the Emperor could issue and enforce laws that were binding to all his subjects without distinction. This, of course, the bishops could not do. He even could approach the Persian King Shapuhr II in order to conclude a treaty with him, and he did so since he felt obliged to extend his all-embracing care over the Christians on Persian soil.[52] Normal bishops could never have taken such a diplomatic step.

Considering this field of force, we can imagine what Constantine had in mind when he used the distinction between 'those inside the Church' and 'those outside'. At the same time, we must note an overlap of authorities, as far as the Christians are concerned, and a lack of clearly defined competencies between ecclesiastical and political leadership. Anyhow, Constantine has made it clear that, although there was no specific rank for him in the hierarchy of the Church, by virtue of his election and illumination by God he possessed an authority and a mission that the bishops had to recognise as equal to theirs. And Eusebius acquiesced wholeheartedly!

Constantine analogous to the Logos

Most significant is the laudatory speech Eusebius was deemed worthy to give in Jerusalem at the dedication of the Church of the Holy Sepulchre, when the thirtieth anniversary of the reign of Constantine was also celebrated. In this *panegyric* Eusebius developed the idea of a remarkable correspondence with the *Logos*/Christ. Under the pagan emperors, festal assemblies (*panegyris*) of this kind had already been usual. On such occasions, an official panegyrist would address the emperor on behalf of the assembly, mostly with a speech in which the emperor's person and the blessings of his reign were applauded in superlatives, but always in a religious language, i.e., referring to his divine protector. Constantine had heard several of such addresses from his early days as an emperor onwards, when he had not yet declared his adherence to Christianity. It is quite correct not to blame Eusebius for exalting the Emperor, since the model was given by tradition. One may even notice that, within the limits of such a speech on such an occasion, according to good Christian tradition, Eusebius emphasised the Emperor's subordination to Christ. Thus, he praises 'our emperor for understanding very well the fact that Christ is the origin of his emperorship', calling him 'the friend of the Logos-Saviour'.[53] What we should notice is not the fact itself of all the laudatory words, but the theology behind them, that is to say, the way Eusebius describes Constantine's relation to Christ and his salutary work. He is doing this by establishing a series of analogies of this kind:

1   The *Logos* reigns eternally with the Father – our emperor reigns for a long time.
2   The Saviour of all adjusts his universal kingdom to the Father – the Emperor adjusts his subjects to the realm of the *Logos*.
3   The Saviour of all judges the demons with his invisible divine power – his friend, the Emperor, restrains the visible enemies of Truth.
4   The *Logos* sows in his disciples the seed of reason and redemption – his friend, proclaiming God's will, exhorts the entire human race to embrace the knowledge of what is best and stimulates them all through the vigour of legislation on religion.
5   The Saviour opens the gates of the Heavenly Kingdom to the departed – he who zealously purifies the Earth from error invites holy and pious men

into his palace and is concerned with the salvation of the entire multitude of his subjects.

Eusebius continues in this way. He makes Constantine a true image and imitator of the *Logos*. Thanks to the virtues that dominate his royal soul, he has become a real sovereign, a copy of supermundane rule.[54] He is 'the one sovereign out of One, the image of the One Sovereign of all.'[55] Here we meet a particularly cherished analogy of Eusebius: the transition, at the religious level, from pagan polytheism to Christian monotheism is, on the political level, paralleled and caused by the passage from the polyarchy (the tetrarchy which in Eusebius' eyes was more an anarchy) to the monarchy. The sole monarch not only reflects the one heavenly monarch, but is also connected with the worship of the only true God, as its stimulator and guarantor.

Problematic appreciation of Eusebius

'Eusebius brought reassurance and evidence of the accessible purpose and power of divinity in a changing world.'[56] This correct but terse appreciation by Lyman points to the effect of Eusebius' theological headwork, 'reassurance and evidence', in addition to which one should specify that reassurance is the fruit of the evidence produced. Eusebius tried to explain embarrassing contemporary events by relating them to biblical parallels and promises, in order to attain (for himself and for his readers) the assurance that the fate of world mission and Church was still in God's hands. Whatever judgement must be pronounced on the outcome of his interpretative theology – and it is difficult enough to do him justice – it is true that his efforts have a strongly con-textualising character. He set out to discern God's continuous and progressive activity in the ups and downs of the Church and to convince both Christians and pagans of the elements of fulfilment in recent developments.

His basic theological presupposition was that from the beginning the *Logos* prepares the world's sanctification and return to God, operating by earthly means and under earthly conditions. This fundamental assumption explains why he was led by an optimistic view of history. His optimism, shaped in the decades in which the situation for Christians was propitious, was dramatically put on trial by the great persecution. But Eusebius did not lose his optimism and, therefore, it came back with renewed conviction when he saw how the mightiest submitted their fate to the God of the Church. With all his emphasis on the Theophany, i.e., the Incarnation of the *Logos*, he was pro-foundly fascinated by the Old Testament: not only because of the prophecies and figures that announced coming fulfilment, but also because it presents God as acting in and through history, both punishing and redeeming. All this meant that Eusebius was eager to discover new signs of progress and fulfilment and prepared to embrace enthusiastically an emperor who engaged the Church in his brilliant successes. Eusebius was certainly not a flat opportunist; he saw his theological presuppositions confirmed by what he witnessed, and he found many good arguments to fit the events of his days into his scheme of progressive realisation of the universal kingship of the *Logos*.

Constantine was pivotal in this scheme of thought. For Eusebius it was evident that the successful Emperor was actuated by zeal to conduct all his subjects to Christian worship and ethics, even when he did so gradually. The Church was invited to be his ally and why should she not assume this mission since it yielded her so many chances and privileges? The role Constantine assigned to the Church presupposed her vigorous unity. This was why he increasingly interfered in internal situations when he feared that they would compromise his ally in the eyes of the still-influential pagan circles and weaken her power. Constantine even had to make choices in the field of doctrine and to help to make 'orthodoxy'. And, however much it is true that not the theological debate but only unity and peace in the Church were of any interest to him, in order to achieve these he had to plunge into theology. So he did and he even acquired some expertise in the matters under debate.[57] All this together could only raise his prestige in the eyes of a man such as Eusebius, who was inclined to see nothing but blessings.

Eusebius was led by enthusiasm for this particular emperor and not particularly interested in drawing up a theory of the emperorship as such or in the relationship between the ruler and the Church. Only after Constantine's death, when he wrote his *Life of Constantine*, he may have meant to lay down the lofty principles that had guided Constantine's policy, anxious as he was about the future of that legacy now that the monarchy was again divided into three dominions. Eusebius could feel famous enough to do that job. In his eyes, the earthly monarchy was part and parcel of the mission of the *Logos*. Bringing to an end a period of anarchy and civil war, the monarchy established by Augustus had proved an important moment in the preparation for the Gospel. With Constantine, history was repeating itself, and this time the Emperor had not only restored peace, but also demonstrated to be a Christian. The polyarchy, which had always been a fine condition for polytheism, had been swept away to give way to the monarchy which, mirroring the heavenly monarchy, was the best condition for further monotheism as propagated by the Church. The existence of one supreme God justified the existence of one empire under one emperor, representing God's sovereignty; on the reverse, the glorious and autocratic style of the earthly emperor was gradually transferred to the heavenly monarch and shaped the image of God and Christ.[58]

In retrospect, it must be stated that Eusebius has contributed much to what may be labelled as the re-sacralisation of the (Christian) Emperor. This seems paradoxical, since the Christian Emperor step by step abolished the pagan cults, depriving them of their socialising and religious function. He acknowledged that he had received his mandate from the Supreme Godhead, whom he pretended to serve by piety and devotion, and no longer by the bloody sacrifices of old. There certainly was, on the one side, a 'demolition of the cult of the ruler'. But Aland, who used this expression, also concluded that 'the Christians took over the adoration of the ruler as representing the

Godhead.'[59] Eusebius wholeheartedly assigned to Constantine the position of mediator between God and all imperial citizens, in a way quite similar to the claims of the earlier pagan emperors. The pagan conception gave way to a Christianised mediatorship, but the old thought structure persisted and, as they inserted Constantine into a biblical thought scheme of promise and fulfilment, theologians who followed the line of Eusebius could hardly avoid re-sacralising the Emperor, having just applauded his desacralisation. It was probably against Eusebius' intention, but nevertheless thanks to him, that the theological appreciation of Constantine led to an ideology of the Christian emperorship which developed mainly in the east.[60] Seeing how Constantine offered a helping hand and, in a way, respected the internal autonomy of the Church, Eusebius could not conceive of a more prophetical and critical attitude. In particular after the Council of Nicaea he felt no discrepancy in being loyal both to his church and to his emperor.

Eusebius has been criticised for that by later scholarship. We will not go deeply into this discussion, but refer to two main positions. On the one hand, he has been denounced as 'the herald of Byzantinism', i.e., a Church–State relationship in which the first is docile and uncritical,[61] and as 'a political theologian [. . .] who prostituted theology to the questionable purpose of providing Roman universal dominion with metaphysical foundation'.[62] But other scholars warn against the application of modern criteria to Eusebius. They rather stress that he (and his fellow believers) faced a completely new situation, with which the Church had no experience and for which it had no reflection at hand.[63] Ruhbach, for instance, denies to Eusebius all political interest, but speaks so much in defence of our theologian that he factually accuses him of theological naivety and one-sidedness. It seems more appropriate to admit that Eusebius brought about happiness with the close alliance with the state power. He was blind to the negative effects such an alliance with this power could have to the Church, because he was caught in the theological presupposition of a progressive conduct of world history by the *Logos*.[64]

Athanasius of Alexandria

An age gap of thirty years separated Athanasius from Eusebius, and our third witness of the Constantinian turn outlived the first Christian emperor by thirty-six years. For one decade only Athanasius had to do with Constantine, and in the present chapter we focus on those years. In his apologetical writings he uses the example of an earthly monarch in order to elucidate monotheism, without reference to Constantine or to any historical event. He was confronted with Constantine's authority in a church-political contention. Athanasius developed a theology of the Incarnation which differed from Eusebius'. It became the base of his later strenuous struggle against his doctrinal opponents and, in the long run, against an emperor who strongly supported the latter.

Harmony and monarchy

Barnard states that up to Constantine's death Athanasius held a conception of the Christian Empire which scarcely differed from Eusebius'. He refers to *Against the Gentiles* 38 and 43.[65] In these chapters Athanasius intends to prove that there can be only one creator and sustainer of the universe. He points to the order and harmony of its many and different parts, invoking 'natural reason (which) knows well that superior to the multiple is the One and Perfect.'[66] Then he elucidates the argument from harmony which logically leads to the existence of one actor or chief, by means of three examples. The first is the city, where people live together peacefully, having equal rights and joining their professional activities in spite of their differences. Then he reminds the reader of the human organism, in which the activities of the different parts are coordinated and, last, of the harmonious sound of music, despite the fact that it is produced by the different strings of a lyre or the different voices of a choir. City life shows that it is coordinated by a governor and so the human body shows the activity of a soul, though both are invisible. In the example of the city, Athanasius refers to what he has said earlier about polytheism, viz., that it produces atheism: 'equally, it is inevitable that polyarchy implies anarchy'.[67]

These last words recall Eusebius, who linked earthly with heavenly monarchy. But that is all these two theologians have in common. Athanasius uses timeless arguments and he does not evoke concrete historical events. His example is not the Roman Empire but a random city. And for his argument that there is one God who in spite of his invisibility is obviously commanding and directing the cosmos, the political example does not have more weight than those of the body and the choir.

With more justification, one could refer to *On the Incarnation*, 27–32.[68] Here Athanasius brings out three arguments in order to prove the truth of Christ's resurrection. They are the contempt of death which Christians show in times of persecution; the spread of Christianity; and the impact on pagan society of the demonstration of the powerlessness of demons and idols. These arguments might implicitly refer to recent changes. But again there is no reference to any of the emperors who organised the recent persecution, nor to the role of Constantine with regard to the second and third proof of the triumphant lordship of Christ. Athanasius saw one parallel between the *Logos* and a lawful king: neither of them would tolerate his subjects to be under the power of a tyrannical intruder. But this argument again is an unhistorical one and, moreover, it is paralleled with two others of general validity. The argument of a vindicating king is also found in *On the Incarnation* 13, where it serves to prove the necessity of the incarnation: God is compared to a king who being just a man would nevertheless not tolerate the occupation of his territory and people by a strange ruler. For a certain time he had been sending dunning letters, but since this proved ineffective, he finally decided to appear in person.[69] None of these arguments and images does relate to one-off events of the author's days.

Negotiations with Constantine

If we must conclude that in his early work Athanasius did not interpret contemporary history but stuck to general parallels, we may ask if his dealings with Constantine in Church politics after the Council of Nicaea throw any light on his views regarding the new relationship between Church and State. This question requires a brief anticipation on the doctrinal conflict which is the subject of the next chapter.

The controversy because of which Constantine convoked a council was caused by an Alexandrian priest, Arius. The Council condemned his Christological theses and sent him into exile. But two years later Constantine summoned Bishop Alexander and the clergy of Alexandria to readmit Arius, whose revised confession of faith Constantine thought quite acceptable. Athanasius transmitted Alexander's refusal to the court. When Alexander died, Athanasius was consecrated bishop, but this caused some local discontent, which would soon be exploited by the opponents of the doctrinal decision of Nicaea. The uncompromising Athanasius held to the condemnation of Arius and his opinions. Both parties tried to win the Emperor's sympathy and support. Athanasius' opponents could hardly use theological arguments, since the decisions of the Nicene Council were Constantine's achievement; therefore, they launched personal attacks, trying to defame the inflexible Alexandrian bishop.

Athanasius on his part did the same thing: he tried to convince the Emperor of the falseness of the allegations against him and to impress him by means of personal visits. In the end, Constantine judged that he was a troublemaker, who did not rely on a majority, and he dropped him. This event justifies the conclusion that Athanasius did not dislike the Emperor's support for the position he thought to be the right one because of conciliar decision and sane theology. In other words, he opposed the Emperor only in so far as the latter did not maintain the decisions of his 'own' council. No less than the others, young Athanasius thought of a harmonious relationship between the Church taking its own decisions in episcopal assemblies and the Emperor defending the Christian faith and watching over the internal peace. The idea that a Christian emperor could either thwart synod decisions or even manipulate episcopal assemblies was a discordant phenomenon Athanasius did not foresee as long as the great Constantine lived.

A different theology of the Incarnation

In *Against the Gentiles*, Athanasius' demonstration of the 'way of truth (that) will lead us to the really existent God' follows the steps of the rational, immortal soul and the order and harmony of the universe as evidence for the *Logos*, 'through whom we may come to an understanding of his Father, God.'[70] Before passing to the second part of his treatise, he resumes his conclusions which concern 'the divinity of the Word of the Father and his providence for and power in the universe'.[71] The first quotation seems to indicate that Athanasius was treading in the footsteps of Origen and Eusebius, suggesting that knowledge of God is the result of an intellectual ascent from the human and the cosmological structures to the *Logos*, and then from him to the Father. The second quotation, however, announces what will appear to be Athanasius' most fundamental theme: the full divinity of the *Logos* in Christ. There are indeed several similarities with the apologetical arguments of Eusebius, but the vigorous stress upon the full divinity of the *Logos* should not be overlooked.

In Athanasius we find an important shift in emphasis with respect to the Salvation through Christ. He first explains that the restoration of what was lost by sin can only be accomplished by the same powerful and divine person who created the human being in his own image. The quality of being 'in God's image and after his likeness' (Gen. 1:26) had been given as a grace added to humankind's biological existence, which is naturally vowed to disappearance but now made susceptible to immortal life. When as a result of human carelessness this grace had been corrupted and humankind was (again) in the power of mortality, the *Logos* took upon himself human flesh in order to achieve two results: first, to overcome 'natural corruption consequent on death,'[72] second, to overcome mankind's 'total lack of understanding and knowledge of its creator'.[73] We see here an inversion of the salvific effects of the incarnation, the primordial renewal of God's merciful design for humankind being incorruptibility. The *Logos* did not assume human flesh merely in order to make his appearance, he assumed it in order to surrender it to death, so that 'as all die in him (2 Cor. 5:14), the intrinsic law of human corruption be abolished, since its power was concluded in the Lord's body and would never again have influence over humans who are his equals; and in order that, as humankind had turned to corruption, he might bring them back again to incorruption'.[74] The way to a restored communion with God is not primarily via illumination and revelation of knowledge, with piety and obedience as good fruits; it first receives an ontological basis by the fact that the Word of God offers his own sinless human nature in order to abolish the verdict on sin and to 'enter' into the realm of death, liberating from its power those he has made his equals by assuming human flesh. It is only in the second place that Athanasius deals with men's irrational fouling of their souls, which exposed them to the deceit of the demons, so that the knowledge of the true God became hidden. Like Origen, Athanasius sees the self-manifestation of the *Logos* as human among humans as the only effective reorientation towards the invisible God of religious search fixed on visible elements and forces.[75] He stresses anew that the restoration of accurate knowledge of God could never have been accomplished by an ordinary, or a particularly gifted, human being but only by him who himself is the Image of God.[76]

The 'demonstrative' aspect, so important in Eusebius, is, therefore, not entirely absent from Athanasius' thought. But it is part of an exchange between divine perfection and dynamics on the one hand, and of human deficiency and weakness on the other. By means of having his divine nature partake in the human condition, the *Logos* operated this exchange once for all.[77] The same words that Eusebius used for the relation of the *Logos* with God (*metadidonai*, to give a share in, and *metousia*, partaking in) Athanasius reserves for the gift of being 'in the Image', which God imparts to human-kind through the *Logos*, first at the creation and then as a result of the incarnation. With Athanasius, fourth-century theology was on the way to postulate an essential gulf between God and creation, which only a divine intervention could bridge.

Conclusions

We paid most attention to Eusebius: of the three, he was the theologian who made the most profound study to situate the transition of Christianity to the victorious side in a theological framework of interpretation. Eusebius has indeed proved to be a contextual theologian, who set out to assist his fellow believers to understand their time and to update their attitude. He shared the sentiments of triumph that pushed Lactantius to picture the political events as divine retribution, and Athanasius to adduce evidence for the reality of Christ's incarnation and resurrection. But above all, Eusebius saw the tri-umph as a 'natural' step in the comprehensive process of salvation that started with the Patriarchs of the first covenant. As he abandoned the apocalyptic scheme, his theology lay open to the idea of continuity and progress, demon-strable in evident and convincing landmarks. Although he is responsible for a 'theology of the emperor' with some grave consequences, he certainly focused on a broader horizon, viz., that of the religious ways of humankind. The totally unexpected and surprising character of the Constantinian turn is an excuse for the ready and eager embracing of the new alliance with Emperor and State. The Church, and even a scholar like Eusebius, had never thought of more than obtaining a de-facto tolerance.

However, the Eusebian construction tended to overestimate the over-whelming changes of the time, seeing them if not as revelatory by their own inherent meaning and message, then at least as keys to a better understanding of biblical revelation.[78] When too great a weight is ascribed to moments in world history, these may influence or even distort the understanding of the biblical message. The danger of such 'demonstrative' theologies certainly is that God's action is too exclusively linked with the visible progress and the social triumph of the institutional Church. An example of this is Eusebius' fascination for the 'monarchy' reintroduced by Constantine. He exalted this imperial monarchy because it fitted so well the scheme of restoration by the *Logos* of true, monotheistic religion among men through a historical process. Under his influence, Church and theology gradually lost their capacity to resist a ruler whom Eusebius, with all his broad knowledge of history, defined as a kind of saviour, invested with the divine mandate to promote true religion and civilisation. For the moment, contemporary developments indeed seemed to work for the better of Christianity. But what would happen when the Church was obstructed again in its ongoing theological reflection or even forced into a false direction by rulers who were following their own interests? Such events would inevitably affect the optimism in our theologians of Constantine's period, viz., their tenet that worldly support for Christianity and auspicious changes prove the truth of its faith. This brings us to the main crisis of the fourth century, the Arian struggle.

4 Defining Christ's relation to God

Introduction: two tracks of investigation

Constantine had bad luck. His wish to cement the unity of the Empire with the help of a united Church and to see the Christian religion become an efficacious substitute for the official cults, which were falling into desuetude, ran up against dissent in the Church. This led the Emperor to intervene more directly and deeply in the internal, in particular doctrinal, affairs of the Church. His sons and successors, above all Constantius II, followed the same conduct: they intervened no less than their father had done and influenced the process of doctrinal, viz., Christological clarification. All the time, ecclesiastical parties and bishops solicited support for the consolidation of their opinions and influence, and the willingness of the emperors to promote one group at the cost of another became no doubt a great temptation. On the other hand, the leaders who failed in winning imperial support gradually experienced the burden of the State's interference in theological issues and this helped them to reconsider the relationship of the Church with the Emperor and to develop a critical attitude. The general enthusiasm for Constantine gradually gave way to a new sense of identity and self-determination vis-à-vis the imperial power, but the way proved to be long and hard. The fact that the last emperor from the Constantinian dynasty turned away from Christianity and tried to restore paganism shocked all Christians. But Julian's reign did not last long enough, neither to crown his religious policy with success, nor to free the church leaders from their looking out for the powerful hand of the State. The only benefit of Julian's keeping aloof was that some important parties found ways to join each other and to discover common ground. Thus, the end of the Constantinian dynasty and era became the beginning of a new period and the present chapter consequently runs from the year of the transfer of power in the east (324) until the death of Julian (363).

The imperial rulers of the period we are dealing with are:

324–37: Constantine I, *sole monarch*

temporary subdivision

the east, 337–61: Constantius – the centre, 337–50: Constans
the west, 337–40: Constantine II – 340–50: ruled by Constans

350–61 *east and west combined under* Constantius, *sole monarch*

361–3: Julian, *sole monarch*

The above tableau implicitly shows the following proportion of strength: after Constantine's death none of his sons was strong enough to impose himself as ruler of the whole empire. After three years, the western emperor Constantine II tried to eliminate Constans but failed and the western prefecture was added to the centre. Up to the year 350 he was more powerful than his eastern brother, but then he was worsted so that Constantius alone remained in power, reuniting all territories into one empire.[1]

State and Church politics should not obscure our view of the *doctrinal dimension*. At the beginning of the fourth century, many questions about the nature and work of Christ were still undecided. The east, especially, was conserving the rich theological and exegetical legacy of Origen, but Antioch had its own exegetical school tradition. This left the door open for different approaches and accentuations. The conflict, which would dominate six decades of the fourth century, had started some years before Constantine invaded the east.[2] The theological reflection on this central issue followed its own dynamics, independently from the Emperor's meddlings, although he did not wait long to intervene as soon as he was confronted with the struggle. Neither the imperial policy, however much involved, nor the power politics of the important bishops suffice to explain the vehemence of the struggle. Every student of the fourth century should take seriously the theological positions that were at stake, since they always express a particular understanding of the salvation through Christ, in connection with the cultural and spiritual transformations. The political and the doctrinal tracks are intertwined and often cross over one another. It would be a mistake to see the one as only a by-product of the other. However much connected and confused, both lines and their respective dynamics should be discerned.

Since the doctrinal discussion had its roots in the period before 324, we will first pay attention to this level. This will enable us to answer in the end our fundamental questions about the contextualisation that has been brought about. A central question in this respect is the *making of orthodoxy*: was there already an orthodox conception of Christ, which just had to be adapted to the new context of the fourth century? If such was the case, the theological achievement would have lain in the fresh contextual expression of a traditional truth. The alternative is that orthodoxy was the result of a quest that absorbed unconventional insights but was edged with 'errors made by all schools of thought'.[3] In that case, the real achievement lay in a process of clarification, which obtained approval and authority only afterwards. Here we choose the second alternative. This line of investigation asks which were the new needs the achievement of an orthodoxy was satisfying? It will also help to indicate where decisive points have been crossed.

This chapter is divided into the following sections:

1   The theological and ecclesiastical situation Constantine was confronted with in 324.
2   The Council of Nicaea and the discord it left behind (324–40).
3   Progress in theological reflection under a twofold imperial authority (341–53).
4   Breakdown and resurgence of the Nicene Party (353–63).
5   Survey of the contextualisation process in the period 324–63.

The critical theological situation in the east and its causes

When Constantine entered the eastern provinces he was confronted with a seriously divided Church. Backgrounds of this doctrinal division go back into the final decades of the third century, since the Origenistic legacy, on the one hand, and the rejection of two extreme answers to the secret of the person of Christ, on the other, had left the Church with the question of the exact relation between the Saviour and God. Though rejected, these two answers continued to work as approaches of the Christological problem, departing either from the man Jesus as God's true servant or from a pre-existent divine being who had assumed human form. Those coming from the broad central line of Origenism proved able to incline to either of these approaches: 'left-wing' Origenists assimilated the *Logos* to a human being with an alterable nature and will, whereas 'right-wing' Origenists attributed to the *Logos* a shared essence with God the Father, which he preserved during his incarnation. A middle course held to the genuinely Origenistic idea of derivation (of the *Logos* from God), but showed sympathy for the left-wing group, because the opinion of the latter preserved the proper selfhood of the *Logos* better than the idea of his natural sonship.

Constantine's hopes and general measures

After Constantine had won his final battle against Licinius, he did not wait long to introduce in the eastern half of the Empire the same laws on religion he had promulgated before in the west. Religious freedom, social rank and confiscated land and property were immediately rendered to the Christians and their communities. Since he had taken possession of the provinces with the largest Christian population, he could lay off his previous caution and use 'every opportunity to stress the truth of Christianity'.[4] But he still refrained from coercion on pagans to pass over to the Christian religion. Since Christianity was being favoured to such an extent, a social urgency to embrace it automatically did its work.

Not only the Christian centre of gravity, but also the economic and military main points were in the east. Therefore, Constantine looked for an excellent site to build a new capital. The choice was fixed on Byzantium, a fishing port on the Bosporus, on the spot where the Asian and European coasts are most near to each other. An imperial residence there was near the permanent Germanic and Persian battlegrounds and it was situated at the crossing of the sea channel from the Mediterranean to the Black Sea and of the overland route from Italy to Asia. Diocletian had built his capital at nearby Nicomedia on the Asian side, but Byzantium was an ideal site to control the turbulent east. Without delay, constructions started in 324 and six years later the new capital was officially inaugurated as Constantinople ('Constantine city').[5] The city was modelled upon 'Old Rome' in order to have the prestige of being 'the second Rome'. It was, however, from the beginning provided with church buildings, of which the Church of the Apostles was the most important and beautiful. Twelve cenotaphs remembered the twelve who were sent out by Christ; a thirteenth empty sarcophagus waited for Constantine's body – the apostle of a new age and of equal success.

From his sense of a divine mandate and his high missionary expectations, it was quite logical that Constantine was annoyed when he found a divided Church: a hot theological dissent had started in Alexandria in 318 and had spread all over the eastern regions. Bishops opposed each other, communities were in disorder and pagans had a joke at their expense. Constantine was far from pleased by this humiliating spectacle and he immediately took action. As we will see, this conflict did not have its origin in matters of personal conduct, like in the Donatist quarrel in Africa. It was a theological conflict, touching at deep religious convictions about salvation. But initially, Constantine could not see it that way and, in a letter, he blamed the two Alexandrian protagonists for the futility of their disagreement. In his eyes it was just an academic dispute, injustifiably disturbing the unity of the Church, which is the basis of correct worship and concord between people.[6] To Constantine, only appropriate worship and the settlement of a Christian public order through legislation were of importance. But his adviser Hosius, Bishop of Cordoba (Spain), whom he had joined to his court and brought along to the east, soon made him understand that this was not the way to handle the affair and that he had to go deeply into the theological issues which were at stake. Circumstances persuaded the Emperor that this would be the only way to fulfil his mission of conducting the Church on the right path.

Theological situation at the beginning of the fourth century

The appreciation of Jesus Christ as a divine figure who for the salvation of humankind had appeared on Earth was still open to different approaches and tentative definitions. Before the year 300, three extreme opinions had provoked repudiation by the mainstream Church and had been condemned by local synods. Synods used to communicate their decisions to other important

Christian centres so that in most cases a common feeling about important issues got established. These three definitions of the extraordinary and saving 'actor' in Christ were docetism, Sabellianism and dynamism.

Docetism, was the idea that, because of his divine nature, Christ could only have appeared in a non-real corporality. His 'body' was just the semblance of a human body, not susceptible to real humiliation and suffering. Or Christ himself must have been so distinct from the body that none of its experiences affected the heavenly person, who was only loosely connected with it. Docetism was found with Gnostics, to whom the presence of divine elements in the material world was a kind of accident.

Sabellianism was named so after a certain Sabellius, whose teachings were rejected in Rome under Bishop Calixtus (*c.* 217). Sabellius taught that the divine person, who had assumed human flesh, was not distinct from God himself. The title 'Son of God' was just indicating another stage of God's self-revelation. This Christology fitted strict monotheism but was incompatible with all those texts in the Gospels that speak of Jesus addressing God as 'his Father' and of his wrestling to remain true to his mission. After Sabellius had returned to his native country Cyrene, his doctrine resurged there *c.* 260 and started influencing Egyptian minds. Though officially condemned, Sabellianist thinking continued to be attractive for some bishops in the fourth century. It corresponded with the way in which Christ was worshipped in liturgy and experienced as divine Saviour. This type of thinking is often characterised as a 'Christology from above'.

Dynamism is the name given to the opposite extreme, and it was equally monotheistic. But it approached the extraordinary in Jesus starting from his humanity. According to the dynamists, the *Logos* is God's outward-directed force and wisdom, a force identical with himself and without a proper personality.[7] This *Dynamis* has been active at all moments of the history of Salvation, but did most specifically so in Jesus because of his outstanding moral union with God. The man Jesus proved himself 'Son of God' since he allowed the Spirit or Virtue of God to take full possession of him and to act through him. This doctrine was rejected in 268, when a synod in Antioch condemned Paul of Samosata, who was no less a person than the bishop of that city. The feeling was that the dynamist conception did not sufficiently mark out Jesus over and against Moses and the Prophets, since they, too, have been 'inhabited' by the same force, be it to a lesser degree. Dynamist Christology also embraced so-called adoptianist views, i.e., the idea of Christ's sonship as result of progress and reward of his perfect obedience. It can be typified as a 'Christology from below'.

The positions of Sabellianism and of dynamism were officially condemned. Yet they persisted as basic approaches to the problem of Christ's relation with God, and during the fourth century they reappeared again and again in new tentative formulas. But for the moment we have to point at a large middle course of Christological reflection and definition with *subordination* as a common feature. Its characteristic is the hierarchical conception of the relation of God and his *Logos*/Son. In Egypt, Palestine and elsewhere there was a strong legacy of Origenistic theology. Origen had taught an eternal generation of the *Logos* by the Father, the Scriptures presenting him as God's Image. In Origen's thought this meant that the *Logos* is the single and only true Image of God (constantly expressing himself in his direct image), but at the same time the transition to the many logical beings, which are only *in* God's image.[8] He is the intermediary, so to say, the first 'step down' from the One and Highest to the plurality of other beings. This conception of the place of the *Logos* in the whole cosmological framework fitted with the Middle Platonic vision of the world and its subsequent strata, stretching down from the purely spiritual Being to the low level of matter, from the One to the confusing diversity of corporeal existence. *Emanation* was the basic structure of this world-view. Origen did not shrink from defining the *Logos*/Christ as 'our second God', which was exactly what Sabellius and Paul of Samosata sought to avoid. But Origen did not mean this in a numerical way, as if Christians believed in two Gods next to each other: he saw a direct derivation of Christ from God and an essential unity between the two divine persons in their distinction. In his view, monotheism was not at all imperilled.[9]

Subordinationist Christology left room for Christ as a person distinct from God the Father and yet uniquely related to him. This type fitted most the cosmological and anthropological views of contemporary Platonic thinking. Nevertheless, the hierarchical and emanational concept came to be under the pressure of a growing conviction, both in philosophical and in theological thinking, of God's transcendence over against all secondary and created being. In the Church, the debate on the consequences of this changing presumption was provoked by the teachings of an Alexandrian priest, whose name Arius became that of a long-time and vehement struggle.

The Christology of Arius

Arius (256–338) was of Libyan origin and under Bishop Alexander (313–28) became a priest at the Church of Baucalis in Alexandria. Because of the city's largeness, priests enjoyed a greater liberty to advance their opinions in sermons than they had elsewhere. Arius took this opportunity and by the year 318 he had a large constituency, composed of people from different social classes. We shall first look at his doctrinal views and then see why this priest found supporters from many sides.

In order to understand Arius, two contexts to which he was indebted should be discerned. The first is the thought frame of Middle Platonism. The concept of a chain of emanations linking the One and Highest with the lower and diverse beings was leading to the awareness that finally a deep rift separates God from all the rest. The expression of this awareness was a theology of negations: God is absolutely transcendent; nothing can be stated about him if only that he is not like us and not like the intermediary beings who fill the gap between the 'Only one' and the 'Plurality', which is the gap between spirit and matter. In Christian terms, this rift distinguishes God essentially from creation. He alone is 'Unbegun', not conditioned by anything outside himself and, consequently, eternal and immutable. Now the question arose whether the *Logos* belongs to the divine or to the created level of being. Were he uncreated, this would imply the existence of a Second Principle, in every respect equal to the first, i.e., equally 'unbegun' and immutable as God the Father. But this assumption was vulnerable because it appeared as a contradiction in itself, for there can only be one single unconditioned principle. If one would say that the *Logos* is a creature, that would lead to the consequence that, against scriptural evidence, Christ was not truly the Son of God but one who shared creational instability.

The other context that has shaped Arius' thought was that of the school of Lucian in Antioch that Arius had attended *c.* 280. Here the students were trained in methods of literal exegesis. Arius' attention was, therefore, drawn to those texts in the Gospels that present Christ as inferior to God – as his servant who had to fight Satan and to remain obedient to the Father's will, and who admitted not to know God's sovereign decisions.[10]

Scholars differ on the question whether Arius' Christ is conceived from a metaphysical or from a soteriological concern. Gregg and Groh strongly defend the soteriological understanding of Arius.[11] Hanson confirms that 'one cannot understand the former until one has grasped the latter'.[12] Both, however, recognise in Arius a metaphysical axiom, viz., that God cannot have a direct contact with the material or with suffering and, consequently, needed 'another'.[13] At this point the two motives converge.

Arius' Christ was a created *Logos*, embodied in a human flesh without a rational soul. According to current psychology of the soul as the vitalising and steering force of the body, Christ's body was inhabited and conducted by the *Logos* instead of by a soul. This means that Christ had the same faculty of thinking and willing as anybody. Only in him, it was the *Logos*, and that made some difference since the *Logos* is God's first and most perfect creature. Like all subsequent creation, he had been created by an act of God's will. As there can be only one Unbegun, he had no common nature with God and was, consequently, neither eternal nor immutable. As a matter of fact, Arius clearly stated that God is without anything equal or similar or worthy of the same honour.[14]

Arius liked to combine all this into the slogan: 'There was a time when he did not exist'. He even taught that God always had his 'proper' *Logos*/ Wisdom, but that this property was not identical with the Word or Wisdom he later created in order to create all other things through this external intermediary. His key text was Proverbs 8:22 where Wisdom says: 'The Lord created me at the beginning of his work, the first of his acts of old.' If the Scriptures call Christ God's Son, he argued, this must be the recompense of his faithfulness. But, since Christ presented himself as 'Son' before he had completed his ministry, Arius took recourse to God's foreknowledge: God knew that Christ would be faithful and gave him the dignity of Son beforehand.[15] Arius 'conceived of all of Christ's major titles, including even that of "Son", as proleptically given by virtue of God's foreknowledge. Thus, Christ's titles and highness were dependent upon his fulfillment of the path of obedient sonship'.[16]

It was, indeed, essential to Arius that this faithfulness by a creature made Christ our forerunner on the way to the sonship of God, a way that every person can go. This is why Hebrews 12:2 calls Christ 'the pioneer and perfector of our faith'. Being a creature and, consequently, of changeable nature, he had an alterable will like all humans. Arius attached great importance to this freedom of choice, which made the incarnated *Logos* susceptible to moral advance and growing steadfastness and, thus, of recompense with the rank of 'Son'. Not that Arius ever thought of the possibility of a failing, disobedient Christ; God would have known that. Only theoretically he had the freedom not to fulfil God's will.[17] He therefore truly deserved the dignity that God had given him beforehand. It was a common assumption of both Arius and his later opponents that mutability is inherent to all created nature and goes hand in hand with moral changeability.

Gregg and Groh consider it the 'constructive' side of Arius' Christology that he laid so much emphasis on Christ's sonship as recompense for his faithfulness. This should be acknowledged over and against the usual complaints about the denial of a truly divine subject in Christ. The Arian redeemer is, indeed, 'one of us' and, at the same time, 'more than we', since God has given him the grace to pave the way of adoption. But these authors have to admit that such a redeemer 'was not entirely unique' and that he, rather, was a 'representative creature'.[18] Arius' construction clearly leads to a Christ who is neither fully God nor fully human, though he possesses some attributes of both. Other inherent weaknesses of his Christology are the distinction between Word/Wisdom as God's eternal property, on the one hand, and the Word/Wisdom that God has used as his instrument in creation and salvation, on the other. The other inconvenience is the hermeneutical trick of explaining the scriptural references to the sonship of the *Logos* as proleptic reward for the faithfulness he still had to prove during his life on Earth.[19]

In spite of these inconveniences, Arian Christology did appeal to many, to dockers as well as to high-class ladies, to fresh converts as well as to Origenist bishops. They either appreciated the pure and logical monotheism with a created 'servant of God' acting in the external works of creation and redemption,[20] or welcomed the strong appeal to the human free will for the sanctification of life. Arius was an ascetic offering himself a fine example of sobriety and steadfastness. He and his followers went on the streets of Alexandria (his parish church was near the docks) and asked average people whether, in their opinion, Christ had been unchangeable like a stone or able to fulfil his mission by free will. The numerous converts from paganism to Christianity were probably attracted by the cosmological structure that was familiar to them, whereas the picture of Christ as God's faithful servant, rewarded with divine sonship, resembled the ancient representation of a divinised hero.

Arius popularised his central thesis with rhymed slogans. No wonder that the spread of his ideas alarmed Bishop Alexander, who held a different opinion of the person of Christ.

Opponents and supporters

Alexander's hermeneutic reading of the Scriptures resulted into a differentiation between two kinds of sonship: a natural one, which is by 'property of nature', and one by adoption, dependent on moral advancement. Contrary to the latter, the first is not subject to changeability. The adoptive sonship is the result of both 'fitness of character' and 'free gift of God', and, as such, it is 'changeable'.[21] Alexander stressed the biblical descriptions of Christ as the Image of God (Col. 1:15), 'reflecting the glory of God and bearing the very stamp of his nature' (Heb. 1:3) and the prologue of the Gospel according to John: 'the Word was with God, and the Word was God' (John 1:1). He drew the conclusion that Christ as the 'Word [that] became flesh' (John 1:14) could not have had an essence inferior to the Father's.

On the basis of the same separation between the Unbegun and all that had once come to exist, Alexander drew the conclusion that the Word must belong to the creative and not to the created side of the ontological rift. He has not been created but begotten by the Father. Alexander modified the Arian thesis that God alone is the Unbegun into the statement that he is the only Unbegotten. Two almost identical Greek words: *agenètos* (unbegun) and *agennètos* (unbegotten), which so far had not been distinguished in philosophical language, now became a means to make a distinction between what Christ as Son shares with the Father and what not. He is equally eternal and unbegun but not unbegotten. Over and against Arius, this means that there has never been a time when the Son did not exist, since everything, including time, has been created through him. But the Father is his origin and eternal begetter. In order to explain an eternal fatherhood, reference was made to the sun, because it constantly originates its radiations. The idea of God, always expressing himself in his son, image or radiation was found in Origen. But the more flowing transitions from higher to lower being, which characterised both his view on the world and on the way of salvation, were now replaced by a sharpened dualism, which necessarily urged the theologians to situate the redeemer either clearly on the divine side or on the same level as the rational creatures. Exactly this opposed Alexander to Arius, though to a large extent they were both heirs to Origen.

Alexander excommunicated Arius and his Egyptian partisans, viz., five priests and six deacons of the Alexandrian clergy and, moreover, two bishops of Cyrene, Arius' native area. Convinced of the congruity of his teachings with those of most eastern bishops, referring first of all to Eusebius of Caesarea, Arius sent a letter to another Eusebius, who had been his fellow student in the Antiochene School of Lucian.[22] He complained of being 'unjustly persecuted by our bishop Alexander'. The appeal to the other Eusebius, rather than to the famous bishop of Caesarea, was not without reason: his college friend was occupying the see of Nicomedia, the residence of Emperor Licinius. But at that time, Licinius no longer protected Christianity and forbade the assembling of synods, and the interference of bishops in the Egyptian conflict could spread like a savannah fire. Eusebius, an ambitious intriguer, did not wait long to side with Arius: in 319 Alexander wrote to all bishops (in the east) to defend his decision and to protest against the meddling of Eusebius, whom he criticised as someone who thought that all church affairs hang on him. As bishop of the capital, Eusebius took pleasure in importuning the mighty head of the Egyptian-Libyan Church.[23] One year later, Arius and his partisans canvassed for support by publishing a confession of faith. Provincial synods in Bithynia and Palestine, i.e., in those regions that stood under the leadership of the Nicomedian and the Caesarean Eusebius, approved this confession and blamed Alexandria for its unjustified dismissal of Arius. Such was the situation when Constantine took possession of the east.

Eusebius of Caesarea supported Arius as well. He certainly did not agree with all Arius' theses. In the following decades, it would become characteristic of the 'Arian party' to be a rather occasional alliance of those who, in one form or another, rejected the idea of a shared essence of the Father and the Son. Palestinian Eusebius was the first to take Arius' part on theological grounds. When dealing with Eusebius' theology of history (see above, Chapter 3, pp. 54, 56) we saw his soteriological emphasis on the world-embracing and continuous activity of the *Logos*, both in his pre-existence and his incarnation. This activity is mainly that of a universal 'instructor', but his instruction is not thought of as merely external: by the power he deployed during and after his presence on the Earth, he has achieved real transformations in the souls of men as well as in the social and political sphere. The start and the example of this moral improvement have been set by 'the dominance of (the) *Logos* over (his) body'.[24] Eusebius does not refer to a human soul of Jesus, but sees the *Logos* as the vitalising power of his body. But instead of ascribing the human characteristics of Christ to the created nature of the *Logos*, by which Arius could explain Christ's imperfections, Eusebius stressed that the human body does not detract from the qualities of the *Logos* as the *Logos* of God!

Here we see a clear difference between Eusebius and Arius. The biblical titles Word, Wisdom, Power and Will of God point at an essential unity between the Son and the Father. But – as Lyman says – 'he is not this on his own, but only from the Father.' And she concludes that the truly unique relation between the two divine persons is not one of 'shared essence' but of 'derivation'. The Son is not created like all the rest; he is a second God, directly derivated 'from the first, with an emphasis on separation and likeness'.[25] This sounds genuinely Origenistic and, to a certain extent, Eusebius was more traditional than were left-wing Origenist Arius and right-wing Origenist Alexander. But Eusebius was so far post-Origenistic that the emanationism of the master had yielded to a voluntaristic approach: God wanted an image of himself to be his servant in creation and salvation, not as a mere agent but in a unique relation to himself. The Son is not a separate person because of an ontological axiom; he is so by intention and choice of God. In spite of his indebtedness to Origen, Eusebius could not keep out of the general climate of a sharpened distinction between the two kinds of being, unbegun and created. Thus, he accentuated an essential identity, but at the same time tried to maintain a subordination of the *Logos*. Lyman therefore judges Eusebius' Christology as half and half: 'Because the Son was not fully divine, he was unable to divinize, and because the flesh was only an instrument, genuine human obedience was impossible.'[26]

The definition of the *Logos* as product of God's will, as universal instructor and as subject of the sanctification of his own body, must have been the reason for Eusebius' sympathy for Arius, even though by his Origenistic conservatism he would not agree with Arius' most extreme assertions. He repudiated both provocative theses that 'there had been a time when the *Logos* did not exist' and that 'he was created out of non-being'. Instead he held that the Son was 'begotten before all ages by a process beyond man's understanding'.[27]

The Council of Nicaea and its aftermath (324–40)

Constantine's method of solving discord in the Church was the assembly of bishops, since most of the leading opinion-makers were now of that rank. However, the views of an Alexandrian priest on the nature of Christ caused a vehement debate among the eastern bishops, which had already escalated when Constantine came to power there. He convoked at Nicaea an assembly of 300 bishops, preponderantly easterners, and urged them to adopt a formula that could unite the largest possible majority. A few recalcitrants were dismissed, but even these Constantine tried to have reintegrated after some time. The conflict blazed up again. Finally, Constantine switched to the side of the supporters of Arius and sent his main opponent Athanasius of Alexandria into exile in Gaul. As this exile effected the involvement of the western church, by the year 340, the 'Arian crisis' was affecting the whole Church.

The Council and its resolutions

Constantine's prompt reaction to the Christological controversy in the east was – as we have said – an admonition to the Alexandrians not to disturb the Church and the faithful by a sophisticated dispute about details. He sent his adviser Hosius to the main centres Alexandria and Antioch to deliver his blame and to size up the situation. On the spot, Hosius must have understood the gravity of the controversy. As a westerner, he approved of Alexander's decision, recognising in his theology the Latin conception of one *substantia* common to the Father and the Son. In Antioch he assembled a synod, which, for the time being, excommunicated Eusebius of Caesarea and two other bishops until such time when a larger assembly would examine their opinions on Christ. This greater synod was planned to take place at Ancyra (modern

Ankara), but Constantine wanted to have it closer to his residence, and, thus, the bishops were convoked to Nicaea, situated 50 kilometres south of Nicomedia. He also placed on the agenda other issues that eventually would create further dissent.

In later periods, the First Ecumenical Council is frequently called the meeting of 'the 318 fathers'. The exact number of participants and voters is unknown. But the meeting had an overwhelming participation of eastern bishops and only six delegates from the west, one from each large area.[28] The Bishop of Rome did not attend. As for the Arles synod (314), the bishops were granted the facility to travel without charge on the coaches of the imperial post, and, arriving at Nicaea, they were lodged at public expense. The meeting was held in a palace of the Emperor, who acted as its host and gave the opening speech. He impressed the bishops by giving a special and respectful welcome to members who still bore the scars of torture incurred during the persecutions, which had been so cruel in the east.

The bishops felt that a totally different era had begun. They applauded the glorious Christian emperor as God-given, and most of them were willing to accept the steering role he intended to play. As Honorary Chairman, he did not directly preside over the discussions (after all, it was a synod of the Church!), but many a time he intervened and admonished. The first ecumenical council of the Church was an invention of the first Christian emperor and it was supposed to come up with his wishes for unity and peace. This 'imperial' character was to endure as long as east and west held common councils.[29]

As there were no clearly defined positions but rather a multiplicity of individual opinions and nuances, Constantine's intention was to bring together the largest possible group of one mind and to compel the others to assent. Only a few bishops had a good theological basis. Prominent among them was Eusebius of Caesarea, whose first concern was, of course, to have the provisional excommunication of Antioch removed, so that he could participate as a member in his full rights. He therefore submitted the confession of faith of his community, saying that this was what Caesarea had believed since apostolic times and to which he concurred. Without allowing any discussion, Constantine judged it sufficiently correct to readmit the influential man, whose cooperation he eagerly wanted. Thus, Eusebius got his rehabilitation and he could deliver a speech to the Emperor to thank him on behalf of the whole church. After a long and vivid debate, in which Constantine took an active part, a commission was charged to elaborate a formula, which he urged the members to adopt as the common faith of the Church. To this 'Nicene Creed', a number of anathemas were added, in which the provocative theses of Arius were explicitly repudiated. This meant that Arius was condemned and exiled from his church, and so were two bishops from Arius' native region Cyrene. Eusebius of Nicomedia and Bishop Theognis of the council's host town Nicaea were also exiled, not because they refused to sign the creed but because they made contact with Arius and his companions. We already know that Eusebius of Caesarea, moved by his admiration for Constantine's efforts for the protection and the unity of the Church, signed both documents, yet felt obliged to explain and justify his vote before his confused community.[30]

Here are the Eusebian confession and the Nicene Creed:

Eusebian confession	Nicene Creed
We believe	We believe
in one God the Father almighty, maker of all things visible and invisible	in one God the Father almighty, maker of all things visible and invisible
and in one Lord Jesus Christ, the <u>Word</u> of God,	and in one Lord Jesus Christ, the <u>Son</u> of God, begotten from the Father, only-begotten, <u>that is from the substance</u> [*ek tès ousias*] <u>of the Father,</u>
God of God, light of light, only-begotten Son, <u>first-born of all creation, before all worlds</u> begotten of God the Father	God from God, light from light, <u>true God from true God</u>, begotten <u>not made, of one substance with the Father</u> [*ou poièthenta, homoousion tôi patri*],
through whom all things were made;	through whom all things were made, <u>both in heaven and those on earth;</u>
who for our salvation was made flesh <u>and lived his life among men</u>, and suffered,	who for <u>us men and</u> for our salvation <u>came down and</u> was made flesh, <u>entered humanity</u> and suffered
and rose the third day and ascended to the Father and shall come <u>again in glory</u> to judge the living and the dead.	and rose the third day, ascended into heaven, is coming to judge the living and the dead.
And we believe in <u>one</u> Holy Spirit.	And in the Holy Spirit.

The anathemas define more precisely:

> But as for those who say that there was a time when he was not, and that before he was begotten he was not, and that he came into being from things that were not, or who affirm that the Son of God is of a different subsistence or essence [*hypostaseôs è ousias*], or created, subject to change or alteration, them the Catholic and Apostolic Church anathematizes.[31]

The underlined words indicate the mutual divergences and the additions in the Nicene Creed. It is important to note that Eusebius' expressions 'Word' (*Logos*) and 'First-born of all creation before all worlds' were judged insufficient to exclude an Arian interpretation and have, therefore, been replaced by 'Son', by the statement that he is truly God and not a creature and by the repeated affirmation that his being (or substance[32]) is from God and the same as God's. In the anathemas, Arius' favourite theses are easy to recognise. No distinction is made yet between 'subsistence' and 'essence' (*hypostaseôs è ousias*), a parallelism that was to create much confusion and discord afterwards.

Two council resolutions validated for the entire Church what the west had already decided: no rebaptism of heretics (see Chapter 2, p. 39) and an indulgent treatment of the lapsed (see Chapter 1, p. 18). Another decision made an end to the celebration of Easter on two different dates and another enhanced respect for the clergy. All these decisions fitted Constantine's endeavours to unify and consolidate the Church. The council ended with a banquet, hosted by the Emperor. He judged that 'some persons had shamelessly blasphemed our Saviour, our Hope and Life; in defiance of the divinely inspired Scriptures and the holy Faith'.[33] Constantine had understood that the crisis, provoked by Arius and Alexander, was not about philosophical futilities, but about something deeper: the understanding of Christ and of salvation.

An anti-Nicene opposition gets the upper hand

Constantine granted to the Nicene Council validity that did not exist before. By a decree of 326 he declared heresy illegal. This meant that the State obliged itself to suppress the doctrines that had been anathematised by a synod, above all when the assembly had been enacted under the supervision of a high state official and the Emperor himself had been present. But, as we will see, the Emperor reserved to himself the right to keep an eye on the application of the council's resolutions and to verify the decisions of subsequent synods. This meant that those who felt themselves the doctrinal victims of the exclusions formulated by the Nicene Council could not, with any hope of success, attack the creed itself. What they could do, and actually did, was to hand in professions of faith, by which they intended to prove their basic conformity with the creed, in the hope to be reinstated in their functions. Another weapon was to attack their opponents on the level of their moral conduct in order to make them undefensible. As a matter of fact, the aftermath of Nicaea shows a period of struggle in which theology was hardly at stake, far from it: opposing parties solicited the Emperor's favour – a situation that the strong interference of the Emperor had made more or less unavoidable, both for the soliciting party and for the Emperor himself.[34]

Thus, by 327, Eusebius of Nicomedia and Theognis of Nicaea, and even Arius and his Egyptian companions, managed to convince Constantine that the faith they held was not incompatible with the Nicene Creed, though they attached to it their own interpretations. Constantine, who wanted nothing better than peace in the Church, was willing to allow the return of those who had been condemned and removed. A new assembly of about 250 bishops gathered at Nicaea in December 327 and annulled the dismissals. Eusebius and Theognis could reoccupy their sees. Profiting from his proximity to the court, Eusebius succeeded in eclipsing Hosius as adviser of Constantine and set out to assemble under his leadership all those who were dissatisfied with Nicaea. But Alexander of Alexandria refused to come and also refused to comply with Constantine's demand to reintegrate Arius and his friends into the Egyptian clergy. Alexander died soon after and, as the reader already knows, his young deacon and secretary at the Council Athanasius became his successor, though not without some local opposition. By the fact that Athanasius maintained the hard line of his predecessor, he became for many years the principal target of the Eusebian or 'Arian' party.

In 330, a synod met in Antioch. Eusebius of Caesarea presided over this meeting and managed to have Antioch's own bishop, the anti-Arian Eustathius, dismissed. He did so by accusing Eustathius of 'Sabellianism' (see this above, p. 73) and of moral depravity. Eusebius himself was nominated to take over the see of Antioch, but he refused, taking care that this important see would go to an outspoken pro-Arian. From then on, the attacks concentrated on Egypt. Eusebius' good fortune was that there was some opposition against the choice of Athanasius. By the end of the persecutions, something had happened that was similar to the events in Africa. A group of bishops and communities had accused the successor of martyrised Bishop Peter of lack of courage during the persecution, and they had chosen another, Meletius by name, as Bishop of Alexandria. They established a schismatic church and the Meletians were the Egyptian 'Donatists'. A doctrinal question was not at stake; it was just a quarrel about the moral qualifications for leadership. In the beginning, Arius had joined the Meletians, but a rupture followed this. Nevertheless, by the year 330, Eusebius of Nicomedia succeeded in matching these local Egyptian schismatics with the anti-Nicene opposition: more than any other, they should be able to provide him with details of misbehaviour of Athanasius that could be used as allegations against him.

The Meletians indeed reported several cases of violence to Athanasius' henchmen. It was said that when chasing away a celebrating Meletian priest from his church, the bishop's people had thrown over the altar and had broken the chalice of the Eucharist. It was even said that one of the Meletian priests had been assassinated by order of Athanasius; but the man in question, hidden in a monastery, was found and triumphantly brought out alive by Athanasius. Although Athanasius was still thwarting Constantine's order to readmit Arius into the Egyptian clergy, his ability to prove the falseness of these mean allegations rather strengthened his position. The ongoing enmity finally urged Constantine to convoke another council, which was to assemble at Tyre in May 335.

Knowing there would be a large Eusebian majority, Athanasius refused to attend. The synod sent to Egypt a commission of inquiry, composed of Athanasius' enemies. Meanwhile, Constantine summoned the bishops to Jerusalem for the dedication of the Church of the Holy Sepulchre – a state act to honour the crucifixion and resurrection of Christ – and for the celebration of his own thirty regnal years.[35] It was at that occasion that Eusebius of Caesarea pronounced his famous laudatory speech.[36] The members decided to admit Arius to their meeting on the basis of a new profession of his faith. Back at Tyre, they heard from the commission the evidence about the broken chalice and for this reason, and for the refusal to appear before the synod, they deposed Athanasius from his see and appointed another in his place.[37] But these decisions were only effective with the approval of Constantine. Therefore, a heavy delegation, including the two Eusebiuses, Theognis of Nicaea and two bishops from the Balkans[38] went to see the Emperor in his new capital, Constantinople. When they arrived, they found Athanasius already using all his influence to thwart the execution of the Tyre resolutions. Indeed, Constantine did not agree with the dismissal of Athanasius, who in his eyes still was 'a man of God'. The Eusebians had to play high: they told the Emperor that Athanasius had threatened to blockade the export of Egyptian corn on which the capital was dependent. Only then, Constantine, aware of the power of the Alexandrian 'pope',[39] concluded that Athanasius was a troublemaker and not the right person to represent the majority of eastern bishops. He exiled him to the out-of-the-way corner of Treves in northern Gaul. However, since he did not confirm the appointment of the chosen successor, it is probable that he only wanted to make Athanasius sing another tune.[40] When Constantine died on 22 May 337, having received baptism from the hands of Eusebius of Nicomedia, the situation was that those who, for one reason or another, supported Arius 'enjoyed a supremacy in the eastern Church which appeared almost complete'.[41] But Arius did not enjoy a triumphant reinstatement in Alexandria, where an outraged majority of Egyptian Christians continued to reject him.[42]

The western Church gets involved

Athanasius was kept in Gaul until 337. After the death of their father, Constantine's sons allowed the exiled to return to their posts. Athanasius was not a man to keep quiet about the reasons for his exile. He informed and involved the Bishop of Treves, went to see Constantine II, the ruler of the western prefecture (Britain, Gaul and Spain) and obtained from him a letter of recommendation. Then, on his way home to Egypt, he spent six months contacting Constantius, the ruler of the eastern Mediterranean, and potential supporters in the east. In Alexandria, a synod met, welcomed Athanasius as legal bishop and informed Rome. But Eusebius, eager to remain Bishop of the Imperial Residence and, thus, changing Nicomedia for Constantinople, expelling the legal bishop, organised a synod at Antioch (338/9). In presence of Constantius, the members deposed Athanasius anew and appointed in his place a certain Gregory, an undefiled outsider from Cappadocia. When the latter was actually enthroned under military protection, the situation became so oppressive for Athanasius that he fled Egypt and returned to the west.[43] Another anti-Arian bishop, Marcellus of Ancyra (d. *c.* 374) arrived there soon after. The same synod of Antioch had dismissed Marcellus, who was suspect since at Tyre he had refused to vote for Arius' rehabilitation.[44] We shall deal with him below because of his theological views which eventually would compromise Athanasius' position.

For the moment, Rome's bishop, Julius (337–52), received both. He considered the dismissal of Athanasius questionable in every respect, judging that it was incorrect and based upon false charges. He wrote to the eastern bishops that Athanasius and Marcellus had been unjustly dismissed by the Antioch synod and that their enemies had caused quarrels and schisms by not keeping to the decisions of the Nicene Council. He invited all to Rome for a new general council to settle the affair. The eastern bishops did not react before they had first organised their own internal meeting. It took place in early 341 at Antioch on the occasion of the dedication of a splendid church Constantine had ordered built. Athanasius and Marcellus had to wait in Rome for about a year and a half. The first used his time for writing an *Encyclical Letter*, in which he described in violent colours the injustices inflicted upon him; as well as letters to the Emperors Constans[45] and Constantius. Probably he also made a start with his great doctrinal work, the three *Orations against the Arians*.[46]

So far, the struggle that followed Nicaea had been about persons and their sees. But now Julius made faithfulness to the Nicene decisions a point, Marcellus' theology had been critically examined by old Eusebius of Caesarea,[47] and Athanasius assimilated the attacks against his own person with an abandonment of the adopted creed! As a result, the controversies turned again to a theological debate. Before dealing with this next phase of the struggle for a definition of Christ's relation to God, some remarks should be made about the actors.

Bishops on the front line

The result of the Emperor's meddling in the clerical and doctrinal controversies was that one party requested his support against the other. Bishops tried by all means to obtain from him the backing they needed to get rid of an opponent. Constantine expected the Church leaders to secure unity and peace. But they, the 'metropolitans' above all,[48] put him to inconvenience by their quarrels and forced him to intervene. When provincial synods became a regular practice, the metropolitan was their normal chairman and, owing to this function, obtained superintendence over the other bishops. We have seen the extent to which Alexander and Athanasius asserted themselves as heads of the Egyptian-Libyan church province and how their actions were crossed by Eusebius of Caesarea, Head of the Palestinian Church, and by his namesake, Bishop of the Imperial Residence. They all were well matched in appealing to the Emperor, Eusebius of Nicomedia being the most successful intriguer. As soon as Constantine had passed away, Athanasius did not wait long to involve the successors in his contest with the Eusebian party. The Emperor was caught up in a spiral that he had started himself. Constantine was all the more obliged to look out for majorities since he did not want to coerce the Church. All he did was to recommend, admonish, menace and, eventually, remove a clergyman from his function.

But other factors contributed to the importance of bishops in the controversies of the fourth century:

1   Their courageous example and responsible leadership in times of persecu-
    tion. When these were over, they continued to be determined, sometimes
    even aggressive, against their adversaries, whether doctrinal and factional
    opponents within the Church, pagans or Jews. On the other hand, many
    of them were prepared to suffer hardship and exile for their standpoints.
2   Their public and acknowledged function as priests of the cult that was
    generally supposed to ensure divine blessings to the Empire. The trad-
    itional exemption of the pagan priesthood from civil duties and from
    taxes had been transferred to the Christian clergy. They could invoke
    with success support from the State.
3   Residing in a city, the bishop 'became a symbol not only of the spiritual
    community, but of the diverse social elements within it [changing] from
    local teacher to cosmopolitan representative of ecclesiastical and often
    secular authority'.[49] Bishops exercised influence on public morals and
    organised assistance to their poor. Since they usually had their constitu-
    ency, they were also able to mobilise the crowds against their adversaries,
    the more so as religion was a matter of common interest. A bishop
    enjoyed additional support when a holy monk stood on his side.[50]
4   By their position and social power, bishops assumed a leading role in
    theological disputes. They considered themselves as 'examiners and asses-
    sors' in matters of the faith.[51] The times of Tertullian, Hippolyte and
    Origen, who were creative theologians without being bishops, were over.
    But if every important theologian of the fourth century was a bishop, this
    did certainly not mean that every bishop was a theologian!

Development of Christological reflection (341–53)

The defining of viewpoints in the Christological debate reveals a deep-lying
difference between the eastern and western parts of the imperial church. The
east sticks to the maintenance of a clear distinction between the divine persons of the Father and the Son, risking the latter's subordination. The west,
including eastern defenders of Nicaea such as Athanasius and Marcellus of
Ancyra, apprehends the dissolution of the essential unity between the Father
and the Son, risking their identification – a view which Marcellus' opinion
fostered indeed. Without following Marcellus, Athanasius developed his
theology on the principles of a full and essential unity of Christ with the
Father, of an ontological cleft between the divine persons and all creatures,
and of a 'wonderful exchange' of divine forces against human weaknesses,
thanks to the incarnation. His implicit repelling of the Platonic thought
about the structures of cosmos and humankind make Athanasius a contextual
innovator rather than a traditionalist. Beginnings of a dissociating from
docile applauding of the Christian emperor and Christianised society are also
discernable.

New synods and refining of the issues

The period from 341 to 353 is characterised by a revival and a refining of the theological debate. This does not mean that church politics do no longer play a role, but the research into the proper definition of Christ's relation to the Father is taken up, since the formula of Nicaea had not set the minds at rest. In these years, roughly speaking, the east stands over against the west and the exiled eastern bishops who had sought refuge and support here. We have seen how this involved the church of Rome and its bishop Julius, who not only admitted into his communion front-rank figures such as Athanasius and Marcellus, but who also wanted the Roman voice to be heard on the issue itself. His local synods sent letters to the east. Rome judged that Athanasius was the legal bishop of Alexandria and that Marcellus had irreproachable theological opinions. The interference of the west was new. Until Athanasius' flight to Rome, it had shown no deep interest in the controversies that shook the east. An independent western position was also owing to the balance of power between the two parts of the Empire, the western emperor Constans being stronger than his brother until he was overthrown in 350.

In spite of this bipolarity of the east and the west, there is a certain rapprochement on the level of the credal definitions. Conducted by the Eusebian party,[52] successive synods of the east brought out new formulations, leaving out those formulas that had proved provoking and dividing. This may look conciliative, but in the west it raised the suspicion that the new definitions were intended to cover Arian Christological conceptions. This suspicion was not necessarily justified since the so-called 'Arian Party' is 'better understood as a loosely allied group of people with overlapping but by no means identical concerns, held together more by their opposition to certain Marcellan and Athanasian tendencies than by a single specific theological platform.'[53]

The series of synods was opened with the 'Dedication Synod' at Antioch, already referred to above. It gathered in early 341 and answered to the synodal letter of Julius about Athanasius and Marcellus by issuing a confession, which actually did not sound heretical but nevertheless was tendentious by what it left out. Julius, far from being impressed, complained of the arrogance of the Antioch Council to dishonour 'the over 300 Fathers' (i.e., the Council of Nicaea) who had condemned Arius. He justified his decision to take Athanasius and Marcellus into his communion, arguing that he had looked at the grounds on which the first was deposed and had discovered that they were false, and that he had found no offensive elements in the theology of the latter. He repeated his earlier proposal to hold a council that would have to reexamine both cases on an ecumenical scale. Constans supported this plan and pressed his brother to convoke together a general council. In 343, eastern and western delegates assembled at Serdica.[54] The meeting resulted in a failure and almost in a schism: both parties held separate meetings and accused each other of holding heretical views, although each group cleared itself from the extremes the other was laying at its door. We shall discuss the real issues and fears below. The Council of Serdica manifested that there was a deep rift between the eastern and the western church. The main causes of this lack of harmony were the differences in theological skill and in language: the west was far behind the east and Latin could not always offer the correct synonyms for the subtler and scientifically developed Greek conceptions. Therefore, the westerners failed to see the real issues that worried the eastern-ers. For the time being, they had no fine theological leaders of their own,[55] but only eastern refugees such as Athanasius and Marcellus, who were rejected by the majority of their home regions. These did not regard Athana-sius as the legal bishop of Alexandria and judged Marcellus' theology as 'Sabellian'. The western delegates approved of the Roman decisions in favour of Athanasius and Marcellus; thereupon, the easterners broke off their com-munion with the western church leaders.

Nevertheless, after two years, the east sent a delegation to the west with its written standpoint, amplified by specific declarations. In this document they stressed that by confessing Father, Son and Holy Spirit according to the Scriptures as distinct persons, they do not introduce three gods. And when they say that the Son exists on his own, this is not meant to separate him from the Father, to whom he is united by nature forever. But instead of the Nicene terms 'from the substance of the Father' and 'of one substance with him', they wanted to define the Son's relation to the Father in the formula 'similar to the Father in every respect', leaving out all terms speaking both of his 'being' and of his inferior rank.[56] By such reassurances the east tried to reconcile the west, but it was in vain. Under Constans' pressure, Constantius acquiesced in the reinstatement of Athanasius as Alexandria's bishop. The intruder Gregory was removed and after seven years of exile Athanasius made a glorious re-entry into his city, where he would remain in office for ten years (346–56) before he was expelled again. A renewed action against him was prepared by a synod of the east at Sirmium in 351,[57] which rejected the use of all Nicene Christological terminology and, once more, deposed Athanasius. By then he had lost his western protectors, Constans and Julius. For some time, his position in Egypt was strong enough to maintain himself. This situation lasted until Constantius had managed to isolate Athanasius totally from the west and then could deal a heavy blow to him (see below, pp. 97–9). The now-unconcealed rejection of the decisions of Nicaea put the Nicene Creed at the centre of the theological and political struggle. It made Athanasius, who thus far had avoided binding up his Christology with the term *homoousios*, a frenetic defender of the definitions of Nicaea. He wrote a second doctrinal work in which he defended the council's decisions, aligning them with his own thought.[58]

Which were the deeper motives of the dissension between the 'Arian' party, showing surely some moderation since the death of Eusebius, and the westerners? The parting of the minds was due to the different approach to the mystery of three distinct 'actors' in God's dealings with humankind. It was the theology of Marcellus, whom the west accepted and the east anathematised, which revealed the respective preoccupations and fears.

Marcellus stated that the Christian faith could never imply the existence of two Gods, the Father and Christ, nor accept that the latter was just a creature. It was the old dilemma of the 'Monarchians' of the third century. Marcellus solved the problem in a way that inevitably recalled to his contemporaries the already condemned 'Sabellianism', though he denied that his views were identical with those of Sabellius. As God's own Word and *dynamis*, Jesus Christ must be inseparable from God. Consequently, there are not two divine persons, God being just one person together with his Word. Marcellus founded his opinion on the relation of Christ with God on Johannine texts such as: 'I and the Father are one' and 'the Father is in me and I am in the Father'.[59] These words – he thought – attested that before his incarnation, the *Logos* was God and that it was only by becoming man that he became Son. His distinctness from the Father is only temporary: beginning with the incarnation it will come to an end when, as Paul says, 'he will deliver the kingdom to God the Father'.[60] Marcellus' Trinity was not eternal but conditioned by the history of salvation and, therefore, subject to extension and reduction.[61] In supporting such a trinitarian doctrine, the west made it clear that its concern was to avoid ditheism (or tritheism[62]), whereas the east feared whatever kind of denial of a distinct, personal subsistence of the *Logos*. The idea of one common essence of the Father was repugnant to the east as well, because it could suggest a material partition of the one divine being into two and offend the axiom of God's immutability and impassibility. Such was the difference in approaching the relationship between God and Christ: does the way lead from the three divine 'actors' of salvation to the definition of their harmony and likeness? Or should one go from their basic unity to their distinctive actions?

The theological and soteriological structure of Athanasius' Christology

Though Athanasius published several church-political apologies in relation to the vicissitudes of the Arian struggle, some of his doctrinal works on the Christological debate also appeared in the years 341–53. We already mentioned that the three *Orations against the Arians* might have been composed in the early 340s. They continue the basic thoughts of his theology of incarnation, already laid down in his treatise on this subject (but then without reference to Arius' Christology). According to Athanasius, all those who sought to define Christ's relation to God without making use of the term *ousia* simply were 'Arians', even if some were moderate and – as we have seen above – did not share the extreme theses of Arius himself. Without manifesting a special preference for the term *homoousios*, he insisted on the expression of the Son as 'belonging properly to the Father's essence' (*idios tès ousias tou Patros*) and synonymous wordings.[63] Here follows a brief outline of the central themes in Athanasius.

Essentialism, no voluntarism

Athanasius' conception of God is characterised by essentialism. This distinguishes him from Eusebius as well as from Marcellus, however much these two were each other's opponents.[64] The Son has not been begotten by an act of God's will, he rather *is* this will, and to the same degree God's own Word, Wisdom and Truth. There is absolutely no moment of deliberation or decision in God preceding the generation of the Son.[65] If at any moment God had been without his *Logos*/Son, this would imply a change in his being. 'Thus "begotten" was above decision, and meant a whole participation – that is, essential communication. The Son's nature was therefore not determined by his priority or proximity to the Father, but by their shared divine essence.'[66] The Son is God's image in the full sense: he is the constant expression of God's being. This not only implies eternal being but essential goodness and faithfulness as well. God is essentially good and faithful: it belongs to his nature to be so and it does not depend on a contingent decision. God did not need a son as a being lower than himself, as a safeguard against too direct a contact with the material world and against his involvement with humankind.[67] The prevalence of a hierarchical structure would encroach on God's essential goodness and faithfulness. Athanasius starts from the principle that nature precedes will.[68] When dealing with human nature we will find the same.

Division between uncreated and created being

If in Athanasius there is no 'hierarchy of decreasing essences intervening between the Father and the world', there is, however, a deep and fundamental 'division between uncreated and created being'.[69] Those two are of a radically different, even contrasting, order: the uncreated is by itself the fountain of life and, thus, eternal, immutable, completely independent of any external condition or will; on the contrary, all creation has been brought into existence out of nothing, is changeable and has no everlasting vital power in itself. Athanasius is putting aside the last remnants of the emanative world-view, which from the beginning of the cross-cultural contact had been questioned by the biblical concept of a God who is active in creation and sustainment of the world but was still in the mind.

No creature really has vital and ethical stability in itself, but everything is subject to transitoriness and unsteadiness of the will. The unsteadiness of the will, i.e., the choice between good and evil, between orientation towards God and turning away from him to idolatry, is the corollary of the physical instability. On the created level, as much as on the uncreated, nature precedes will. In his *On the Incarnation of the Word*, Athanasius has presented human goodness and orientation towards God, which were part of the first people, as a grace bestowed on their weak nature, as a safeguard they only had to conserve in order to reach full communion with God.[70] The disobedience to the commandment that God had given in Paradise turned out to be the beginning of a slippery slope, along which human beings became totally enslaved to religious blindness, moral depravity and to the dominion of death over them. Athanasius fosters a rather pessimistic view of man, as far as man's own possibilities are concerned. He does not consider the individual but the human family as a whole, which has lost the notion of the Creator, has lowered itself to divinise heroes, powers and desires, and has become totally submitted to these created forces. Before the coming of Christ, humans were, in fact, deprived of sound reasoning and of the grace of bearing God's image.[71]

A *soteriology of exchange*

Athanasius' Christology is elaborated upon the consequent idea of 'the wonderful exchange' between Christ and humankind.[72] By assuming and appropriating to himself the human nature, Christ has produced a far better situation than the original creation. Communion with God has now become guaranteed. In the *Orations*, Athanasius emphasises that the incarnation has once and for all established a connection that is firm and lasting.[73] He writes:

> If man just receives [God's grace], he also can be deprived of it, as has happened to Adam, who received and lost again. But in order to make grace inalienable and guaranteed to men, he [Christ] appropriated the gift to himself. For indeed [. . .] since it was him who as a man received [. . .], the gift will be permanent in us as well.[74]

Athanasius speaks of grace, which has become 'unshakeable and irrevocable' for us.[75] Communion with God in both an ontological and ethical sense can nevermore be lost by the human race in its corporative totality, like Adam lost it for himself and for his posterity. As divine person in human flesh, the 'new Adam' secures to mankind the gracious gifts he brings. The transformation of unstable human nature has been given a better and far more real basis than it ever had before:

> We no longer die by virtue of our former birth in Adam, but since from now on our birth and every human weakness have been transferred on the Word, we are raised from the earth, the curse of sin being abolished because of him who 'became a curse' in our midst.[76]

Describing the radical change in the human situation, brought about by the active presence of the Word in our flesh, the Alexandrian theologian uses bold expressions like: 'The Word became flesh in order that we be deified' and 'Our flesh is no longer earthly, but has been "made Word" by the Word of God who became flesh for our sake.'[77] One remark should follow at once: this deification does not mean the abolishment of the ontological distance between God, the Unbegun and the human nature that is created, and it can never cease to belong to that level. Men never become God or melt with him. Their new position is that of adoptive children of God, never of 'sons by nature'. What Arius attributed to Christ as created *Logos*, Athanasius assigns to the Christian. The highest possible elevation of man as a created being is to be endowed with participation in divine properties, by an act of grace and on the irreversible basis of the incarnation. This irreversibility is stressed by the numerous ways in which Athanasius expresses that the ground of our redemption and endowment with God's gifts lies in our kinship with the Word, which has been established through the incarnation: 'consequently we are being saved on account of our being in a similar body as he has.'[78]

By virtue of the concept of 'exchange', which implies that the Word appropriated to himself all failures of human existence, Athanasius won a hermeneutical instrument to combat the seeming scriptural basis for the correctness of the Arian Christology. The Arians had looked up all the Gospel texts that seemed to give evidence for Christ's inferiority with respect to God. We have pointed above to the Gethsemane story where the Gospels read that Christ 'began to be greatly distressed and troubled' and prayed 'that if it were possible the hour might pass from him'.[79] They referred to other texts that suggest a limited knowledge of Christ[80] or speak of privileges and powers the Father has given to him.[81] Their conclusion was that Christ gave evidence of fear, of ignorance and of the capacity to 'receive', so that one ought to say that the *Logos* was imperfect and, therefore, capable of improvement and reward.

Over and against this exegesis, Athanasius starts from a different hermeneutical point of view, which he calls the 'principle and character of the holy Scriptures, viz. that they contain a double message about the Saviour: 1) that he always was God and Son, being the Word, the radiance and the Wisdom of the Father; 2) that, later on, he took the flesh on behalf of us and became a man.'[82] John 1:1 and 14 are the basis on which all statements pronounced by Christ or made with regard to him should be examined and classified, according to their illustrating either the first or the second reality. This division enables Athanasius to ascribe each evidence of 'imperfection' in the life of Christ to his humanity and to make clear that such a human 'weakness' was a necessary part of the Word's objective to heal the human nature and to expel all shortcomings from it. The presupposition of this Christology is that every deficiency in human existence was borne by the Word and that, on the rebound, every victorious transformation of these deficiencies by his power is henceforth communicated to his fellow humans through the medium of the common flesh. Lyman correctly says: 'Because revelation and transformation lie at the heart of Athanasius' Christology, an obedient human will, if implying a created nature, was largely extraneous.'[83] Because of Arianism, Athanasius was allergic to the slightest semblance of adoptionism in Christology. He was no less averse to the idea that salvation only consisted of instruction and example, put before men by Christ. The result was a picture of

Christ in whom a unilateral, divine action of redeeming and transforming was executed, without real cooperation of his human will.

Individual sanctification

Athanasius nourished a conception of the human race which we may call 'corporate' rather than 'collective', because, although non-individualistic in its essence, it certainly does not exclude the individual's faith response and progress in sanctity. In the same passage of the *Third Oration* in which Athanasius speaks of our 'logofied flesh' and of our birth in Adam, transferred upon the Word in order to be transformed, he also refers to the 'water and the Spirit' (John 3:5) as an included moment.[84] A question that bothers many students of Athanasius is how much room his corporate conception of human nature leaves for an individual role in sanctification. All redemptive moments, from the removal of fear, ignorance and temptability to the endowment with steadfastness, wisdom and everlasting life, seem to be rooted in the incarnate life of the Word, who infuses his brothers and sisters with these transforming forces through his kinship with them. Even the descent of the Holy Spirit on men is assured by the fact that in the waters of the river Jordan, the Spirit came down upon the Son, i.e., on his human side, since as Son he was not in need of the divine Spirit: 'For because the flesh was first sanctified in him and he is declared to have received the Spirit on account of that flesh, we have the gift of the Spirit, which proceeds from that moment, "receiving from his fullness".'[85]

Schwager puts the question how human freedom can be guaranteed when salvation is ensured in such definitive terms, and he points to the fact that in Athanasius, Christ is also an example to be followed. He suggests that the soteriology of the *Orations* received supplement in the doctrine of the Spirit which Athanasius was to later develop in his *Letters to Serapion*.[86] Lyman suggests that Athanasius implicitly meant all these massive soteriological assertions to come true within the realm of the communion of the Church and that by insisting upon an ascetic form of Christian life (as he regularly did in the *Festal Letters*[87]) he 'sharply defined the Christian community over against Graeco-Roman culture'.[88]

Contextual significance of Athanasius' theological principles

Athanasius has often been presented as the defender of orthodoxy against Arianism as heresy. As a corollary, Arius' Christology was marked as devi- ation and modernism. The reality was just the reverse: although Athanasius, when opposing the Arian Christology, constantly referred to a 'standardised' reading of the Scriptures by the Church, from the angle of contextualisation (as we have defined it), it is rather him who framed a new course in theology. I suggest that a step further should be made beyond those who 'portray him as a "Catholic traditionalist" prodded to new reflection by controversy, rather than an academic and a philosopher like Arius.' It is this non-philosophical approach that made him 'an authority in conflict with his own tradition',[89] a renewer. He was someone who met the challenges of the profoundly modified religious and political context of the century, notably that of the post-Constantinian decades.[90] At the end of this chapter, we will give an appreciation of the theological significance of the central period of the fourth century, seen as a process of searching. But, as far as Athanasius is concerned, since his theology will not change in its essentials after 353, we may already draw some conclusions about its degree of contextualisation. We bring out three aspects:

First, Athanasius was indebted to the *Platonic conception of being* in following the idea of the precedence of nature over ethical qualities. But more consistently than his predecessors, he was drawing consequences from the biblical conception of creation, viz., that reality must be seen as divided up into two spheres of being: creative and created, communicating and receiving, stable and mutable. This radical contrast excluded emanationism, which rather made God the summit of a cosmological edifice in which a hierarchy of degrading perfection and diversification should explain why lower forms are both united to him and moving away from him. Athanasius corrected the Origenistic tradition, i.e., the Middle Platonist influence on Christian theology. Eusebius as well as Arius also weakened Origen's emanationism by stressing the moment of willing in the generation of the *Logos*/Son; but the way in which they did so reinforced his subordination, making him the intermediary agent between God and his works. Over and against a divine sonship, conditioned by God's will to act externally, Athanasius identified the Son with the intrinsic divine qualities of life, love and compassion.[91] Every kind of Christology which put the Son 'somewhere in between', was to him 'Ariomania' (Arian madness), because it reduced the Son to the ranks of creation, even if he was seen as the summary and executive of all God's designs for (the rest of) creation. This intransigent, in many eyes intolerant, standpoint, by which all his adversaries are assimilated to one once-condemned person, can also be evaluated as a farewell to the traditional apologetic theology, which over a long period had been tied up to the inherences of the cosmological categories it had used for its Christology.[92]

Second, Athanasius adopted from Platonism the ideal of contemplation of divine and spiritual goods as the *true destiny of human life*. This implied the call to spiritual ascent by renouncing the lower, bodily appetites. But this current conception of man was also deeply modified by his 'verticalism'. As he relates man's vocation to be in God's image and likeness and to act according to his *logos* consequently to the unique and natural image and reason of God, the highest characteristic of humans coincides with grace, which can only be safeguarded through an undisturbed relation with the *Logos*.[93] A complete restoration of this relation was needed to enable humankind anew to contemplate and to serve God in the right way.[94] This was done by the *Logos* in the beginning. And it was done again in the incarnation, for an unshakeable and transforming salvation can only come from one who fully shares God's nature. We have seen how strongly Athanasius stressed man's natural weaknesses; his anthropological pessimism is overcome by a Christocentric optimism. Man is, by the Word's life in the human flesh, graciously divinised. Divinisation by Christ in such radical terms means at the same time a reduction of the whole human being to creational proportions.

Third, Athanasius prepared a critical distance vis-à-vis the hopes for an emperor-led civilisation. This working element in Athanasian thought was not at once explicit. In Chapter 3, p. 65, we saw that Athanasius quite naturally embarked on negotiations with Constantine. He continued to do so with Constans as long as this emperor controlled the west. And he headed for Constantius as soon as the latter was in power.[95] He addressed Constantius as an emperor who 'loves truth and God'.[96] But the tyrannical policy of this emperor with regard to the doctrinal issues and the sudden rise of the pagan emperor Julian would lead him to change his mind and to become really critical about the interference of an emperor with the Church.

> Athanasius' complaint that the emperor interferes in the affairs of the church is not in fact directed against interference as such, but against imperial actions of which he disapproves. Athanasius implicitly asserts that emperors have a right to overrule church councils – provided that they do so in the interest of orthodoxy rather than heresy.[97]

His criterion was, indeed, the emperor's stance for or against the doctrine of the Church as the Nicene Council had fixed it.

Yet there is some progress if we compare Athanasius with Eusebius of Caesarea. Eusebius saw the Church as a culture-shaping factor in a great historical process of civilisation. In this process, the Christian emperor was the pre-eminent ally of the *Logos*. Quite remarkably Athanasius saw not the emperor in the centre but a monk – Antony of Egypt, on the fringe of society – as a principal ally and conductor of the Christian people, and the Church as the proper space for the life of the redeemed. Lyman calls it ironical that 'in a setting of increasing social legitimacy for Christianity, [Athanasius'] incarnational view cast Christian identity in starker form over against the larger world or its history.'[98] The real progress of the Church was not connected with the alliance of Christianisation and civilisation, led by the emperor. Salvation is given by the recreative and transforming effects of the incarnation, not by its educational forces and, therefore, not dependent on the political and cultural downwind. Its truth does not need to be confirmed by historical processes. It is typical that Athanasius composed a biography of a monk, whereas Eusebius wrote a biography of an emperor. Both are presented as leader of a 'Christian city', but how great is the difference! In the *Life of Saint Antony*, the community of hermits is described as a 'city of perfection', secluded from society.[99]

Breakdown and resurgence of the Nicene Party (353–63)

As unassailable sole monarch from 353 onwards, Constantius energetically set himself the task to restore peace and unity among Christians. Having already ruled the eastern part for fifteen years, he knew well the forces of opposition against the Christological formula of the Nicene Creed, viz., the consubstantiality of the Son with God the Father and against the person and the trinitarian doctrine of Athanasius. His first objective, therefore, was to break down the support Athanasius was enjoying in the west and in his home base, Egypt; by 356 he had succeeded. Ongoing theological diversification in the east pushed Constantius to impose a neutral and unsatisfactory formula, invented by his court bishops and pushed through on a series of state-organised synods. Christ had to be confessed as 'similar to the Father according to the Scriptures', and all other definitions were prohibited. A few courageous opponents had to suffer exile, but the theological process could not be stopped by this coercion. It found a new centre in Asia Minor. During his short reign, Emperor Julian tried to revitalise Hellenistic paganism and, by releasing all its fighting cocks, help the Church to founder. On the contrary, the sudden absence of state interference gave way to a new majority which searched for ways of formulating a more-than-ethical bond between Christ and God.

Constantius' tyrannical church policy (353–61)

From Athanasius' theological principles underlying his position in the Christological debate, we turn again to the game of political forces. All through the decade during which Constantius was sole monarch of the Empire, there was intertwinement of imperial interference and theological precision. Constantius used strong-arm methods to achieve his end, which was religious unity. He pushed the Church to subscribe to a credal definition, vague enough to be acceptable to the great majority of bishops, and he removed by force those who resisted. Constantius continued the line of Constantine, but he did not possess his father's political skill or his extraordinary authority.

We summarise the positions as they were in 353: the line of reasoning of the east departed from the scriptural evidence of three divine persons acting in the process of salvation and came from there to a definition of their mutual harmony and likeness. The assumption of a common divine essence and, consequently, all formulas that made use of the term *ousia* were felt as an infringement on the distinction between the three divine persons, and on their individual properties. The east hung on to the term *hypostasis*, 'subsistence'. The westerners, on the contrary, departed from one divine essence as basis of God's different actions for the benefit of humankind and the created world. Their key word *substantia* covered the meanings of *ousia* and *hypostasis* as well, which made it difficult for them to grasp the thought associations of the Greeks. Moreover, they considered Athanasius unjustly dismissed.

However, they were not in the first place concerned about the person of the Alexandrian metropolitan, but about the proper definition of the faith and the correct application of church order.

For that reason, the new Bishop of Rome, Liberius (352–66), wanted a new general council of east and west in order to overcome the differences. He advanced his request to Constantius, after the Church of Rome had declared, once again, Athanasius legal bishop of Alexandria, and had dropped Marcellus, whom Rome had been protecting for several years but whose views it knew to be too offensive for the east. But even so, Liberius could expect irritation. Nevertheless, he felt urged to make a countermove since the east had held a synod in 351 at Sirmium. This synod had laid the foundations for the actions Constantius was prepared to undertake as soon as he could. The foundations were:

- The renewal of Athanasius' dismissal. The result was the consecration of a new bishop for Alexandria, a certain George from Cappadocia, whose consecration had to take place in Antioch,[100] Alexandria still being strong enough to refuse him.
- The dismissal and exile of the city's own bishop, Photinus, because as an adherent of Marcellus he could be easily targeted as 'Sabellianist'. The next step was to bracket Athanasius together with both heretical thinkers who now had been condemned.
- The adoption of the creed which in 345 had been presented to the west as a proposal. As we saw above (Chapter 3, p. 88), this confession carefully left out those terms that were offensive to the east. This creed was again meant as an opening to the west.

The Sirmium decisions equated Athanasius with the old Nicene Creed and its most remarkable key word 'consubstantial' became controversial, being a target for the one party and a rallying cry for the other.[101] Strengthened by Sirmium, Constantius set out to remove Athanasius from his see, but he could not succeed as long as the west was supporting him.[102]

As soon as Constantius had defeated his last opponent in the west, he responded to Liberius and, indeed, convoked a synod to Arles. However, it was not a general council, as Liberius had wished, but a provincial synod with a limited number of participants from Gaul only. The Emperor did not allow a debate on the controversial matters of faith. The main point on the agenda was the condemnation of Athanasius. The bishops submitted, even Liberius' own delegates. The only bishop who opposed was sent into exile.[103] After the synod had spoken as he wanted, Constantius issued an edict that all western bishops should see local state authorities in order to have their personal subscription registered.

Liberius was quite upset. Together with three Italian bishops he insisted anew on the necessity of a general council to deal with matters of faith. To this end, they sent a delegation to Constantius, suggesting that the decisions of Nicaea would be the best basis for negotiations. Constantius agreed and appointed his new western residence Milan as meeting place. The synod was held in the summer of 355, with a mainly western participation. The bishops were on the point of confirming the Nicene Creed when two court bishops from the Balkans, Valens of Mursa and Ursacius of Singidunum,[104] ordered to transfer the assembly from the church to the palace, where Constantius increased his pressure. Athanasius reports that during the session the Emperor exclaimed, 'Whatever I wish must be considered church law; so you either obey or go into banishment'. Athanasius was not present and those words may not have been what Constantius said literally, but they surely record what he intended and what the bishops understood as his implacable will.[105]

Now it was the turn of the rest of the western episcopate to be purged. Seven bishops were dismissed and replaced by 'Arians'. Among them was Milan's own bishop, Dionysius, who was forced to cede his see to a man from faraway Cappadocia, Auxentius, who vigorously promoted Arianism in the west, although he knew absolutely no Latin.[106] Liberius himself was brought to the Balkans and exposed to such heavy pressure that after two years he gave up his resistance and declared himself willing to break with Athanasius. Had his spirit been broken? Or had he come to the conviction that the stubborn Alexandrian metropolitan was impeding the building up of a broad mediation group?[107]

Ninety-year-old Hosius of Cordoba, Constantine's adviser in the old days of Nicaea, was dragged all the way to Sirmium and kept there until he put his signature under the new formula, which was intended to do away forever with the Nicene Creed. But before he died, he recanted, stipulating that, if he had been mistaken, he had never assented to condemn Athanasius. His friends excused him, referring to his age.[108] Perhaps he had not seized the meaning of the Greek formulas in question. But in one thing the old man saw very clearly, and he bequeathed to Church and Emperor a guideline for their relationship, which was going to be tested and developed in the last decades of the fourth century. Athanasius preserved what Hosius wrote to Constantius:

> Stop [your compulsion], and remember that you are a mortal man: fear the day of judgement and keep yourself pure for it. Do not intrude into the affairs of the Church, and do not give us advice about these matters, but rather receive instruction on them from us. God has given you kingship, but has entrusted us with what belongs to the Church. Just as the man who tries to steal your position contradicts God who has placed you there, so you should beware of becoming guilty of a great offence by putting the affairs of the Church under your control. It is written: 'Render to Caesar the things that are Caesar's and unto God those that are God's' [Matt. 22:21]. Hence neither do we [bishops] have the right to rule over the world nor do you, emperor, have the right to officiate in the Church.[109]

In early 356, Constantius felt ready for his final blow against Athanasius. A large military force was needed for the raid on the church where Athanasius was celebrating a service, in order to seize him and to install waiting George in his place. Athanasius escaped and for the next six years was hidden by the Alexandrian churchpeople and by the Coptic monks. George did not enjoy his episcopal function, since the Egyptians rioted against him.[110] There was much violence against the authorities which returned to persecute and torture the followers of Athanasius to such a degree that the days of Diocletian seemed to have recurred. From his hiding places, Athanasius intensively followed the events and wrote his ample and one-sided comments. It was then that, after a last appeal to Constantius, he explained to the monks that the Emperor was no more than a tyrant and an enemy of Christ.[111]

Constantius, however, approached the moment of his victory. After the regional synods, he judged that the time had now come to unite the whole church by means of a definition that had been prepared by his court bishops. But still he did not have enough confidence in the positive outcome of a truly ecumenical council and, therefore, convoked the west and the east to separate synods. In 359, the westerners were summoned to Rimini and the easterners, two months later, to Seleucia.[112] Only in the next year, the results of the two meetings would be combined in a council in the imperial capital city.

Both synods showed discord among their members. The delegates, especially those from the west, had to be 'standardised'. The meetings were enacted under heavy pressure of the court bishops and of high state officers. No free discussion was allowed: the only decision requested was adhesion. Since the great majority of the Rimini synod still held to the Nicene formula, its 400 members were detained on the spot, in the heat of summertime, while two delegations went to see the Emperor. He received the one with the compliant minority, while refusing to meet the representatives of the reluctant majority. Waiting and threats led the latter to accept the formulation that Christ is 'like the Father, according to the Scriptures'.[113] The closer definition 'in all things' after 'like the Father', advanced by a rising group of eastern theologians (see below, p. 101) was omitted, and all use of the disputed terms of *ousia* and *hypostasis* simply forbidden. The central term for the relation of Christ with God should be 'similar', in Greek *homoios*. The subscription took place at a small town called Nike (200 kilometres west of Constantinople). This was intentionally done in order to promulgate the new 'Homoean' confession as 'Nicene Creed', so that the first Nicene Creed with its *homoousios* would be wiped out and uninformed bishops would be deceived.

The same game was played at Seleucia. Here, too, was a strong group that felt that 'like the Father' would only refer to Christ's will and obedience and not express his profound essential and existential unity with the Father. As we will see in the next section, this group around Basil of Ancyra meanwhile had proposed to define Christ as 'of similar essence with the Father', *homoiousios*. What had happened in Rimini recurred: both factions sent their delegations to Constantius; they were detained until all resistance was broken. In the end, indeed, the representatives of both synods had complied with Constantius' demands and had subscribed to the 'Homoean' Creed.

In early 360, this glorious result of tyrannical religious policy could be ratified in Constantinople by a meeting of bishops, who this time were selected from both parts of the Empire: 'Nike' was confirmed, all earlier and eventual new creeds were interdicted. The meagre result of forty years of research and discussion on the nature of Christ's relation with God seemed to be the declaration 'that the Son is like the Father as the divine Scriptures declare and teach'.[114] In order to achieve peace, the terms *ousia*, *hypostasis* and *substantia* were simply dismissed as 'non-biblical'. The escape of a non-precise reference to the Bible meant the giving up of any attempt to express in contextual wordings the uniqueness of Christ as Saviour. It meant that the ongoing clarification of the biblical testimonies relative to the incarnated Word and his redemptive work in a society that had become much more receptive was buried. The whole affair was no less a capitulation to an emperor, who pretended that he was able to settle controversies in the sphere of faith and played the game to let the Church itself take the decisions he wanted.

But there were still forces in the Church that would not let themselves be silenced. 'The craven acquiescence he [viz., Constantius] extorted was short-lived'.[115] Things changed when, after a battle with the Persians, Constantius fell ill and died in November 361, only forty-four years old.

New need of a definition including ousia

The policy of Constantius and the personal service and carriage of the court bishops were intended to quiet down the theological controversies. But the peace achieved through the almost general acceptance of the *homoios* formula was only on the surface. We already referred to the rise of a group in Asia Minor that was unsatisfied with the prohibition of any statement about the divine origin and character of the Saviour, fearing that 'similarity with the Father' was giving way to a mere conformity of Christ's will with God's purposes. They were advocating a new formula that included a reference to Christ's essence, convinced that one could not do without *ousia*. For that reason, they advanced *homoiousios* as a middle-course solution.

Their position was strengthened by the revival of a purified Arianism. We have mentioned earlier that 'Arianism' and 'Arians' had become a collective term for a loosely connected group of those who, fearing 'Sabellianism', opposed Marcellus and Athanasius.[116] Athanasius himself was contributing much to this generalisation of his opponents, many of whom did not share all Arius' proper viewpoints. In the course of the 350s, a left-wing Christology came up, which showed many similarities with early Arianism. Their key word was *anhomoios*, i.e., Christ unsimilar to the Father. There is a discussion among scholars, whether these 'Anhomoeans' are rightly to be seen as 'New Arians', or not. Thümmel points at several similarities with the theses of

Arius.[117] Barnes judges the anhomoean approach a 'new phenomenon, whatever its similarities to some of the propositions which Arius had advanced.'[118] What turns the scale for Barnes is the application of formal logic – an element absolutely absent in Arius. Moreover, the doctrinal protagonists of the new persuasion, Aëtius and Eunomius, did not refer to the old heresiarch. The discussion, however, is mainly on the starting point, since neither Thümmel nor Barnes denies that there are indeed similarities with Arius' propositions.

The 'anhomoean' approach was strictly logical and rejected the assignment of definitions from one object to another. The primordial definition of God should be that he is 'underived': not only is he himself unbegotten, but no being can ever have been begotten by him, since that would imply partition. The one who is called 'Son', therefore, has come into existence and has no similarity with his Creator except in his willing: 'his sonship is constituted by his obedience to the Father, by his willing God's will, that enables him to save us into a sonship in the same mode'.[119] Only in his willing and acting Christ is like the Father, but no more than that. It is true that, according to Eunomius, Christ in his pre-existence had been creator as well, but there is no essential difference between him and all other creatures except his precedence.

The 'Anhomoeans' were not without influence on the scene of church politics since they had a stronghold in Bishop Eudoxius, who got hold of the see of Antioch in 358 and of that of Constantinople in 360, maintaining himself in that important post for ten years. The significant effect of the promotion of their Christological approach was that in the next period they became the adversaries, against whom all the other groups joined forces.[120]

The 'anhomoean' Christological approach made it clear that the 'homoean' definition was not sufficient to keep out a mere similarity or accordance between Christ's and God's will. Over and against this extreme position, the group around Basil of Ancyra took advantage of the fact that their *homoiousios* or 'Christ being of similar essence with the Father': (1) implied a statement on Christ's more-than-human essence and expressed that his belonging to the Father was of a more profound nature than of an agreement of will; (2) implied a safeguarding of the proper identity of the Son against any 'Sabellian' interpretation by the use of *homoios* (similar) in *homoiousios*, instead of the old Nicene *homos* (identical) in *homoousios*. Lietzmann draws the conclusion that it was in fact a revival of the conception of Eusebius of Caesarea.[121]

Basil assembled a synod at Ancyra in 358 in order to legitimate his definition in spite of earlier prohibitions. He stated that if it was inevitable to maintain the *homoios* formula, then this definition should at least be specified by the addition 'in his *essence* and in all things'. The remarkable fact about the synod of Ancyra was that, unlike all the other assemblies of the 350s, it was a free meeting, not convoked and manipulated by the Emperor or his henchmen. Basil's action had a transitory success: Constantius did not want a resurgence of what looked like Arianism. If Christ was 'unlike the Father', he could no longer be confessed as 'Son'. The 'Anhomoeans' had no real chance. But, as we have seen, on the synods of 359–60, it was the colourless Homoean

Creed that won, thanks to the manipulations of the court bishops. For the moment, Basil was unwelcome, and in 360 he and the excellent bishop of Jerusalem, Cyril, were dismissed.[122]

Basil's town Ancyra was the main city of Galatia, a region adjacent to Cappadocia. By this time, adjacent Cappadocia turned out to be the cradle of a series of three fine and influential theologians, adhering to the Christology of the *homoiousios* formula. They are commonly identified as 'the three Cappadocians': Basil of Caesarea in Cappadocia[123] (b. *c.* 330 and bishop *c.* 364), his younger brother Gregory of Nyssa (b. 335) and their friend Gregory of Nazianzum. Both Basil and Gregory of Nyssa refuted the Christology of Eunomius. Basil's criticism was that Eunomius had presented a (perhaps logical but) cold image of God, just telling how he is (viz., underived, eternal, etc.) but not what he is (viz., the God of Abraham, of the Alliance and of salvation).

These three are also called the 'New Nicene Group'. Apart from them, the old partisans of Nicaea such as Athanasius and some westerners still survived and were to appear again as soon as Constantius was dead. We now have to look at the cores of resistance in the west.

Opposition from the west: Hilary of Poitiers

Hilary (*c.* 315–67) was not the only person in the west who resisted Constantius' church policy, but for two reasons he was outstanding: he was the first western theologian to produce a systematic refutation of the Arian Christology; second, he played a conciliatory role between east and west and between old and new adherents of Nicene theology. According to Borchardt, the value of his theology 'can hardly be over-estimated' and his efforts for conciliation 'must be regarded as the chief merit of his work'.[124]

Hilary was elected Bishop in 353 and after three years deposed and exiled by a provincial synod because of his theological opinions, which he was not given the opportunity to expound. Following the Emperor, intolerance reigned in Gaul and Hilary was sent to Phrygia in Asia Minor, where he was retained until 360. From his exile, he admonished the bishops of Gaul not to sign the Sirmium formula, which other prominent western bishops such as old Hosius of Cordoba and Liberius of Rome had accepted under pressure. An equally important fact was that, during his exile, Hilary obtained fine knowledge of the eastern theological discussion. So far, the west had shown no ability to join in the current debate. Hilary was the first to fathom the implications of the genuinely Arian, and the various semi-Arian, views on the nature of Christ. Like other western bishops, the faith question was his primary concern. But Hilary was convinced that the elimination of Athanasius was only meant to achieve a complete rejection of the Nicene Creed and its Christological passage. The results of his research and of the development of his own opinion are found in a voluminous work *On the Trinity*.

Hilary wanted the confession of Nicaea to be the theological standard.

Divine fatherhood and sonship are both eternal. This eternal generation of the Son by the Father implies the transference on him of a fully equal nature. Being the Spirit of God and the Spirit of Christ, the Holy Ghost also shares full divine nature. In spite of the identity of divine substance, there is a distinction between the three persons, each of whom having a proper and specific existence. Hilary adopted the image of the fire, which causes another fire without partition or diminution of intensity. Consequently, the Son is of no lesser nature than God is. Because the Son shared true, divine essence, he was not capable of suffering, but his body was. The similarities with the theology of Athanasius are obvious.

Phrygia, where he wrote his great work, was not far from Galatia. It is no wonder that during his exile Hilary made the acquaintance of Basil of Ancyra and his group. Hilary put his trust in Basil's trinitarian theology and saw him as an ally. He thought that a consistent interpretation of the *homoiousios* formula they advocated could not but lead to an acceptance of the Nicene *homoousios*. Both expressions were sane and of identical meaning in his eyes, and he hoped that his friends in the west would not cling to the old formula as the only banner of correct Christology. Hilary conceived the plan to reconcile the Asians with the members of the western opposition.

After the débâcle of the double synod of 359 (Hilary attended the one that was held at Seleucia and the combined synod in Constantinople), he was allowed to return to Gaul. He organised a synod in Paris in 360, which took measures to reestablish the supremacy of pro-Nicene bishops in Gaul. This shift was now possible thanks to the political and military crisis that had forced Constantius to transfer powers to his young cousin Julian. In spite of his deep devotion to his philosophical studies in Athens, Julian was obliged to protect the Empire against German invaders. He turned out to be such a successful commander that his victorious troops proclaimed him Emperor. Constantius was unable to prevent this. In his heart, Julian had already abandoned the Christian religion (see the next section) and he was not minded to pursue Constantius' religious policy. This gave Hilary and his companions a free hand.

Like Athanasius, Hilary did not produce any theory about the relation of Church and State. But 'he did contribute towards this by the boldness with which he opposed the emperor'.[125] It was important that he did so in the years when so many knuckled under Constantius' tyrannical policy and Athanasius had been pushed into the background. By his conciliatory action, he prepared a new climate in which Athanasius was soon to join, when Constantius' death paved the way for him to reappear on the scene.

The turn under Julian's reign (361–3)

Julian was the last surviving member of the Constantinian dynasty and thirty years old when he took over the whole empire. He was a 'philosopher on the throne' and wanted the State to be governed by philosophers, as Plato had advocated. He purged the court of eastern pomp and protocol and dismissed all superfluous, honey-tongued officials. This sobriety was, however, counterbalanced by a reinstatement of the splendid and wasteful pagan ceremonies of old: temples were reopened and restored, bloody sacrifices reintroduced for which numberless animals were seized; Julian loved sacrificial ceremonies. He even planned to have the Temple of Jerusalem rebuilt; he liked the Jews because they had had a splendid temple and a rich ritual of offering to a national God and yet were monotheistic.

What Julian intended was to restore to the leading social circles their old Hellenistic self-respect and pride. The binding religion of the Empire should be again the 'monotheistic' solar cult. Julian had turned his back on the Christian religion already, *c.* 350, but it was only as monarch that he openly confessed his change of religion. He certainly did not order a persecution of Christianity but tried to take the wind out of its sails by frustrating its influence over the people and, especially, over the youth. He was the first to promulgate an Education Act that stipulated that the traditional curriculum should be taught only by teachers who actually respected its contents and agreed with the classical philosophy of life. This was a way to remove Christian teachers who were supposed not to reconcile this to their conscience. Julian introduced a state inspection on the appointment of the teachers. He also introduced a new-style priesthood: priests had not only to be correct celebrants of the old rituals, but also examples of a 'philosophical', i.e., ascetic and ethical, lifestyle. Julian wanted his Hellenistic priests to surpass the Christian clergymen in moral integrity.

In 362 Julian moved to Antioch, a city he thought more inclined to the pagan cults than Constantinople. He was mistaken. The progress of Christianity and the abandonment of paganism had already gone too far to reverse, so that Julian's efforts were an artificial and rather tragic enterprise. Neither the slaughter of animals by their hundreds, nor the philosophical reinterpretation of old myths could enthuse the populace, which laughed at their moralistic and dull emperor. In June 363, Julian was killed in a lost battle with the Persians. All his measures were revoked by his successor, Jovian.

Nevertheless, his short and unsuccessful reign was of great importance to the Church. In their violent posthumous reactions to Julian, whom they called 'the Apostate', they showed that they had been shocked by the perspective that history of salvation could be turned back and the 'Christian times' would be over. The Eusebian view of history as the progressive and victorious revelation of the *Logos* did not leave any room for a repaganisation of Roman civilisation and emperorship. The prospect of an eventual rebuilding of the Temple in Jerusalem horrified them most of all, since its destruction in the year 70 was always seen as historical proof that the coming of Christ had for ever abolished the cult of the Old Covenant and had spread the new worship 'in spirit and truth' (John 4:24). The Christians would indeed have been profoundly embarrassed if they had to conclude that God allowed the restoration of the Jewish Temple and cults.[126] They were relieved by

Julian's early death and comforted by thinking that God had intervened in time.

The second effect of Julian's reign was the consolidation of a broad alliance of all those who felt their theological conscience violated by the tyrannical policy of Constantius and by the frustration of ongoing and refining research for correct definitions through the interference of servile court bishops. In 361, the peace and unity Julian inherited from his predecessor were only apparent. The brutal interdiction of going beyond the flat formula of Christ's similarity to God, based upon a vague reference to the Scriptures, was far from stopping the debate on the mutual relationships of the three divine persons. Like in the years following Nicaea, a definition of the faith that had been imposed by the Emperor in order to force unity, was repugnant to the hearts and minds of many church leaders as well as to communities that had seen the dismissal of their appreciated bishops. Hatred had accumulated against a Christian emperor, but Julian's neutrality in doctrinal matters allowed the return of the banned bishops and the formation of new alliances on the base of an essentialist and not merely voluntarist Christology. The Church was free to take up again and to pursue its own theological discussions without interference from the State. In spite of the frightening aspects of Julian's religious policy, this was the great advantage of his short reign. No doubt the Emperor expected something different to happen. He hoped that the release of all leaders would weaken the Church, since he knew that 'Christians can be to each other worse than wild animals'. And, though this was not far from the truth, there were also conciliations that brought about a new, influential majority.

In Alexandria, pro-Athanasian mobs lynched Bishop George soon after he had ventured to show himself in the city. Julian thought that pagans had killed the Christian bishop and was not eager to blame them for their violence. Athanasius could now come back from his hiding place and reoccupy the see. Having been an outlaw for six years – his longest exile! – he made a triumphant re-entry. Without delay, he set himself to assembling a synod and to building up a common front of those who were willing to reject the Arian Christology and more recent views on the Holy Spirit as a subordinate angel-like spirit. Preferring the old definition in the Nicene Creed of the Son being *homoousios* with the Father, he accepted the good right of the Cappadocian proposal to define him as *homoiousios*. He even accepted the new language of *three hypostaseis*, stating that *one hypostasis* as held by himself and by the westerners was justifiable as well, provided that it should not cover any 'Sabellianist' confusion of the three divine actors. This attitude could not fail to rally westerners, such as Hilary, and those easterners whom the anhomoean position and the imprecise reference to 'the Scriptures' (always remaining open to different interpretations) had brought to include *ousia* into the definition of Christ's relation to God. The synod of Alexandria and its document, the *Tome to the Antiochians*,[127] offered a valuable model for reconciliation and the joining of forces, as well as for rallying those who under the pressure of

Constantius but with bad conscience had signed his formulas. It is to be considered a great merit of the thus-far-intolerant Athanasius[128] that he forged a new unity, without requiring a strict allegiance to the letter of the Nicene Creed. After the almost complete breakdown of the Athanasian or Old Nicene party, this was the moment of its resurgence and, at the same time, of the start of new developments.

Retrospective view on the period 324–63: evidences of contextualisation

Our method of investigation of the stirring times of the Arian crisis is to distinguish and follow two tracks of contextual impact and response, the political and the doctrinal developments. It was clear in advance that they were intertwined from the beginning and would remain so all along the period. The doctrinal controversies, already emotional by the fact that different underlying perceptions of salvation were at stake, were once more envenomed by the new chances to engage the state and its instruments for a particular party or opinion. By their wish to see the Church contribute to the unity of the Empire, the Christian emperors not only got increasingly involved in doctrinal questions, trying to suppress divisions, but they also paved the way for the temptation for ecclesiastical parties to seek their force in imperial support rather than in theological arguments. These were, however, not absent. Synods and innovating theological thinkers pursued a process of independent reflection on the basis of which the three divine actors, to whom the Scriptures bear witness, belong to each other and form a unity. Therefore, the theological, i.e., predominantly Christological, reflection was not by any means a by-product of a struggle for more power and influence between mutually contending bishops or between these and the Roman State.

Church and Emperor

In the preface to the fifth book of his *Ecclesiastical History*, fifth-century historian Socrates explains why he repeatedly includes the emperors in his story. It is 'because, since they begun to be Christians, the affairs of the Church used to depend on them, and the greatest synods have proceeded and proceed at their will.'[129] The synods that exceeded local or regional scale were, indeed, instruments of imperial authority over the Church. We saw how Constantine started the use of this means, first with a general council of the west (Arles, 314) and then with an 'ecumenical' council, i.e., an assembly representing the entire Church of the Empire.[130] This use increased under Constantine's successors and, therefore, the large synods are an important aspect of the new balance of power and influence between the Church and the Christian emperor.

It was a matter of give and take. The Emperor gave the consent and facilities to assemble as (great) synod, the confirmation and carrying into effect of its decisions by the means of state power. Many church leaders of the epoch got rapidly accustomed to these new possibilities, solicited the Emperor's support and used it to strengthen their position. From its side, the Church gave the ecclesiastical sanctioning of judgements on persons and opinions that would handicap the Emperor's objectives. Constantine had introduced this cooperation with statesmanship and led by motives of political and religious prudence. His example had been set with such vigour that Constantius had to take all the pains to force the church representatives of east and west to subscribe to the formulas and condemnations he wanted, using his court bishops as executors. The emperors never abandoned the principle that the Church took its decisions by the voice of its own representatives, however heavy their pressure to march in this or that direction may have been.

So, if the give-and-take model followed the rules of the game, the intention got corrupted, both as a result of the less scrupulous style of interference of Constantine's successors and of the temptation of power to which a number of bishops yielded. This context furthered a mixing of interests, and it took several decades before some responsible leaders came to discern that drawing the emperor into the matters of faith could as well be detrimental to the nature of the Church. There was no feeling at all that it was not up to an emperor to convoke synods and to urge for decisions.

These remarks are certainly critical but do not pronounce a severe verdict, since the fourth-century Church and theologians were without any experience of an alliance with the State. The ethics, developed in a spirit of distance and mistrust face to a pagan and sometimes hostile state, could only gradually be transformed into ethics of social and political co-responsibility, for which the Church had no ready theory at hand. The way to a greater independence vis-à-vis the emperor's interference began by judging the policy of the emperor of the moment by what one felt as sane doctrinal tradition. It was by trial and error that the Church had to learn that the standards of its preaching must be fixed by itself.

The exceptions we see in the period dealt with in this chapter are all the more remarkable. In this respect, Constantius' tyrannical policy moved an old man like Hosius of Cordoba, once Constantine's principal adviser, to formulate a maxim for the separation of the competencies of the emperor and the bishops. By virtue of his own conviction of having a divine mandate and of his being confirmed in this sense of vocation by church leaders such as Eusebius, Constantine had concerned himself with the finding of a doctrinal statement about Christ that could oblige the largest possible majority. After some bad experiences with less talented rulers, the Church discovered to which extent its own confession and reflection could as well be hampered by an emperor who pretended to competence in matters of faith. Whereas several bishops still welcomed the convergence of their opinion with the powerful assent of the court, others started to feel uncomfortable. It was no doubt because

Constantius did not back them up that Athanasius and Hilary in the long run saw the tyrannical side of this Emperor. This was the result not so much of a theory about the Church–State relation as the experiences that had opened their eyes. No more than anybody else in the Church would they give up the advantages for Christianity of the secular arm: the protection of the Christian religion over and against pagans, Jews and heretics, and the execution of its decisions and wishes.[131] But, thanks to Constantius, there was an increase of self-consciousness and determination among a number of bishops who felt that they were the guardians of the Church's traditions and convictions and that the fixation of these should not be left to a worldly ruler and his concerns. Therefore, the end of the eventful period 324–63 showed an increasing 'attitude of independence and even defiance' on the side of the bishops.[132] This new trend held a promise for the contextual profile of the Church in the following years (363–97).

The role of synods

If 'the greatest synods have proceeded at the will of the emperors' (Socrates),[133] there were more and different synods in our period. 'There were numerous councils between 324 and 361 which met without seeking imperial permission to do so.'[134] Synods already were 'a long-standing practice. The novelty was that after 324 the emperor sometimes summoned a council and set its agenda.'[135] Barnes also admits as 'new in the Christian empire [. . .] the automatic enforcement of the decisions of church councils.'[136] It is true that, in spite of formal freedom, the proceedings of synods were at least influenced by the tempting perspective of the emperor's approval and the effects this would have. Even when the emperor or his officials pulled the strings, discussions and block formations were not excluded. It was only in the 350s that Constantius showed a determination to extort, at any cost, the result he wanted.

In spite of this, quite a number of synod meetings followed their own line. In the first place, not all the synods that dealt with the Christological problem had an ecumenical and imperial character. There was a distinction between provincial, regional and ecumenical synods. Some met by order of the emperor or at his instigation – these were mostly the greater ones – whereas local and provincial synods assembled on the initiative of the metropolitan. We saw Athanasius and the Roman bishops Julius and Liberius and Basil of Ancyra take initiatives to assemble such synods. And in the second place, we may notice that these synods were not only free from direct state pressure but often had room for manoeuvring against the emperor's wishes, as happened on the Egyptian and Roman synods that defended the legitimacy of Athanasius' episcopal function and his doctrinal position.

Though the official doctrine of the Church was finally fixed by synods of the imperial and ecumenical type, the smaller meetings often had the function of being stepping stones in the process of theological clarification.

They contributed to the marking out of concerns and fears and of untenable positions such as the 'anhomoean' extreme. It is only natural that synods were often opposing each other. Alexandrian synods stood over and against those of Antioch; at Serdica (343) the delegates met in two separate groups; and from 345 onwards the western synods reacted to the eastern (Sirmium) by advancing their own proposals. Was there a super-synod to arbitrate or harmonise?

It is only in retrospect that it can be said that the status of the Council of Nicaea stood supreme above all the following synods of the period we have been discussing here. It is totally incorrect to attribute a dominating authority to Nicaea and its decisions, for we have seen that the Nicene Creed and its key word *homoousios* came to be the heart of the controversy only after 351. Only after Athanasius had set himself to defend the decisions of the Nicene synod and after his deposition had been renewed by the Sirmium synod, the Alexandrian bishop and the Christology, which he identified with the Nicene formula, became from then onwards the target of those who sought to define the harmony between Christ and God without any use of essentialist notions (*ousia*). Likewise, it became the rallying cry for those who wanted to emphasise a full unity between Christ and the Father. We gave the reasons for the comeback of a formula containing *ousia*, thanks to the opinion and action of Basil of Ancyra. This meant the beginning of a revaluation, however critical, of the Nicene Creed.

But there was still a long way to go before Nicaea regained the ecumenical authority it had only had during a few years after 325. By 360, its definition seemed to have been wiped out forever. But by the 'conversion' of Basil and his friends to a definition that included *ousia* (like their new key word *homoiousios*), the Nicene formula was given a chance to become the expression of what large majorities believed. We can, therefore, not join the view that at Nicaea a clearly defined doctrine of Christ had already been laid down and that, consequently, its aftermath was a conflict between 'orthodox' defenders and heretical assailants of that ecclesiastical faith. Nicaea was the beginning of that 'process of trial and error' (Hanson), which by a gradual clarification was leading to the authoritative status accorded to its creed by hindsight.

Excursus: the Bishop of Rome

Before we close this section on the role of synods, we must make a few remarks on the position of the Bishop of Rome in the doctrinal and canonical controversies. When they were deposed or expelled from their sees, Athanasius, Marcellus and other eastern bishops turned to Rome, where the Bishop, or a local synod convoked by him, took a decision after examination of the case. We saw that for many years, viz., from the arrival of Athanasius and Marcellus in 340 until Liberius' capitulation in 357, Rome defended the legitimacy and the theological views of Athanasius (and in a first stage also of

Marcellus). It was under the leadership of Rome that the west reacted to the creeds issued by the synods of Antioch and Serdica. Both Julius (in 341) and Liberius (in 353) called upon the Emperor for an ecumenical council in order to settle the questions about the creed and about Athanasius' position. These facts may suggest that Rome already enjoyed a special status and that its bishop had the position to play a central role.

No doubt the Bishop of Rome was a prominent figure in the church of the west. Constantine called upon him for arbitration at the beginning of the Donatist quarrel, although together with three Gaulish bishops (see Chapter 2, p. 39). In the Church as a whole, however, the bishop of Rome was no more important than were his colleagues of Alexandria and Antioch. He enjoyed a slightly higher authority than the bishops of other western capitals such as Carthage, Arles and Treves. This was due to the importance of the city of Rome as the old imperial capital. Rome conserved its prestige even after Constantinople had become the new capital, since Constantine's city was called 'the new or second Rome'.[137] The Christian community of Rome was numerically strong and well organised and, moreover, it had often taken the lead in doctrinal and disciplinary dissensions.[138]

However, all this does not imply that the bishop of Rome had any particular authority over the ecumenical councils. It was the emperor who convoked them, and the bishop of Rome could do no more than ask the emperor to do so when, as to Julius and Liberius, this seemed important. The Roman Catholic scholar Goemans, who studied the general council in the fourth century,[139] came to the conclusion that there is no evidence for a special role of the Roman bishop in relation to the ecumenical councils. His cooperation or convocation was not indispensable. He had neither the right to preside over the meeting nor, since he never attended any council in person (he used to send delegates), was his ratification of the council's decisions afterwards requested. This situation changed under Liberius' successor Damasus (366–84) who, with all proper reserves, may be called the first pope.[140]

The theological process

Hanson called the process that led to the doctrinal definition of the Trinity 'a process of trial and error – with error on all sides'. From the beginning of the Arian struggle, nearly all eastern theologians[141] were frightened by the spectre of Sabellianism, viz., of any formulation of the relationship between the Father and the Son that would obscure their proper and distinctive personalities. Besides this fear, we find such a spiritual conception of God that any definition that could suggest a partition of his being into two equals was repugnant.[142] Therefore, definitions that made use of the term *ousia* (essence) were for decades a great stumbling block in the debate. The Nicene *homoousios* ('consubstantial to' or 'of one essence with the Father') was one such, though it was not the only use of *ousia*.

Three successive waves manifested the determination to get rid of this term:

- Arius and his companions, immediately after the Council of Nicaea;
- the 'Arian Party', i.e., the eastern majority, on successive synods which started with the 'Church Dedication Synod' at Antioch (341) and culminated in the Sirmium meetings which prohibited all use of *ousia* and compound words;
- the 'Anhomoeans', sometimes called 'Neo-Arians', of the late 350s.

Therefore, the definition of a full communion of essence and attributes seemed to menace the scriptural distinction of the persons of God and Christ. The most sweeping utterance of this fear was the anhomoean position, but this approach could hardly do justice to the idea of 'sonship' and to the New Testament appositions of Christ, such as 'Image of the invisible God, in whom all the fullness of God was pleased to dwell' (Col. 1:15–19) or 'He reflects the glory of God and bears the very stamp of his nature' (Heb. 1:3). As a result, *ousia* became a target to the intellectual theology, on the one hand, and the indispensable expression of Christ's unity with God, which was more and deeper than one of good will and perseverance, on the other. It was for that reason that eastern theologians such as Basil of Ancyra and Cyril of Jerusalem, though coming from the ranks of the 'Arian' middle party, changed their mind and, after all, preferred the inclusion of *ousia* into the definition of Christ's relation to God. The result of this consideration was the term *homoiousios*. It was a compromise, forged in order to confess, on the one hand, that as God's image Christ has more in common with the Father than a harmony of will,[143] and, on the other, to have a safeguard against too great an identification.

All through the twentieth century and still today we can hear criticism on the fact that Christ's uniqueness and salvific significance has been expressed in Greek philosophical terms. But in the context of the fourth century it was a significant way of confessing that Christ is 'fully and unequivocally God, although distinct from him as person and in his actions'. These actions consist, in particular, in the capacity of suffering death, i.e., in a divine solidarity with the human condition, in spite of the unassailable axiom of God's impassibility. Men like Athanasius wanted to give full weight to the current axiom of God's eternity, immutability and immateriality, as well as to his compassion for the creatures endowed with reason. But how could an immutable and immaterial God be in saving solidarity with humans if not when his essential goodness and love had fully been dwelling in the man Jesus and had been at work in all his deeds? Thus the pre-existent subject in Jesus Christ, i.e., the Son or the Word, must have been sharing God's nature by virtue of a generation that assured to him an identical and not a lesser quality of essence. Being declared 'of one essence with the Father', Christ was proclaimed the direct expression and guarantor of God's love and fidelity.

It is true that terms such as *homoousios* belonged to the ontological language of the Platonic tradition, where it was used to express a same level of being, implying full congeniality. We said that the tendency in late third- and early fourth-century philosophy was to widen the distance between a transcendent God, on the one hand, and the cosmos with all its plurality and variety, on the other.[144] In this context, the explicit Christian conviction that God willingly decided to create, required a choice between the alternatives of the Son who was the outcome of the same will to create (Arius) or who was fully congenial to God (Athanasius). The priority given to a soteriological approach necessarily led to the blowing up of the traditional cosmological doctrine of the *Logos*. If Christ was conceived of as the first emanation from God or the first product of his will, it would result into a Christology that corresponded with a hierarchical order of beings. In such a structure, he could play a central role in creation and in the instruction of humans who, by following his example, would develop a determination to force back bodily appetites and to ascend to the harmony of their soul with the spiritual world. In this conception, Christ would be a frontrunner who clears the way to the adoptive childhood of God. Over against this optimistic anthropology we have seen the rise of theologians inspired by a more total and radical view on Christ's redeeming work. According to the perception of the latter, Christ has made the Father known because he came from 'the bosom of the Father' (John 1:18). Thanks to the fact that he partakes in God's life, his incarnation not only brings salvation for the body as well as for the inner life, but even takes the physical as entry and stable base for a complete and irrevocable transformation of human nature, both physical and ethical. The 'Christology of exchange' only makes sense if Christ is both fully God and really man. We saw how consistently Athanasius explored this way of thinking, though there was also 'error on his side', since he did not give Christ room for a real increase in wisdom (Luke 2:52) and assimilation of his human will to the Father's (Mark 14:36).

There is another element in the change of orientation that Athanasius brought into theological thought and in which he would be followed by other prominent theologians of the century, notably by the rising generation in Asia Minor.[145] We mean that Athanasius, though he was imbued with philosophical culture and terminology, was not really philosophically minded, but rather echoing the voice of the community's experience of salvation in Christ. He and the next generation shared the piety of their local churches. It was the living faith of these communities that, through them, corrected the achievements of conceptual logic.[146] The faithful were not interested in precise and justifiable formulas that ranked the person of Christ in a metaphysical scale, they experienced him as divine Saviour and worshipped him conformably. Athanasius saw the Christian community as the place where the new life installed and guaranteed by the divine Christ was realised and from where it was leavening the world. Much more than that, he would appreciate its religious civilising within the framework of a Christianised empire. This impact of the communities' belief on leaders such as Athanasius and the

Cappadocians should not be overlooked. Their frame of reference was the faith by which the Church was living, rather than the adjustment of biblical data to formal logic or to the Empire as reflection of Christ's kingship. Taking all this into account, it seems justifiable to see Athanasius as an innovator rather than a conservative mind, since his theological ways were a response to a changing cosmological and political context.

5   Christianity matures

Introduction to the last decades and the emperors (364–97)

Julian's reign had been no more than a short interruption of the growing alliance between Church and State. His successors were Christians again. This does not mean, however, that they shared identical opinions on the doctrinal issues, which were still under discussion. Some of them preferred a watered-down Arianism, shorn of the extremes, judging it to be the most, elastic and unifying basis for a state religion. Others turned to tolerance. And, finally, Christianity met emperors who wanted the Nicene Confession to be the base of ecclesiastical consensus. They all had one target in common: imperial unity, consolidated by a unanimous church. We therefore must expect a continuation of the controversies of the preceding period on the relation of Christ to God the Father, and of the wrestling between emperors and bishops for the discretionary power in doctrinal affairs. The extension of the debate to the status of the Holy Spirit introduced a new element.

After Julian's defeat against the Persians, the next emperors had to face the military threat in the east, to which were added the incursions of German tribes, notably the Goths, on the northern border. Jovian (July 363–February 364) had no choice but to make peace with the Persians by parting with some eastern territories. As a consequence, the Romans were no longer able to protect the Christian kingdom of Armenia, which was invaded by the Persians and suffered their revenge (see below, Chapter 6, pp. 153–5). After Jovian's death, an army commander, Valentinianus, took power, choosing for himself the west and entrusting the east to his brother, Valens. In 378, Valens was slain in a battle with the Goths at Adrianople (as little as 200 kilometres from Constantinople). This shameful defeat obliged the Roman leadership to incorporate Gothic detachments into the army and to admit Goths into their administration; it was a blow to the Roman feelings of superiority, still nourished by traditional minds. Only capable army commanders and reformers of the administration found ways to maintain a form of Roman supremacy, provided they took account of the new balance of power. After Valens had died, Valentinianus' western successor, Gratianus, chose one of his successful generals to save the endangered east: Theodosius, born of a Spanish military family, won a surprising battle against the Goths and, on the base of this relief, Gratianus made him Emperor of the east. Theodosius reigned in total from 379 to 395. In 388 he helped young Valentinianus II to shake off a usurper. But he then took up residence at Milan and in the following year even made his solemn entry into the city of Rome. Being in fact the ruler of the prefecture of Italy, he left to Valentinianus the prefecture of Gaul only.[1] Formally, the latter remained the emperor of the whole west till his death in 392. During the final three years of his reign, Theodosius ruled the whole empire before its definitive division into two empires that were to follow different courses.[2] This provides the following tableau:

Jovian 363–4

East	West
Valens 364–78	Valentinianus I 364–75
Theodosius I 379–92	(son and co-regent) Gratianus 367–83
	Valentinianus II 375–92

Theodosius I 392–5

When Valentinianus II succeeded to his father, he was only four years old. He could only play a role after his elder brother Gratianus had been killed by mutinying troops. He still was no older than twelve and stood under the influence of his mother Justina, who sympathised with the Arian party. During the late 360s and the 370s, the events of the Church were, therefore, largely dominated by a pro-Arian Valens and by a toler-ant Valentinianus I. The religious policy of the latter was continued by Gratianus, until a sudden change in 379, certainly under the influence of Theodosius who now was his powerful colleague and who was strongly in favour of the Nicene Christology and maybe also through the theological instructions he received from Ambrose, the pro-Nicene Bishop of Milan since 374. The renewed support of Arianism by Valentinianus II and Justina in the 380s provoked a harsh confrontation with this highly qualified church leader. When Theodosius came to reside at Milan (from 388 onwards), this favoured an excellent relationship between him and Ambrose.

The political alliance between Gratianus and Theodosius is also responsible for the stabilisation of Nicene theology in the Church and for the monopoly of a Catholic orthodoxy in the whole empire. They broke the power of both the Arians and the 'Pneumatomachians', i.e., those questioning the divine status of the Holy Spirit.[3]

They also excluded from influence other Christian heretics, Jews and pagans. By a decree, issued in February 380, the Christian religion in its Nicene form was established as state religion and was given the exclusive right to be called 'catholic'.

Christianity passed to the comfortable status of the only permitted religion, and the stream that had proved resistant against the pressure of many emperors was now recognised as the exclusive form of its confession and institution. At the same time, the leading theologians of the epoch integrated the harvest of classical Greek culture into this victorious Christianity. The centre of new and contextual theology shifted from Egypt and Palestine (homelands of Athanasius and Eusebius) to Asia Minor and Syria. The three so-called Cappadocian Fathers played a dominant role in the reaffirmation of the Nicene Christology and, by developing a doctrine of the Holy Spirit, in the completion of a trinitarian model of thought. As we said above, the theological discussions about God, who manifests himself in more than one single individuality, had been extended to the Spirit. When the question was debated whether he is just one of God's servant ghosts or a divine person of the same nature and rank as the Father and the Son, this debate caused a new controversy among those who otherwise agreed upon the full divinity of the Son.

General decisions on the official doctrine of the Church and on the filling of important sees were taken at the instigation of the emperors and sanctioned by them. The custom, which Constantine had introduced with reluctance,[4] had set. It was to Constantinople that in 381 Theodosius convoked a synod in order to reaffirm the faith of Nicaea against the Arians, then mostly 'anhomeans' led by Eunomius, and to reconcile the Pneumatomachians. Though this Constantinopolitan synod was a meeting of the east and its decisions had to wait a long time for western approval, it later won the status of Second Ecumenical Council. Its creed, which was both a confirmation and an extension of the old Nicene Creed, was predestined to enjoy the most ecumenical recognition ever given to any Christian creed. It now plays an important role in the search for Christian unity. We therefore have to give full account for its production and content, as well as for the effects of the Constantinopolitan council in the context of the period we are examining. However determinative the concern for political unity was in the emperors' minds, theological clarification was no less a real concern of the Church itself, since it had gone through so many and bitter controversies.

This brings us back to the relations between the Church and the Roman State. The brutal interference of Constantius and Julian's subtle repression had excited a fresh self-consciousness among a number of bishops, notably when they experienced oppressive actions that attacked convictions they considered as the proper and correct faith of the Church. This self-consciousness increased. In this respect, the west produced an impressive model in the person of Bishop Ambrose. He courageously resisted 'Arianising' emperors such as Valentinianus II and in a remarkable case even dared to subject the great protector of orthodox Christianity, Theodosius, to the rules of ecclesiastical discipline. The relations, and even confrontations, between a prominent church leader and three different Christian emperors show a development, the implications of which should not be missing in any picture of the contextualisation in the fourth century.

This introductory overview leads to the following subdivision of this chapter:

1 The final phase of the Arian struggle; the external events (364–82).
2 The final phase of the Arian struggle; the doctrinal results.
3 The reception of the Creed of Nicaea-Constantinople; its ecumenical status.
4 New trends in the relationship between the Church and the emperor.

The final phase of the Arian struggle; the external events (364–82)

The division of the Empire that followed the period of three monarchical rulers favoured the conflicts between old and new ecclesiastical parties. Arianism found imperial support or tolerance. In the east, the debate on the divine relationships was extended to the Holy Spirit. Each doctrinal group tried to get hold of important sees so that capital cities had two (or more) contending bishops, each with local constituencies and support from outside. The years 379–81 brought a great change when the two emperors united their forces and proclaimed one specific theological trend 'catholic' and made this form of Christianity the sole state religion. When an imperial synod restored the validity of Nicaea and rejected three contemporary convictions about Christ and the Spirit, an 'orthodoxy' was established and confirmed by the State. The 'Theodosian era' replaced the 'Constantinian' times. The preponderance of Constantinople in these events prevented the west as yet from acknowledging the doctrinal results, which were mainly due to the work done by the Cappadocian Fathers.

The balance of power: emperors and ecclesiastical parties

The reign of Julian had been too short, and his measures in order to re-establish a Hellenistic religious society too artificial to impede the process of Christianisation of the Graeco-Roman world. Jovian restored the previous relationship between Church and State. Members of the Arian Party and Athanasius went to see the new Emperor in order to win his support. Thanks to Jovian's sympathy for the Nicene Party, Athanasius could regain his see. But Jovian's reign was even shorter than Julian's: it only lasted eight months. In the west, Valentinianus I turned to the tradition of religious tolerance, whereas the eastern ruler Valens revived the policy of Constantius: he supported the (Neo-)Arians and pressed for elastic theological formulas. The east, therefore, went through an ascendancy of Arianism again. Athanasius was sent into his fifth exile; Cyril of Jerusalem suffered his third dismissal. But the impact of the theological achievements, in particular the convergence of old and new supporters of an essential unity of Christ and the Father, could no longer be silenced.

In the preceding chapter (pp. 105–6) we have referred to the reunification of parties that Athanasius achieved in Alexandria in 362. As a result of the previous party-building, the congregation of Antioch, the third city of the Empire and capital of the diocese *Oriens*,[5] had split into no less than four factions: a 'Eunomian' or 'Anhomoean', an 'old-Nicene' under Bishop Paulinus, and a middle group, following the Cappadocians, i.e., the position of reconciling unity of essence with clear distinction of their individualities. The fourth group followed Bishop Apollinarius of Laodicea, whose Christology was perfectly Nicene but confused the minds because he taught that Christ had not had a complete human nature.[6] Antioch thus counted three communities that were equally attached to Nicaea but were nevertheless separated from each other owing to ingrained office-holdings and personal constituencies. The major faction took its stand by Bishop Meletius, a real leader who also enjoyed the recognition of the churches of Asia Minor. But Paulinus was at the head of a strong community as well, and he was enjoying the support of Alexandria and Rome. The significance of the Alexandrian synod in 362 was that Athanasius, although preferring the Nicene formula of *homoousios*, proved to be sufficiently broad-minded to accept the similar key word of *homoiousios*, because in his view it complied with the criterion of the full divinity of Christ.[7] This toning down of the shibboleth by those who held to the strongest unity between Father and Son cleared the way for a reconciliation of all who were abhorrent of the anhomoean doctrine of a merely ethical and metaphorical 'sonship' of Christ.

The presence of some old leaders and their constituencies complicated the political side of the controversy. The situation in Constantinople was similar: one bishop, supported by Alexandria and Rome, rivalled with another, Macedonius, pro-Nicene as well, but even so leader of the 'Pneumatomachians' and, therefore, the target of those who, following the three Cappadocians, advocated a fully divine nature of the Spirit. Any future settlement, therefore, had to include not only the reconciliation of theological formulas, but also solutions for the occupation of the sees of the two capitals.

Athanasius died in 373 and was succeeded by Peter. Meanwhile, the leadership of the Nicene party had gone over to Basil of Caesarea, the frontrunner of the three Cappadocian theologians, who in course of time were also appointed bishops in their native regions. Basil's town was the metropolis of Cappadocia and he became its bishop in 370. Although his college friend Gregory of Nazianzum and his younger brother Gregory (who was to become Bishop of Nyssa) were productive theological thinkers and authors of equal quality as Basil himself, he was the leader. He died in 379, but through the two Gregorys and through others whose minds he had shaped, his legacy influenced the synod of Constantinople (381), the future Second Ecumenical Council. Basil showed the same firmness as Athanasius, but no doubt his character and culture were broader (see below, pp. 129–30).

Catholic Christianity raised to state religion

As under Constantius, Valens' repression of the Nicene Creed provoked firm opposition in the eastern part of the Empire. His policy reinforced the conviction that, after the many tentative Christological formulas of the preceding decades, the Nicene Creed, with its clear confession of a common *ousia* of the Father and the Son, was not so bad after all. Polarisation therefore increased, and even more because of the debate regarding the status of the Holy Spirit. When, after Valens' death, the exiled bishops returned to their sees, ecclesiastical unity became more than ever before the urgent task of the new imperial tandem. Of these two rulers, Gratianus preferred to continue the policy of his predecessor, Valentinianus I. In a declaration given at Sirmium in 378, he proclaimed a limited tolerance; limited, because the Eunomians and the Marcellians – one could say the two extremes in Christological thought[8] – were excluded. But these exclusions still left plenty of room for contrarieties.

Early in 379, Gratianus suddenly modified his religious policy in a strictly pro-Nicene direction. Two influential characters are probably responsible for this turn: Bishop Ambrose of Milan and Gratianus' co-emperor Theodosius. Ambrose had been asked to advise Gratianus on current faith issues, but these explanations may have come to his knowledge somewhat later.[9] The impulse rather came from Theodosius, who not only was a devout Christian but who also strongly sympathised with the Nicene faith.

Theodosius set himself to secure the unity of the Empire on the basis of the Nicene faith and made Christianity the official and exclusive religion of the Empire. Although not yet baptised, Theodosius was a convinced Christian and, as soon as he had pacified the Goths, on 28 February 380, he and Gratianus together issued the proclamation by which it was ordered that

1 Christianity would be the only religion to which all subjects were bound to adhere.
2 The faith as taught by the present bishops of Rome and Alexandria, Damasus and Peter, would be the only confession entitled to be called 'Catholic', since it is identical with the one preached by the Apostle Peter.[10]

Gratianus soon deposed the title of 'Supreme Pontiff', which in pagan view indicated the traditional care of the emperor for the religious obligations of the State.[11] The proclamation of 380 was soon followed by legislation against pagans, Jews and Christian heretics. Tolerance had come to an end; the coercion of the imperial measures led to a massive catholisation of the society.

The edict was promulgated at Saloniki, Macedonia, a frontier town between west and east. Coming from Spain and having waged war on the Balkans, Theodosius made a stop here. He raised to state religion Christianity in its Nicene form, explicitly referring to the axis Alexandria–Rome, i.e., to the theology of Athanasius (Bishop Peter's predecessor) and to the doctrinal stand of Pope Damasus. The latter had taken action against the Arian Bishop of Milan, Auxentius,[12] and followed Basil of Caesarea's convictions concerning the nature of the Holy Spirit. These two princes of the Church expressed what was Theodosius' own conviction, and he made it the starting point for ecclesiastical peace. But he had not yet made a real experience of the hornet's nest of the east and all its passionate doctrinal and personal controversies. The situation Theodosius was going to face was far more complicated and explosive than he had presumed. Anyhow, it could not change his main objective, which was unity as ever before.

The new emperor could not hope to rally the whole east with such a terse definition of the Holy Trinity as was given in the Saloniki edict, especially not since this referred so explicitly and exclusively to the theological standpoint of Rome and Alexandria. Something more sophisticated had to be done. As we have said, besides the doctrinal issues, there were the controversies about persons since Rome and Alexandria were still supporting those bishops in Antioch and Constantinople whose legitimacy was disputed in their own cities. But an event of the year before gave him good hope: in the autumn of 379 a synod had met in Antioch under the leadership of Meletius (the bishop who was supported by large eastern groups but not by Rome), and this meeting had accepted a faith declaration of Damasus, in which he confessed a detailed Nicene Christology and the divinity of the Holy Spirit. This declaration was a possible basis for reconciliation between the east and the west. Actually, the synod of Antioch offered real, ecumenical expectations.[13] Theodosius, therefore, ventured to convoke to Constantinople a broader synod, which in the first instance should be a platform for the reconciliation of the different eastern parties, but which he probably expected to have an ecumenical result, engaging the west as well.

The proceedings of the synods of Constantinople in 381 and 382

If such were the expectations of Theodosius, two of them were not fulfilled, one at least not during his lifetime. The Constantinopolitan synod did not succeed in rallying the Pneumatomachians, nor did it acquire the agreement of the west for the next seven decades. Yet it was a high-level assembly in which most of the leading theologians of the east took part, especially those coming from the diocese Oriens.[14] For some unclear reason, the delegates from Egypt and Macedonia arrived with a delay of one month. The west was not invited at all, but it had its observer in the person of the Bishop of Saloniki. The number of participants was 146 and the synod was later referred to as 'the Assembly of the 150 Fathers'.[15] The assembly was in session from May until July 381.

It is only logical that the Emperor also appointed the Chairman: he was Meletius of Antioch, who had successfully presided over the synod in his city in 379. This move promised conciliation. Meletius enjoyed large support from Asia Minor. Unfortunately, he died before the first month was over. Gregory of Nazianzum, one of the three Cappadocians, replaced him. In order to give him status, Gregory was first consecrated Bishop of Constantinople, although he had already a small bishopric in Asia Minor, which he had never thought good enough to fill. This irregularity, the sudden irruption of the delegates from Egypt and Macedonia (whom Gregory hoped to win because of their solidarity with the west, but who opposed his office) and Gregory's own scholarly but idealistic standard made him unfit to lead the turbulent and thwarting assembly. Soon he resigned both as Chairman of the Synod and as Bishop of Constantinople, uttering bitter reproaches to the synod members. Nevertheless, he did not step out without having exercised some influence upon the debates. The synod found its third chairman in the person of Nectarius, who was able to finish the job. Nectarius, still a layman, had to pass quickly through baptism and consecration before he could actually take the twofold office of metropolitan bishop of the capital and president of the synod. No doubt Theodosius wished that things went that way.

The Emperor had also summoned a large representation of the Pneumatomachians, hoping to rally this group with the new definition of the faith that was to be adopted. Although the synod avoided extending the *homoousia* of the Son to the Holy Spirit, this reserve did not persuade them. The Pneumatomachians, therefore, left the meeting dissatisfied. Their dropping out did, however, not lead the synod to the adoption of identical wordings for the relationships of the Son and the Spirit with the Father. In the Creed the Spirit is confessed to 'proceed from the Father', whereas the Son is 'begotten of the Father', 'lordly' – distinct from Christ who is 'the one Lord' – and 'worshipped and glorified together with the Father and the Son' without being declared 'of one substance with the Father'. These cautious distinctions may have been introduced with the intention to accommodate the Pneumatomachians.[16] This was in vain, but the chosen wordings were maintained.

The first objective having been missed, the synod wanted to reaffirm the trinitarian faith over and against all the aberrations that had come about since the days of Nicaea. Next it had to clear the situation in the central cities of Antioch and of Constantinople itself. Before we examine the doctrinal result of the synod, we shall cast a glance at its decisions, contained in four so-called *canons*.

1 The first canon confirms the doctrinal decision of Nicaea and rejects four Christological aberrations, viz., those of radical and moderate Arianism, of the recent forms of Sabellianism (so to say, the opposite extreme), of Apollinarism[17] and, of course, of the unwilling Pneumatomachians.[18]

2 The second canon forbids the bishops of one diocese to interfere in another. This measure furthered the assimilation of larger ecclesiastical units with the imperial dioceses and the formation of the eastern *patriarchates*.[19] More specifically, it meant barring the heads of the Egyptian Church from their usual power politics outside their province –

a curtailment which, for a long time, the Alexandrian 'popes' were not inclined to accept.[20]

3   Canon 3 meant a further humiliation of Alexandria. It was stated that 'the bishop of Constantinople should have pride of place directly after the bishop of Rome, his city being the New Rome'.[21] Alexandria, until then boasting the second rank, was going to be counted out as an important centre of the Church as a whole. Old Rome was not pleased at all by this canon, because it positioned Constantinople almost at the same rank as itself. Nectarius, the rapidly consecrated bishop and (third) chairman of the synod, knew well how to rise to the stature of true 'patriarch' of Constantinople, becoming the eastern counterpart of the Roman pope.[22] But the church of the new capital could not boast of any apostolic founder or martyr, whereas Rome could point to the work of the apostles Peter and Paul;[23] it derived its prestige only from its foundation by Constantine in 330 and from lodging the imperial court. This canon thus shows how much the apostolic origins and features of the Church became overshadowed by its close alliance with the Empire: more and more the Church adapted its territorial and hierarchical organisation to that of the state.

4   The last canon decreed who should be recognised as the legal bishop of Constantinople: Gregory of Nazianzum (the second chairman of the synod), and definitely not the man who thus far had been supported by Alexandria and Rome. It was another slap in the face of both these cities. It shows how little ecumenical the synod in fact was: it rather reshuffled and stabilised the balance of power in the east and was hardly concerned about good relations with the west. In spite of all this, in Constantinople 381 became recognised as the Second Ecumenical Council.

In a final address to Theodosius, the synod thanked God for having established the emperorship in order to maintain peace within the Church and to consolidate the true faith. At the same time, they asked him to confirm their decisions, which Theodosius indeed did before the end of the month. This time he nominated a larger number of 'norm bishops' for the east than he had done in the edict of 380, adding five bishops who had actually played an important role at the synod, and six other, rather insignificant, bishops – nearly all from the dioceses of Asia and Oriens. Alexandria and Rome were no longer mentioned as standard for orthodox and legal Catholicism, and that was a remarkable shift.

However, an ecumenical gesture towards the west was made in the following year: a new synod, convoked by the patriarch Nectarius, assembled in Constantinople and sent a letter to the western leaders, Ambrose of Milan and Damasus of Rome. The easterners rendered account of the proceedings of the previous synod, qualifying that meeting straightway as 'ecumenical', which it had obviously not been. The westerners rightly felt it that way. Their grievances concerned above all Canons 2 and 3,[24] whereas they kept a complete silence about the doctrinal decisions. As early as September 381, Ambrose, acting also on behalf of Pope Damasus, had lodged a protest with the Emperor against the synod's nominations on the important sees and required that a truly ecumenical council be held in Rome. When Theodosius refused, Ambrose reiterated this request and then he and Damasus convened a synod, which most of the invited eastern bishops refused to attend. The west pretended it to be an ecumenical council (instead of the one at Constantinople), but it never obtained this status since it was held without the Emperor's approbation. On the contrary, it was the synod of Constantinople that, against the will of the Roman pope, later rose to that status (see below, pp. 138–42).

But before we discuss that development we will give ample attention to the creed of 381 and the doctrine it represents.

The final phase of the Arian struggle; doctrinal results

In comparison with the Nicene Creed, the one of Constantinople has a number of additions that implicitly reject the classification of Christ and of the Holy Spirit on the level of God's creation, despite the acknowledgement that they have been and still are subservient to his purposes. It also rejects the idea that at the end of time Christ and the Spirit will lose their proper characteristics. A lasting conceptual apparatus has been developed for safeguarding both the essential unity and the distinction of the three divine persons. This achievement was mainly the result of the work of the three Cappadocians, whose pertinent theological contributions are visible in all debated issues and, predominantly, in an elaborate doctrine of the Holy Spirit and his role. Spiritual contemplatives by inner liking, these three men did not shirk back from church leadership and responsible action. Sprung from the upper class, they were at home in Greek culture, which they appreciated as leading to the Christian faith, and they were able to integrate the best of its harvest into their modes of expression. But in their conception of God and of Man they gave prevalence to biblical, notably ethical, traits and values. Besides Asia Minor, Syria also produced great masters. Rooted in the tradition of literal exegesis, Theodore emphasised the growth in willpower and in active trustfulness, both in Christ as man and in every Christian.

The Creed of Constantinople: confirmation and elucidation of the 'Nicene Faith'

The official doctrinal document issued by the Constantinopolitan synod has been lost. It is very likely that it contained the text of the creed that the Fourth Ecumenical Council (Chalcedon, 451) has transmitted as 'the same Faith [viz., as was proclaimed at Nicaea], which the 150 Fathers, who assembled in the great Constantinople, have approved of.[25] We reproduce its text, printed next to the original Nicene Creed, and then comment on the new elements.

The Creed of Nicaea, 325	The Creed of Constantinople, 381
We believe in one God, the Father, almighty, maker	We believe in one God, the Father, almighty, maker
of all things visible and invisible.	of heaven and earth, of all things visible and invisible.
And in one Lord Jesus Christ, the Son of God, begotten from the Father, only-begotten, that is from the substance of the Father, God from God, light from light, true God from true God, begotten not made, of one substance with the Father, through whom all things came into being, things in heaven and things on earth;	And in one Lord Jesus Christ, the only-begotten Son of God, begotten from the Father before all ages, light from light, true God from true God, begotten not made, of one substance with the Father, through whom all things came into existence;
Who because of us men, and because of our salvation came down and became incarnate, becoming man,	Who because of us men and because of our salvation came down from heaven, and was incarnate from the Holy Spirit and the Virgin Mary and became man, and was crucified for us under Pontius Pilate,
suffered and rose again on the third day,	and suffered and was buried, and rose again on the third day according to the Scriptures
ascended to the heavens,	and ascended to heaven, sits on the right hand of the Father and will come again with glory to judge
will come to judge the living and the dead.	living and dead, of whose kingdom there will be no end.
And in the Holy Spirit.	And in the Holy Spirit, exerting lordship and spending life, who proceeds from the Father, who is glorified and worshipped together with the Father and the Son; who spoke through the prophets; in one holy Catholic and apostolic Church. We confess one baptism to the remission of sins; we look forward to the resurrection of the dead and the life of the world to come. Amen.[26]

It is obvious that the Creed of Constantinople (C), although it has the same sequence of faith articles, is too different to be considered as a repetition of the text of Nicaea (N) with the addition of closer definitions of the salvific work of Jesus Christ and of the Holy Spirit. As a matter of fact, C has been identified as an amalgamation of baptismal confessions, used in the churches of Jerusalem and Rome with, of course, additions that react to new doctrines.[27] Although it is true that C was later presented as a confirmation of N – and even came to be simply called 'the Nicene Creed', this does not mean that N was literally reproduced in C with some extensions: by 'Nicene' the contemporary authors meant 'according to the theology or the character of N', or to put it otherwise, in accordance with the 'Faith of Nicaea'.[28]

The sections about God as Father and Creator, and about the Son, his origin and equality with the Father, do not show any substantial alterations. Arianism, both in its original and in its more recent 'anhomoean' form, was rejected as before. Obviously the wish not to mitigate the theology of Nicaea was so strong that *homoousios* was not even modified into *homoiousios*, though the latter would have corresponded much better with the prevailing theological mind.

There are significant additions to highlight:

First, the emphasis upon the way the Son became incarnate, viz., 'from the Holy Spirit and the Virgin Mary'. This sentence had a bearing on a contemporary Christological controversy, viz., the standpoint of Apollinarius, who detracted from Christ's humanity by denying him the leading functions of the human soul (reason and will), arguing that these were assumed by the *Logos* himself. Opposing this view, the synod puts in parallel the divine and the human origins of Christ, implying that neither of them is to be seen as incomplete.

Second, the addition that the kingdom of Christ will have no end, not even after he will have completed his final work, the judgement of all, is doubtless a refutation of Marcellus' and Photinus' conception of the Trinity, which was a stumbling block for most eastern theologians, who suspected a resurgent Sabellianism. In the preceding chapter we saw how sensitive the east constantly was on this point, much more than the west.[29]

Third, the main task of the assembly was to reconcile the Pneumatomachians. In comparison with Nicaea, in the third section the creed presents an important extension. It has statements about (a) the nature of the Spirit and his relation to the Father; (b) his right to the same adoration by the Church as the Father and Christ receive; and (c) his activities before and since the coming of Christ, in the Old Testament prophets and the Church. These elements intended to put the Spirit on a same level with the two other divine persons. On the other hand, as we pointed out earlier, the synod avoided identical definitions for the Spirit as were used for the Son, viz., 'being begotten from the Father' and 'being of one substance with him'. Christ being the *only-begotten* Son, the Spirit is called *proceeding from the Father* (since he is not another Son), he is not *the Lord* (Christ being the one Lord), but 'lord-like',[30] and instead of insisting upon an equality of nature (*ousia*) an equality of adoration is stated. These subtle differences were probably meant to persuade the Pneumatomachians, but – as stated above – without success.

It may be concluded that, all causes combined, three extreme positions regarding the status of the Son had been rejected: (a) the idea that he was of a lesser rank and nature than God the Father (Arius); (b) the idea that he was only temporarily distinct from God during the work of creation and salvation (Marcellus); (c) the view that the incarnate Son did not have a human mind, so that his personality was only divine (Apollinarius).[31] The new creed neither mentions these thinkers by name, nor is it, like N, followed by condemnations (*anathemas*). The names of those condemned figure in the first canon.

The Creed of Nicaea-Constantinople (NC) was the rule of faith that the Emperor could employ to unify the empire on a religious base. It was also fit for liturgical use both as a baptismal confession and as a glorification of the Holy Trinity. The confession of the Trinity had now become the central dogma of Christianity. It is important to note that the original meaning of the word 'dogma' is adoration, besides 'apology', i.e., the intelligible account of the central articles of faith and, besides, the rejection of conceptions felt as aberrances from correct tradition. The doctrine of God, which was helped to victory, implied the full unity of Father, Son and Holy Spirit in such a way that this unity of essence would not obscure the individual characteristics of each person. Though the Father was clearly confessed to be the unique source of the divinity of the Son and the Spirit, the definition was a middle way between obscuring their permanent distinctive properties, on the one hand, and a gradation within the triune God, on the other.

The contributions of the Cappadocian theologians

In the trinitarian doctrine, some clarifications had been achieved. An important distinction had been made between the common divine nature (*ousia*) and three individualities with distinctive characteristics (*hypostasis*). These characteristics could not only be described by the external works of the divine love (creation, incarnation and crucifixion, life-giving and church-building), but also in terms of internal permanent relationships. Thus, the attribute of the Father is his *ingenerateness* or underivedness, that of the Son is his *generation*, and that of the Spirit is his *procession*. These distinctions are the specific theological contribution of Gregory of Nazianzum, whereas Gregory of Nyssa stressed that the definition could never imply the existence of three disjoined gods.

On several occasions above, the role of the Cappadocians has been mentioned. Led by Basil, they took over from Athanasius the leadership in theological consistency and in political influence. This gradual process of the fading away of Athanasius and of the rise of Basil, his friend Gregory and his younger brother Gregory took place in the 360s after the reconciling synod of Alexandria in 362. This synod had still been conducted by Athanasius, but at the same time it showed that the old man in front had to build a bridge to the *Homoiousians* of Asia Minor and that new questions concerning the person of Christ, such as those raised by Apollinarius, were puzzling the minds. With regard to the west, Basil's theological achievements helped its leader Ambrose to shape his theology and, consequently, to stand against the Arian sympathies of the Milan court.[32] We will therefore examine more precisely the contributions of the Cappadocian Fathers by tracing first their common features and then the particularities of each separately.

Common features

First, they were strongly opposed to any form of isolating the nature of the Son from the Father's essence. Their target was Eunomius, whose cold logic made 'ingeneratedness the sole and crucial characteristic of God',[33] and who consequently denied to the Son any real participation in God's *ousia*. The Cappadocians were deeply interested in the properties of the Father, the Son and the Spirit and in their mutual relations, much more than in problems of derivation. Devoted as they were to the thesis of a common and unchangeable essence of the three divine persons, they valued the Nicene Creed as the most correct expression the Church had ever given to its faith. In line with Athanasius, they dismissed the idea of degrees inside the Godhead, as if the Father would be more 'godly' than the Son, and they both more than the Spirit. The hierarchical conception of God, as it had been handed down by Origen and followed by Eusebius, was on the brink of being totally banished from trinitarian thought. The central issue was no longer how to bridge the divide between the transcendental sphere and the visible world, but the reliability and completeness of salvation, accomplished in mutual unity by three distinguishable persons.

Second, in their defence of Nicaea, the Cappadocians were not by any means verbalists. They were well aware of the inability of the human mind to make an appropriate definition of God. Any confession of God will always make use of human analogies. This acknowledgement of the mystery of God's being distinguished them, on the one hand, from Eunomius, whose logical approach and one-track opinion of God's comprehensibility they judged impertinent. But they differed just as well from Athanasius, who continued to uphold *homoousios* as the shibboleth of orthodox Christology. The Cappadocians stressed that God's being cannot be properly defined, but at the same time that the Scriptures witness to three inseparable but not interchangeable divine 'actors'. Basil particularly referred to the baptismal command that had been given by Christ (Matt. 28:19) and was faithfully followed by the Church in every place. As the Scriptures testify to the proper actions of each person, these properties must belong to their eternal being and independent of the requirements of the work of salvation. Consequently, all three Cappadocians rejected the 'Sabellian' solution, which all eastern theologians suspected in Marcellus of Ancyra and Photinus of Sirmium. Another characteristic of the Cappadocians was their profound conviction that the triune God is worthy of human adoration and liturgical worship, as much as of intellectual grasping.

Third, from his soteriology, Athanasius had expelled the idea of any mediating element between God and humankind except the human flesh which the Son had made his own by his incarnation. Consulted by Bishop Serapion on an early occurrence of Pneumatomachism in Egypt, he placed the Holy Spirit on the side of God and not of creation, lest the Trinity should be conceived of as composed of creating and created nature. The multiple actions of the Spirit upon humankind's weakness and imperfection, in order to lead him on the way of sanctification to his divinisation, are evidence of his fully divine rank. On this foundation, laid down by Athanasius, the Cappadocians developed a richer pneumatology.[34]

They confronted the theory, based on a rather partial exegesis of some biblical texts, that the Spirit, may he be divine and eternal, is not fully equal to the Father and the Son, not *homoousios*, but inferior to them, a sort of servant ghost, sent by them to accomplish certain missions. Against this theory, Basil and his companions emphasised that the Spirit is both gift and giver of true life and of sanctification. He is worthy of the same honour as the other two divine persons and should be glorified together with them. He participates in the same *ousia*. Whereas Basil made a halt before the 'manner of subsistence' of the Spirit, i.e., before the mystery of his origin and the relations within the Trinity, Gregory of Nazianzum went as far as defining these as 'procession', differentiating this mode of origin from the 'generation' of the Son.

Fourth, the Cappadocian theology of the Spirit is closely connected with their deep interest in monastic life. Each of them had originally hesitated between a retired and contemplative life on the landed property (they originated from rich families of landowners!) and the endorsement of a public career, either as a secular orator or as a church minister. Finally they opted for responsible functions in the Church, although after his resignation as Bishop of Constantinople (owing to the difficulties he met during the synod of 381), Gregory returned to his estates. It is no wonder to see those who had chosen a high responsibility in the Church respond to the vocation of an ascetic lifestyle. In a way, an idyllic life in the countryside, calmly devoted to personal reflection, was a quite normal desire among the upper classes of pagan antiquity. This pattern was now Christianised by clergymen who also belonged to the higher ranks of society.

Fifth, finally our theologians achieved an integration of the best and noblest of Greek culture into the Christian system of values, although they were not fully aware of doing so. They used to criticise the philosophers for the arbitrariness of their opinions. However, their sermons are orations following the rules of classical Greek rhetoric. They saw classical education as a fine preparation for the acceptance and the methodical scrutiny of the biblical revelation. They set out to provide the now-Christianised Hellenistic world with 'a complete Christian philosophy, not just ethics but cosmogony and physics'.[35] Most Christian thinkers since Origen had laid stress on man's freedom of choice and responsibility. They had done so because of the weight of Greek astrological determinism, which was an attack on both human freedom and an obligatory moral order. We notice a great interest in a theology of creation, often in the form of an exegesis of Genesis 1–3. Both Basil (imitated by Ambrose) and Gregory of Nyssa wrote such a work, whereas the latter devoted another work to *The Fabrication of Man*.[36] The endeavour of reshaping the entire intellectual Greek legacy into Christian thought forms

and ideals marked the generation that had grown up with the Christian faith
and, at the same time, were at home in the pre-Christian culture, without
being afraid of either component.

The contribution of each Cappadocian individually

Basil spent most of his life in Cappadocian Caesarea, where he was born,
c. 330, as son of a public orator, who was a Christian. After studies in Constantinople and Athens he came back to his native town, where he was
baptised, and then turned to an ascetic life. In 364, the Bishop of Caesarea
called upon him, ordained him priest and involved him in the struggle
against the pro-Arian policy of the Emperor Valens. In 370, Basil succeeded
to this bishop and took the lead of the pro-Nicene movement, which received
its full chances when Valens was succeeded by Theodosius (see above, p. 115).
He died in 379, before he could see the affirmation of what he had stood for
on the synod of Constantinople.

Basil was a born leader,[37] a great organiser, disciplined both in his scholarship and his pious lifestyle. He wrote three books: *Against Eunomius*; a splendid treatise *On the Holy Spirit*; a series of homilies on the *Six Days* (of creation),
as well as over 300 letters. In his theology he combined resoluteness in respect
of the issues at stake with reserve regarding formulations.

Basil made a distinction between the public and liturgical confession of the
Church, which he called the *kerygma* (proclamation), and the search for deeper
knowledge and understanding, for which he wanted to reserve the word
dogma. 'Dogma' was not the preparatory stage of the teaching of the Church,
but the refining elaboration of the confession, which itself is deduced from
the Bible. Basil saw the proclamation of the triune God as directly based on
the baptismal command given by Christ. Kerygma is the minimum that
should be taught, whereas dogma is the deeper insight, transmitted and
studied in small circles of initiated believers. In Basil's view, the monastery is
the appropriate setting for working on the dogma. Along with a life of
devotion and soberness, illumination by the Holy Spirit is indispensable. A
low opinion of the status and gifts of the Spirit is, therefore, a serious sin.[38]

This division of the community into shallowly instructed churchpeople
and truly initiated Christians reminds us of Origen, whose thought deeply
influenced the Cappadocians. There is a great difference, however: Origen
limited the Spirit's range of action to the believers alone and emphasised
the relation of the *Logos* with all rational beings, whereas the Father governs
the entire creation. Origen's trinity model is 'funnel shaped'. According to
Basil, the Holy Spirit is, on the contrary, fully involved in all divine works,
beginning with creation, and worthy to be equally glorified with the Father
and the Son.

Through his own retreat and his growing interest in monachism, Basil
experienced the Spirit's actions in the Christian life. When the Pneumatomachians questioned the Spirit's nature, reflection on the specific activities

of the Spirit became Basil's starting point for further reflection on his divinity. Just as only God can divinise man and only the Son can impart adoptive sonship, so it is only the Spirit that can make man free and conduct progress in personal knowledge and holiness. Basil sees the divinity of the Spirit implied in the baptismal command which is, as we saw, the foundation for a sound trinitarian theology. Sound doctrine leads to due adoration, which completes intellectual theology that by its own limited capacities will always fall short. But it is by all means certain that Father, Son and Spirit have a 'communion of nature', which is the basis of their 'communion of honour'. The fact that the Spirit is to be glorified *together with* the Father and the Son already implies a distinct subsistence (*hypostasis*).

According to Basil, the Nicene Creed expresses the Faith of the Church quite correctly: it mentions the Spirit, even when it gives no further precision. Preservation of this faith does not mean to dwell on the letter of the creed, but to unfold its meaning when new contextual challenges urge us to do so. In his own days, this was the case with the appearance of the Pneumatomachians.

Next to these theological contributions, Basil showed himself to be great and influential in shaping forms for monachism. The rule he introduced has become a basic model in the east, just like the rule of Benedict would be for the west. Basil also created charitable institutions for the benefit of the poor and the sick. He showed deep concern about the decline of authentic Christian commitment, which was becoming a general consequence of the Christianisation of society imposed from above (see also Chapter 6, pp. 171–3).

Basil can rightly be considered as a 'pioneer in theology'.[39] Just like Athanasius, he did not intend to be an innovator, seeing his task rather in the protection of the essentials of the biblical message, summarised in the confession of the Church. But he was aware that new aberrations from that confession demanded a new search for a more adequate, though never perfect, perception of the mystery of God.

Gregory of Nazianzum (*c.* 330–90) was of the same age as Basil. Knowing each other from their native region, they were college friends at Athens. Gregory was also fully qualified for an office as orator, but quiet reflection attracted him more than profiling himself under public attention and also more than the strenuous life of a monk. His father, who was Bishop of Nazianzum, ordained him priest by surprise in 361, and in 372 Basil urged him to accept the bishopric of a remote border town which Gregory thought too horrible a place for residing. It remained an open question whether he was holding an episcopal function (and consequently not available for another see) or not. In general, Gregory's character was quite different from Basil's: he was not a leader, he was quick to take offence and inclined to evade difficulties.[40] But he certainly was an excellent communicator of theological issues and for that reason later generations gave him the epithet of 'the Theologian'.

In 379, when the see of Constantinople was still occupied by an Arian, Gregory was invited to give pro-Nicene sermons in a small chapel. These

Theological Orations turned out to be very clear and influential. As soon as Theodosius took over power in the east, Gregory moved from his small chapel to the city's cathedral, the 'Church of the Apostles'. In that year Basil died and Gregory transmitted the ideas of his friend, essentially identical with his own, to a wider public. He soon became the bishop of the capital (in spite of his post in Cappadocia, which he said he had never taken up) and was automatically appointed president of the synod in 381, when its first moderator, Meletius of Antioch suddenly died (see above, p. 121). He was not to finish the work of the synod, because after arriving late, the delegates from Egypt and Saloniki contested the legitimacy of his election as bishop.[41] Losing the support of those who were his strongest doctrinal allies, Gregory felt no longer capable to conduct the synod and resigned from his two offices with a bitter speech. He retired to Cappadocia. The synod accepted his resignation without protest.

In several respects, Gregory was of one opinion with Basil. Confessing God as a 'Trinity' means both to acknowledge the mystery of his being and to proclaim 'the loving outreach towards his creation'.[42] Although the human mind can only grasp something of God's threefold essence when it faces his works in creation and salvation, biblical revelation is leading to the awareness that the three individualities are essentially part of the divine being and have not come into existence because of those works. Creation and salvation are rooted in God's being as it is in itself, but they do not in any way condition his being. According to Gregory, a correct conception of the three persons, eternally existing in an essential unity and mutual relationships, is not restricted to a concealed insight ('dogma' – here he differs from Basil), but is part of the *kerygma*. The material contribution of Gregory to the Creed of Constantinople is found in the expression he introduced into theological parlance: the Spirit *proceeds* from the Father, but is not *generated* by Him. This distinction made it possible to state the divine origin and nature of the Spirit without equalising Him with the Son and his origin. Being one in nature, the three persons should be distinguished by our minds and be 'recognised by unoriginatedness and generation and procession'.[43] Gregory was not reluctant to apply *homoousios* also to the Spirit, but we saw that the synod did not follow him in this respect. After the synod, Theodosius did not class Gregory among his new 'standard bishops' of the official Catholic faith. Gregory of Nazianzum's contribution is marked by success as well as by want of appreciation.

Basil's younger brother Gregory (*c.* 335–95) is known by the name of the small Cappadocian town of Nyssa, where he became Bishop in 372 thanks to an initiative of Basil's, who was building up more support for his pro-Nicene policy. This choice cost Gregory two years of banishment under Valens, after whose death in 378 he returned to Nyssa. From then onwards he enjoyed broad esteem: his contribution to the synod of 381 yielded him a place among the 'standard bishops', as were designated by Theodosius. It was Gregory who, during the synod, was called to deliver the main speech at the enthronement of his namesake as Bishop of Constantinople and also the funeral oration for Meletius, the deceased first president of the assembly.[44]

Gregory pursued the debate with Eunomius, which Basil had begun. He also wrote a work *Against the Macedonians*, i.e., the Pneumatomachians, and many other doctrinal works. His trinitarian theology is not basically different from that of the two other Cappadocians. He described the Godhead as a 'paradoxical unity in distinction and distinctness in union'.[45] He emphasised the incomprehensibility of God's being as well as the Spirit's right to receive equal honour as the Father and the Son. His wordings on this subject make it plausible that thanks to him the creed reads that the Holy Spirit is 'exerting lordship and spending life', that He 'is glorified and worshipped together with the Father and the Son' (Basil's point!) and 'has spoken through the prophets'. Gregory changed the rather formal characterisation of the Father by 'ingeneratedness' (Gregory of Nazianzum) into 'infinity'. 'Infinite' was meant to indicate God as source and ultimate destiny of all human life, rather than as a philosophical definition, postulated in contrast to human finiteness. Sharing with the other two the conception of an essential trinity, the younger Gregory was profoundly interested in man, who was created in the image and after the likeness of God and who, after the Fall, is destined to regain and to develop this quality, still when after death he is received into God's infinity.[46]

Humans are being called and conducted to an ever-increasing participation in God's being. Their destiny is to grow in perfection. Gregory had no difficulty in embracing Platonic anthropology, of which the fundamental idea is that the human being is composed of a higher and a lower part, viz., the mind or reason and the body. The soul as the place where the sense percep-tions are received and the corporeal sensations are felt is swinging: it can allow itself to be pulled down to these lower sensations as well as work itself up to obey its higher element: reason. Christian thinkers easily saw the simi-larities between this view and the biblical notion of man, created after God's image. That means that they located this quality and vocation particularly in the soul, following the idea that it has to free itself from bodily pleasures. In Gregory, this vocation is not just a matter of man's own intellectual and moral discipline, but of guidance of the Holy Spirit. By the indwelling of the Spirit, the power of the Most High merges with our entire nature. The specific appeals of Christian ethics, such as imitation of Christ, obedience to God's will and love for the neighbour, were also implanted into this anthro-pological pattern, so that altruist values were substituted for the philo-sophical ideals of self-control and mental serenity. In this context, the Holy Spirit represented a specifically Christian element, since he was experienced as adding to man's created reason the 'higher' force of divine inspiration and help for progress. This way of enriching the classical concept of humankind demands a transcendental source of life and gifts of grace.

However dualistic, a Platonist is by no means a Gnostic. This is clear in Gregory's thought: for him the beauty and harmony of the world reflect the divine order, to which human intelligence can elevate itself and rejoice both in this and in the higher world. Such dualism is not absolute but relative. Gregory could, therefore, attach great value to the sacraments, in which invisible reality permeates earthly material and the latter points to the former. In his Christology he emphasised the necessity of a complete assumption of all constitutive parts of human nature by the divine Son, since otherwise humankind would not be saved in its totality. He strongly opposed the Christological construction of Apollinarius of Laodicea, who restricted Christ's humanity to his body and soul and substituted the *Logos* himself for the human mind. Apollinarius' concern was to have one single subject or person in Christ. To this Gregory objected that when the shepherd in Luke 15:4–7 goes after the lost sheep in order to save it, Christ 'lays it on his shoulders', entirely and not in part.[47]

In Gregory of Nyssa, the fullest integration of classical inheritance into the Christian faith has been achieved. Although not endowed with the epithet 'the Theologian', he was in fact a greater and more original theologian than his namesake. He has become a very influential and normative thinker for eastern Christianity, in the same way in which Augustine has become so for the western Church.

Another influential theologian: Theodore of Mopsuestia

The great influence of the Cappadocians in the field of trinitarian theology and upon the Christianised culture of the last third of the fourth century should not distort the picture as if there were no other breeding places of theological innovation than central Asia Minor. The west will draw our attention below (pp. 142–51). But in the east, a type of theology emerged that deviated from the dominant Origenistic ways of thinking. It originated in the region of Antioch, and in the days of the Cappadocians its most remarkable representative was Theodore of Mopsuestia in Cilicia. Born *c.* 352, Theodore was ordained presbyter in Antioch in 383 and became Bishop of Mopsuestia in 392. He died in 428. Young calls him 'a man of outstanding influence and importance, with a particularly interesting place in the history of theology'.[48] He should not be missing in this survey of the diversity of contextualisation in the fourth century, though he also belongs to the next century and played a part in the controversies on the unity between the Son and the Man in Christ. Since he shows some affinity with, and also great divergence from, Gregory of Nyssa, we shall compare Theodore with the third of the Cappadocians.

Theodore was held in great respect in the region of Antioch. He received the laudatory surname of 'the Interpreter', since biblical exegesis was his main interest. He wrote a commentary on the Gospel of John (*c.* 385) and on many other books of the Bible. His method of exegesis was literal and historical, not allegorical and mystical. This is a striking deviation from the way Origen and those under his influence used to read the Scriptures. Theodore did not set out to find allusions to Christ everywhere in the Old Testament, e.g., in verses of the Psalms and in the institutions of ancient Israel. For instance, unlike

Origen and Gregory, he did not read the Song of Solomon as an allegory of the love between Christ and his Church, but as a love song of Solomon and nothing else. In his view, the Old Testament did not prefigure Christ on every page, only in some limited details, such as the smearing of the blood of the pascal lamb on the doorposts in order to save the life of the inhabitants (Exod. 12). Even symbolic significance hardly played a role in Theodore's mind: he saw only historical facts. As a result, he could point the more vigorously to the newness of what Christ has brought about. Christ is the new Adam, who has inaugurated a second state for the human race. Theodore was very congenial to Paul in his emphasis on the newness in Christ. The Son of God has assumed a complete man, who of his own accord complied with the aims of the *Logos*, so that Christ could really act as one person. This compliance reached its summit in the voluntary sacrifice of his life on behalf of his fellow humans. Christ's Man has become the first fruits of salvation, receiving for himself what, through him, all human beings will be given.[49] As the new head of humanity he leads them to life, as the first Adam led them to death. The specific gift to humankind in this new phase of history is the Holy Spirit.

Theodore accepted the trinitarian doctrine with all the interest attached to the full divinity of both the Son and the Spirit. We find the most balanced and elaborate exposition of his theology in his *Catechetical Lectures*. Like Basil and Gregory he combatted the anhomoean and the pneumatomachian views. He opposed Apollinarius' Christology as well, agreeing with Gregory of Nazianzum's thesis that 'what has not been assumed is not saved'.[50] But he deepened this thesis by assigning a contributive role to the human will and intention, both in Christ during his incarnation and in his fellow humans. It is here that difference with Gregory comes to light: Theodore's emphasis is upon the human will and obedience and not so much upon intellect and mystical contemplation. He was not under the spell of intellectual and mystical penetration into the mystery of God, but was rather interested in practical Christian action, worked by man's recreation in Christ and the Spirit's guidance. Though he could hardly avoid using Platonic terminology, his anthropology was basically not Platonic, but rather Semitic. This leads us to the contextual aspect of his theology.

With regard to the region of the eastern Mediterranean, a distinction must be made between two subcultures. It is true that Hellenism was the overall civilisation, that Greek was spoken like English today, and that ideas from the classic philosophical schools were common property, thanks to the good general standards of education. Intellectuals could hardly avoid using a Platonic language. Nevertheless, Greek models of thinking were more dominant in certain regions than in others. In our century we find them of course in Greece, and then especially in Asia Minor and Egypt (where from the first century onwards Alexandria had taken over the leading role of Athens as intellectual centre). This state of affairs strongly marked developing Christian thought. A dominant idea was that man has to strive for union with God by giving his rational, spiritual faculties the supervision over his corporeal appetites. True salvation, or deification, mainly comes through insight and knowledge.

Although Greek-speaking, Antioch was the centre of a Semitic-coloured Hellenism. In accordance with the religious background of Semitic culture, union with God here was conceived more in terms of an alliance between humans and a living God who does not fit into one all-embracing framework of Nature. Human beings were seen as partners in God's history with the world and called to faithfulness. Their main vocation was ethical: they have to prove themselves good servants and reliable allies of this transcendent Lord.[51] Therefore, a great emphasis lies upon the soteriological relevance of history and historical action. The merger of Christian thinking with this Semitic background results in a concrete, historical reading of the Old Testament and in proclaiming God's merciful acceptance of imperfect humans in Christ as additional to the efforts of the human will. It is no wonder that in this model Christ's persevering obedience and faithfulness to the Father are much more emphasised than the elevation of human nature by its assumption by the divine *Logos*, permeating humanity with divine forces. In the union with the divine Son, the will of the man Jesus had a role to play, since it was by an act of their will that the first human beings turned away from God and pulled their descendants down into spiritual and physical death. This way of thinking is clearly different from that of Athanasius, who gave priority to the renewal of human nature by force of the incarnation. In Alexandrian thought, the recreation and invigoration of the human will was an effect of the incarnation, not a progressive compliance with God's will, first realised in Christ as 'first-born among many brethren' (Rom. 8:29. See Chapter 4, pp. 92–3).

It is obvious that the theology of Theodore of Mopsuestia fits in quite well with the religious pattern of the Semitic cultural background. It provides not only an interesting alternative to the Alexandrian and the Cappadocian theology, but in its correspondence with that cultural and religious background it also offers a fine example of a contextualising set of views on God, Christ and Man.

Assessment of theological results and progresses

Having examined the outcome of the synod of Constantinople and the tenor of its creed and having sketched the theologies of those who contributed most to these results, we will review the progress made in the field of doctrinal refinement and contextualisation. Three aspects are most striking.

Christianisation of the Greek cultural heritage

The Christians had experienced a brutal shock when the Emperor Julian deprived them of their privileged position. One of his measures was to entrust education, which still followed the classical, i.e., pagan curriculum, only to such persons as would teach it with personal conviction. This restriction would exclude all sincere Christians. They had no schools nor any 'confessional' curriculum of their own, so that every educated Christian, whether bishop or monk, was familiar with the contents and standards of Greek *paideia*. Most of them, therefore, had an ambivalent attitude towards the Greek literature, wisdom and world-view. They were regarded insufficient and full of inner contradictions, since as products of merely human search and understanding they did not rest on divine revelation. But they were not to be disregarded for that. *Paideia* could well be appreciated and used as a preparatory stage for truly Christian knowledge and life conduct. Though insufficient and in some respects misleading, as an introduction, the classical heritage was regarded as helpful. The majority of the important theologians of the last decades of the fourth century did not feel much divergence between the Christian faith and the (in their eyes) best elements of the classical heritage, especially of philosophic traditions. We noticed this in all three Cappadocians as well as in an 'Oriental' theologian such as Theodore, and we will meet this again in the western leader Ambrose. This adoption and integration of the mature Greek reflections on humankind and cosmos (these were the main fields of intellectual encounter!) were no doubt a corollary of the political and social triumph of Christianity, brought about by the proclamation of Christianity as state religion. What had been achieved on the political and social level should logically be extended to the realm of culture.

Transformations in the doctrine of God

The main result of the controversies on Neo-Arianism and Pneumatomachism is the radical elimination of the traditional hierarchical concept of all being, inclusively the divine triad itself. We saw how since the days of Origen, Christian theology had been wrestling with this burdensome legacy of Greek cosmology. In Origen's thought, the creation of the spiritual, logical beings was a more or less automatic unfolding that followed from the eternal generation of the *Logos*. Eusebius introduced the element of will, both in the generation of the *Logos*/Son and in the creation of the world. But the *Logos* was still seen as subordinate to God, playing the role of intermediary between him and the world. This intermediate position makes him 'the protector, guardian, saviour and physician of whatever later received being.'[52]

In the course of the fourth century, the cosmological framework was supplanted by a different soteriological approach. On the one hand, this meant a loss of openness for the dialogue with the philosophical schools and their concerns. This had been the strong side of Origen, although by the end of his life he had argued more polemically with the hostile philosopher Celsus, just as Eusebius later did with Porphyry. On the other hand, an internal Christian debate kindled on the issue whether Christ, and in a later stage the Holy Spirit, belongs to the ungenerated and unalterable level of being or to the generated and alterable nature which are opposites because of the fact that the one is creative and the other created. In the second case, Christ could only be a pioneer – and the Spirit a ministering force – for humankind on its way of return to God and the highest goods. This return depends to a large part on their correct understanding of the world's structure and on their good will to strive upwards. In the first case, Christ – and the Holy Spirit – are by virtue of their divine character capable of establishing in humans a participation in God which, in spite of their weaknesses and sins, enables them to overcome their instability and imperfection.

The traditional concept of derivation, which embraced the whole range of being, gave way to a derivation within God himself. What the Cappadocians preserved from Origen's heritage is the distinct individuality of each person: the Trinity being in itself and eternally composed of three individualities, to which the term *hypostasis* now was exclusively applied. In Eusebius, this distinction still automatically implied subordination; he stressed the distinction between the ungenerated *ousia* of God and the *second ousia*, 'produced from the First Cause'. The *Logos* is derived from the Father's will and power and personifies his 'Word, Wisdom and very Power'. The Spirit is subordinate to the *Logos* and not much more than a ministering power, above angels and men, but lower than the Son.[53]

Athanasius paved the way for seeing all these saving qualities of the Son as operating through the humanity he had assumed for the sake of redemption. But he had brought the three divine persons so close to one another that their distinct individualities do not stand out clearly. His monolithic theology was subtly modified by his Cappadocian followers, who revalued some of Origen's and Eusebius' thought, without returning to their cosmological framework. God's will to save became more directly connected with the Incarnation and with the continuation of its fruits by the actions of the Holy Spirit. It was, therefore, a logical step to assign a proper personality also to the Spirit, who definitely lost his unclear position as an impersonal power or supreme 'Angel'. Therefore, both Athanasius and the Cappadocians combatted the old and new Arians, because they were convinced that only if the *Logos*/Son and the Holy Spirit fully shared God's proper *ousia*, could they meet man's need for redemption to everlasting and uncorrupted life.

Transformations in the concept of human nature

We also notice an ongoing Christianisation of the concept of human nature. Over and against fatalism and astrological determinism, the Church Fathers wanted to emphasise the human freedom of choice and moral responsibility. Platonic ideals of calling upon the 'highest' human faculties of mind and will against what pulls down to an 'animal' level of yielding to greed and lust were seen as helpful. Any argument for making the right choices, stemming from a sound judgement of the affinity of the rational soul with the invisible and eternal One, could be used for the concept of man the Christian theologians wanted to propagate on biblical grounds. However, from the Christian viewpoint of a loving God, who intervenes in order to renew his creature, this philosophical concept had to be corrected and completed. First, in the field of a theology of creation, in which all that exists, and especially humankind as its crown, is related to God's transcendent will and power. Consequently, the soul is not seen as part of the movement of outflow, with an innate longing for God, but as in need of God's self-disclosure.[54] Progress as man's recovery under the Spirit's guidance, is an important issue in both the Cappadocians and Theodorus of Mopsuestia. Christian ethical demands, such as love for one's neighbour, were another essential correction of the rather egocentric Greek ideal of perfecting one's own self.

We find this tension reflected in the unexpected choice of the well-educated Cappadocians against a worldly career in the public sector and in favour of Church service; and in this field for responsible functions (and the consequent conflicts) disregarding the attraction of a quiet and contemplative existence on a family-owned land property. They knew that being a Christian meant to abandon worldly glamour.

The reception of the Creed of Nicaea-Constantinople; its ecumenical status

Creeds were rooted in local churches for liturgical use in worship and baptism. They did not lose these original functions when in the fourth century two new functions were added. They shaped the catechetical instruction that was badly needed to inculcate into the inflowing masses a real knowledge of the Christian religion they were now embracing. By the fourth-century specifications and closer definitions aimed at heretical opinions, they became an identifying mark of orthodoxy. The Nicene-Constantinopolitan Creed of 381 (NC) was issued by an eastern synod. Although reaffirming the Creed of Nicaea (N), the extended NC had to wait a long time before it obtained recognition as ecumenical confession, necessitated by the rise of unprecedented dissensions.

Creed and Dogma

It has become customary to regard the doctrinal decisions of Constantinople 381 as the closing of the Arian struggle and to label its creed as the *Trinitarian Dogma*. However, at that time the word 'dogma' was not used. It was only in the course of the next century that this word came to mean 'doctrine of the Church'. Until then, confessions, used on community level or adopted by regional synods, were not referred to as 'dogma' or dogmatic summaries. The Creed of Nicaea was generally spoken of as 'the *Faith*', meaning both 'confession' and 'doctrine of the Church'.

The creeds that were issued on the numerous polemical synods of our century and those which later received a dogmatic status were generally local baptismal confessions with some extension on the issues under debate. As such, they reflected the opinions of a dominating party. Yet as baptismal confessions they could differ from each other in exact wording and nevertheless have an identical triassic structure. These confessions were used for worship and had a more or less secret character: a candidate for baptism would only learn the exact wording in the final stage of his or her initiation.[55] As long as the Church was illegal and repeatedly oppressed, there was a reticence to expose to non-believers and mockers the texts that most directly referred to the mysteries of the faith. When Christianity enjoyed recognition and support in public, new reasons for this traditional precaution arose.

Basil, as we saw, made a distinction between 'dogma' and preaching (kerygma): in sermons the 'kerygma' is made public, whereas 'dogma' should be enveloped with reticence. Dogma is the deeper inquiry into the faith by initiated and mature believers. It should be kept away from the realm of the 'public relations' of the Church. His brother Gregory warned that the dogma should never be a topic for chatting on marketplaces or in public baths.[56] This view is symptomatic for the situation in which Christianity now found itself: the danger of profanation came no longer from hostile mobs or authorities, but from a superficially Christianised society in which people were annexing the new religion too rashly, without much respect and understanding.

This precaution had yet another reason, the consciousness of God's inscrutability. Those theologians who contributed so much to the definition of the trinitarian faith showed an awareness of the mystery of God that can never be explained by human syllogisms. There is a tension between this reserve and the need to account for the essentials of the Christian message and make them accessible in contextual concepts. In their opinion, credal texts, however, were not just rational accounts, but also words of praise (*doxology*), used by the community to worship God for what humans may know about him as well as for what they will never know. This doxological aspect of the creed – which is a primal aspect of the confession – counterbalances the concern for precise formulation. This concern was, as we said above, on the one hand, related to the urgency of explaining the essentials of the religion which had become everyone's, and, on the other, of concluding six decennia of theological quarrelling.

Although the word 'dogma' was avoided for the creed, the adopted confession was on the way to acquiring the status of 'dogma' in the later sense, viz., of official Church doctrine. There were two factors at work. First, confessions were more and more taken as the basis for catechetical instruction, which developed to keep pace with the increased influx of members from a pagan background. We have already mentioned the *Catechetical Orations* from the hands of Gregory of Nyssa and of Theodore of Mopsuestia.[57] More exact definitions were added to confessions, which originally were concise because of their liturgical function, with the intention to exclude this or that heretical view. But a new creed could also be phrased in affirmative language, since the explicit rejection of those views was given a place in the *anathemas* (Nicaea) or the *canons* (Constantinople). Therefore, the extended creed could retain its liturgical function, as the future would largely impart to the NC.

Ecumenical status

Referring to the proceedings (pp. 122–3) we call into memory that the assembly of the year 381 in the imperial capital was only an eastern synod and not 'ecumenical' as Nicaea had been. We have seen that the western Church, led by Ambrose and Pope Damasus, rejected the second and third canons and protested against the appointment of bishops for Antioch and Constantinople. The western church leaders requested from the Emperor the convocation of a truly ecumenical council in Rome. As the Emperor declined this demand, they themselves organised a synod, which in their turn eastern bishops refused to attend. On the contrary, they assembled anew at Constantinople under the chairmanship of Bishop Nectarius. It was this follow-up synod that straightaway qualified the preceding meeting as 'ecumenical council', soliciting western agreement. The west and Egypt did not comply, because of their grievances mentioned above. Moreover, they kept totally silent about the newly adopted creed, however much it had the weight of imperial law.

Although there are no explicit references to the Creed of Constantinople from the eastern provinces either, there are some indications that it was not only known, but also in use both in Constantinople and in Asia Minor. The NC suffered a further marginalisation at the council of Ephesus in 431, where it was squarely stated that the old Nicene Creed of 325 was sufficient in all respects and that nobody should be allowed 'to bring forward or to compose or to put together any other faith than that which has been defined by the holy fathers who assembled at Nicaea under the guidance of the Holy Spirit'.[58] As long as people used to speak of 'the Faith of Nicaea', the letter of the creed was not so important. The main thing was the conformity with its substance, and so any orthodox formula constructed on Nicene principles could be designated as 'the Faith of Nicaea'. But by the interdiction of the Ephesian Council to 'compose or put together' any faith definition that would be different from Nicaea, a dividing line was drawn between the texts of Nicaea and of Constantinople.[59]

The following council held twenty years later at Chalcedon (a suburb of Istanbul on the Asiatic riverside) abandoned that strict interdiction. Both fifth-century councils as such are beyond the scope of this book. However, it is necessary to pay attention to the question of how these assemblies, the third and the fourth of the series of ecumenical councils, regarded their 'predecessor' and the definition it had issued.

Chalcedon brought a turn. It was not only the most representative council of the early Church because of its attendance (twice the number of Nicaea!); it also had to face new controversial questions, which had still been undiscussed in the first decades of the fourth century. As the delegates at Chalcedon wished to relate their statements as closely as possible to the definition of the first council, which was held in general respect, they could not bypass in silence the status of the two interjacent assemblies with regard to Nicaea. In the introduction to their own definition they said, 'We decree that the exposition of the right and blameless faith of the 318 holy and blessed fathers, assembled at Nicaea in the time of the emperor Constantine of pious memory, should be pre-eminent, while the decisions of the 150 holy fathers should also hold good', specifying further down that their assembly

> has decreed primarily that the creed of the 318 holy fathers should remain inviolate; and on account of those who contend against the Holy Spirit, it ratifies the teaching subsequently set forth by the 150 holy fathers assembled in the royal city concerning the essence of the Spirit, not as adducing anything left lacking by their predecessors, but making distinct by Scriptural testimonies their conception concerning the Holy Spirit against those who were trying to set aside His sovereignty.[60]

This statement makes it clear that the Nicene Creed was regarded as the pre-eminent and basic definition of the faith of the Church. It is 'right and blameless' and therefore 'should remain inviolate'. With regard to N, the decisions of Constantinople, including its new creed, cannot take their place nor have an identical status. This view logically applies to all subsequent conciliar faith declarations, including the one the present text was intended to introduce and to legitimate. The idea that a subsequent council would have to add an essential element, overlooked by the Nicene Fathers, was simply unacceptable. Nevertheless, the meeting of Chalcedon could not deny that after Nicaea a new phenomenon had appeared, viz., the reduction of the Holy Spirit to a lower rank. N only reads 'and in the Holy Spirit'. The fact that the Spirit was mentioned in the creed was felt as an unequivocal equation with the Father and the Son. But nothing was said about the Spirit's status and activities in the history of salvation, or in their words – about his 'essence' and 'sovereignty'. So the solution was that, on the one hand, nothing had been left lacking by the Nicene Fathers, whereas, on the other, their definition could appear not to be explicit enough to settle a dispute that touches the substance of the preaching. Thus, the NC was presented as a reaffirmation of the Nicene *faith* without a literal reiteration of its *credal formulas*. It is justifiable to call the Creed of Constantinople NC (Creed of Nicaea and Constantinople), or according to common parlance simply 'the Nicene Creed'.[61] The reluctance to introduce a new creed besides Nicaea came from the bishops, who were afraid that its authority would be weakened. The insistence that the council should express itself in new declarations on recent disagreements rather came from the Emperor (through his commissioners at the synod), who was, as always, concerned about disunity in the Church.

The general recognition of the doctrinal decisions of the Constantinopolitan synod of 381, signified its definite insertion into the series of ecumenical councils, namely, as the second. The west continued to reject Canon 3, by which Constantinople as the New Rome was ranked immediately after Old Rome (see above, p. 122).[62] In Eastern Orthodoxy, the NC has maintained its pre-eminence, both as theological charter and in liturgical praxis. The western traditions, both Roman Catholic and Protestant, also recognise it as creed, alongside with the Apostles' Creed, of Roman origin. In recent times, the NC is being proposed, with fresh hopes, as a basis for Christian unity and ecumenical dialogue.[63]

New trends in the relationship between the Church and the Emperor

Thus far, the centre of gravity of new, mainly doctrinal, developments had been in the east. Western leaders had to inform themselves about the finer points of the Greek debate. The greatest church leader of the west, Ambrose, also had to take cognisance of the Cappadocian theology in addition to his being at home in the Latin ethical thinking. His originality is in the further-ance of the independence and self-consciousness of the Church vis-à-vis the Emperor. Continuing the line of judging the Emperor's interference by his loyalty towards the mainstream doctrinal standpoint, Ambrose invigorated the normative character of the Church when he subjected even the most orthodox emperor to penitence for an act of atrocious punishment. Because he required imperial support for the interests of orthodox Christianity, Ambrose did not lay foundations for a separation of Church and State; how-ever, he stopped the sacralisation of the Christian emperor that had begun with Eusebius.

Milan and the career of Ambrose

The north Italian city of Milan had become the residence of the western emperors. It was nearer than Rome to the danger area of the northern borders, crossed by invading German tribes such as the Goths. In the introduction to this chapter, we have mentioned the successive western emperors and their attitude towards the predominance of Arianism, left behind by Constantius. Valentinianus I (364–75) followed a tolerant religious policy. This was continued by his son (and co-regent from 367 onwards) Gratianus, who sud-denly exchanged neutral tolerance for supporting the Nicene cause (379), probably under the influence of the successful army commander to whom he had entrusted the endangered eastern empire, Theodosius I (379–95). After Gratianus had fallen in battle against a usurper (383), his twelve-year-old brother Valentinianus II and his influential mother Justina tried to uphold Arian church life over and against the meanwhile-Nicene main-stream. In 388, Theodosius saved young Valentinianus from another rebelli-ous general and in fact assumed control over the prefecture of Italy, leaving to Valentinianus only the prefectures of the Gauls. He took residence at Milan and became sole monarch of the Empire for the last three years of his reign (392–5). In Milan, it was Gratianus, Valentinianus II (with the empress mother) and Theodosius I who met with a strong counterbalance in the person of the local bishop, Ambrose, consecrated in 374 and still in office at the death of Theodosius, for whom he gave the funeral sermon. With each of these emperors, Ambrose, at a given time, had a serious conflict.

Ambrose, born *c.* 339 at Treves, was a son of the Prefect of Gaul. Belonging to the administrative upper class, he read law and, after having practised in the courts of Rome, was appointed, in 370, Governor of the province of Aemilia-Liguria (north-western Italy) of which Milan was the capital. Four years later, its bishop Auxentius, an Asian and puppet of Constantius, died. The Arian and the Nicene parties both tried to get as successor a man of their persuasion, when, as highest civil authority, Ambrose appeared in the church and by spontaneous acclamation, mainly from the lay people, was wanted as the new bishop. It is significant for the status of the bishops at that time that he accepted the change from civil to ecclesiastical service! Like most civil servants, Ambrose had postponed his baptism,[64] so that the rites of initiation and of ordination had to be conferred on him in a tearing rush.

Ambrose understood that in his new job he had to master the details of the trinitarian discussion as it had been carried on in the east and in the Greek language. He basically followed the Cappadocians, but he was a genuine Latin by birth and education and knew both the Latin classics and a western theologian such as Tertullian, who had already reflected on the relation between the Father and his Word. In the preceding chapter, it was said on several occasions that the western church did not produce great theologians and had difficulties in following the sophisticated debates of the east. So far, Hilary of Poitiers had been a rare exception. Ambrose soon turned out to be an excellent preacher, who made thorough studies of the Bible and wrote a lot of commentaries and meditations. He was even one of the first authors of Christian hymns.[65] This well-educated and deeply devoted man was the real spiritual leader of the west during the last decades of the fourth century, overshadowing Popes Damasus (366–84) and Siricius (384–99), who were rather engaged in establishing their power. Ambrose was convinced that the truth, as revealed by God and laid down in the Scriptures, was entrusted to the Church and that, consequently, the Church had to preserve its independence from the State and its constant wish to interfere. We will now look at the four subsequent conflicts in order to examine how Ambrose put his conviction into practice. The courage and tenacity he demonstrated in these confrontations with the highest authority were doubtless the fruit of his own roots in the administrative aristocracy of the Roman Empire. But a deep concern for the liberty of the Church prevented him from being just a tyrannical prelate.

Ambrose and the emperors

A request for the restoration of religious tolerance, 384

The Emperors Gratianus and Theodosius had proclaimed the Catholic Christian faith to be the religion of all their subjects, and the former had deposed the title of Supreme Pontiff, the highest pagan priestly office (see above, Chapter 5, p. 119). Under the pressure of Theodosius, Gratianus had gone further by withdrawing the traditional privileges and state subventions of the Roman priesthood and by removing from the Senate's hall the altar of Victoria, the goddess supposed to assure the supremacy of Rome over the world. These were measures that hurt the feelings of the senatorial aristocracy, which still held to the traditional concept of the link between the old cults and the prosperity of the Empire. After Gratianus' death, they sent a legation to the Milanese court, led by the Roman Prefect Symmachus, hoping to find young Valentinianus II more indulgent than his elder brother had been.

Symmachus made a brilliant speech in which he pleaded for the restoration of tolerance for the religion of the ancestors and of the old privileges and especially asked for the reinstatement of the Victoria altar. He appealed to principles of equity, but he also used the old argument that the actual disasters the Empire was suffering were due to the neglect of the traditional gods of Rome. Not so long ago, this argument had led to the persecution of the Christians.[66]

The Crown Council was prepared to assent to this request. As soon as Ambrose came to know about this, he appealed to the Emperor, urging that, since this matter was about the worship of God, he as a bishop had the right and the qualification to speak. He argued that it is not the task of a Christian emperor to provide altars for paganism. God was leading history forward and Rome was now passing through a historical change for the better. It even was Rome's honour to keep pace with the new times, instead of returning to old customs, which would no longer bring her to greatness. Finally, Ambrose threatened the Emperor that, if he assented to Symmachus' request,

> you will be allowed to come to the church, but either you will find there no priest or you will find one who will gainsay you. What will you answer the priest who says to you: 'The Church does not want your gifts because you have adorned the heathen temples with gifts. The altar of Christ spurns your gifts since you have made an altar for idols . . .'.[67]

In the context of an age-long tradition of a bond between state and religion, Ambrose put that in respect of the recognition of the deity that was to be invoked and worshipped publicly, a Christian emperor could not tolerate pagan cult alongside the religion that rested upon divine revelation. Of this religion the bishops are the warrantors. And, further, he made it clear that an emperor, who by such religious politics was in fact serving two lords, would not be welcomed in church as a believer.

By his admonition, Ambrose attained his object: the request of Symmachus was declined.

The refusal to cede a church for Arian services, 385/6

The next confrontation with the imperial court was about Arianism. The empress mother Justina, the widow of Valentinianus I, adhered to the Arian confession. She had as court chaplain a priest from Illyria, whom she wanted to be Bishop of Milan instead of Ambrose.[68] Moreover, she and her entourage felt frustrated by Ambrose's success in the question of the altar of Victoria. Therefore, the court was looking for a church building where the Arian chaplain could hold services in accordance with the *homoean* confession, which contented itself with saying that Christ was *similar* to God (see Chapter 4, pp. 99–101).

After trying in vain to lay hands on a small chapel outside the walls of Milan, the court claimed by decree the possession of a basilica in the centre of the city. It came to strong tensions during Holy Week 386, between the Emperor who besieged the church building with army and police forces and the community, having Ambrose in their midst and following his admon-itions. They offered passive resistance, encouraging themselves by means of sermons, prayers and hymns. Ambrose went outside and persuaded the military not to enforce an aberrant form of the faith, reminding them of what eventually would happen to their souls. Several soldiers and policemen went over to his side. The authorities tried to overcome the stalemate by inviting both Ambrose and the chaplain Auxentius to a doctrinal dialogue with the court in the role of arbitrator. But first of all, the occupants had to stop their rebellious sit-in and leave the basilica under the promise of an unhindered retreat.

Ambrose sent a letter to the Emperor in which he stated that bishops can only be judged by bishops and that a bishop is holding his office in commit-ment to the community that recognises him as bishop.[69] He was the elected and, consequently, the competent representative of his church. In a sermon, he made a clear distinction between civil and religious obedience, saying:

> The command is given: 'Hand over the basilica'. I answer: 'It is not lawful for me to hand it over, nor is it expedient for you, O Emperor, to receive it. If you cannot rightly violate the house of a private individual, do you think that the house of God can be appropriated?' It is alleged all things are permitted the emperor, that everything is his. To this I reply: 'Do not burden yourself with thinking that you have imperial power over things which are divine. Do not exalt yourself, but, if you wish to be emperor for a long time, be subject to God.' Scripture says: 'Render therefore to Caesar the things that are Caesar's, and to God the things that are God's' [Matt. 22:21]. Palaces belong to the emperor, churches to the bishop. You have been given authority over public edifices, not over sacred ones.

He also told the court officials, who alleged that the Emperor was using his rights inasmuch as all property is under his jurisdiction: 'If he were asking for what was mine – my estate, my money or anything of this sort – I would not resist, even though all my property belongs to the poor; but sacred objects are not subject to the jurisdiction even of the emperor'.[70]

Ambrose's opposition, which was a plain-spoken refusal of confessional plurality within the local church, highlighted two important issues. First, that, with regard to doctrinal or disciplinary questions, clergymen are elected, judged and eventually dismissed by no other than ecclesiastical authority, i.e., independently from the state and its interests. Second, that it is not up to the emperor to decide which doctrine and preaching should be given room in the Church. In this regard, Ambrose gave as his firm conviction that it is 'the emperor's honour to be called a son of the Church'. For, indeed, 'the emperor is *in* the Church and *not above* the Church'.[71]

The result of this uncompromising firmness of Ambrose was that, on Maundy Thursday, the imperial court abandoned its efforts to get hold of the basilica.

The demolition of a synagogue, 388

In this and the next opposition against an emperor, Ambrose had to do with Theodosius. From this Emperor, Ambrose had not to fear support for either paganism or heresy. A new protest from the responsible and far-from-lenient church leader was nevertheless occasioned by the overbold action of a Mesopotamian bishop and his congregation who burned down the local synagogue. Presumably they expected to remain unpunished now that Christianity had become the exclusive state religion. But Theodosius thought their act an offence against the law and inflicted on the community in question a fine and the obligation to repair the building. A normal measure, one would say, but not so in the eyes of Ambrose.

In defence of the Mesopotamian community, he reproached the Emperor that through his order he would give support to the false religion of the Jews and that, since they refused to recognise Jesus as the true Son of God, he would implicitly encourage the Arians, who held a similar position. 'Which is of more importance', he asked the Emperor, 'a demonstration of discipline or the cause of religion? The maintenance of civil law should be secondary to religion.'[72] Ambrose pressed the Emperor, saying that pending the withdrawal of the given order, he would not celebrate mass.

Theodosius gave in. Ambrose had succeeded in establishing the idea of 'the display of the Christian religion [being] of more importance than the display of law and order'.[73]

The condemnation of a reprisal, 390

The fourth and very significant case of confrontation with the Emperor had its origin in a rebellion of the population of Thessalonica against the detested military commander of that city. In this insurrection, the commander had been killed. In his anger, Theodosius decided to punish the city as a whole, without tracing the perpetrators and bringing only them to justice. He ordered to lure a multitude of citizens to the stadium by means of false promises, where they were massacred without distinction, allegedly some 7,000.

As soon as Ambrose heard of this crime, he addressed the Emperor in a personal letter, written in his own hand, lest any other official would also read it. Its tone betrays that the bonds of the friendship and respect between the Emperor and the Bishop make it very difficult for the latter to urge the great protector of orthodox Christianity to an act of reconciliation. But, referring to Ezekiel's appointment by the Lord as a *watchman*, who has the duty to pass God's serious warnings to the wicked,[74] Ambrose did not evade this difficulty and found the right words for appealing to the Emperor's conscience. In a pastoral way, he reminded Theodosius of his quick temper but also of his pious determination to overcome this defect of his character. The important moment in his approach, however, is that in this perplexing matter personal repentance would not be enough. According to the discipline of the Church, Theodosius had committed a manifold murder which, being a mortal sin, excluded him from the eucharistic community as long as he had not expiated it by a public confession. Once again, and with more right than in the preceding case, Ambrose warned the Emperor that if he would come to church he would not have the frankness to celebrate the Eucharist, for 'Can that which is not allowable, after the blood of one man is shed, be allowable when many persons' blood was shed? I think not.'[75]

Ambrose did not hesitate to name the reprisal on the population of Thessalonica 'most atrocious and with no precedent within memory'. Then he made it his responsibility to insist that

> There must be a reconciliation with our God. Are you ashamed, O Emperor, to do what David the Prophet did, the forefather of the family of Christ according to the flesh?[76] [. . .] These things I have written not to disconcert you but that the examples of kings may stir you to remove this sin from your kingdom, for you will remove it by humbling your soul before God. You are a man, you have met temptation – conquer it. Sin is not removed except by tears and penance! [. . .]
>
> I urge, I ask, I beg, I warn, for my grief is that you, who were a model of unheard-of piety, who [. . .] would not allow the guilty to be in peril, are not now mourning that so many guiltless have perished. [. . .] Do not add another sin to your sin nor follow a course of action that has injured many followers.[77]

Theodosius granted that Ambrose was right and he came to church as a penitent. In his funeral oration, Ambrose has reminded his audience of this moment, praising an emperor who was not ashamed to submit himself to a public penitence, whereas shame dissuades a lot of ordinary people from doing so.

Evaluation of character and actions of Ambrose

The opinions on Ambrose and, notably, on the new elements he has brought into the relationship between Church and State are not unanimous. We will bring out three main aspects.

The elimination of religious tolerance

We have seen Ambrose's intransigence in the matter of leaving space for either the traditional pagan, or the Jewish religion, no more than for Christian heresy. Since the emperors of east and west had legalised the sole right of the Nicene form of Christianity (see above, p. 119), Christian leaders and mobs were eager to draw the consequences from their new status. Anyhow, Ambrose did so when he strongly opposed the request for the restoration of the Victoria altar in the senatorial hall in Rome, the surrender of one of the Milanese churches for Arian services and the sanctions inflicted upon the community in Mesopotamia that had destroyed a local synagogue. In all these cases, Ambrose required an uncompromising application of what the imperial decree of 380 meant. For him it was beyond doubt that it was the duty of a Christian emperor to promote the true religion, which could be no other than the faith founded on divine revelation. The emperor had not to decide on the content and form of this faith; that was within the competence of the bishops only. But the emperor and his means of power were supposed to carry into effect what the bishops had decided with regard to religion. His impatient spirit and actions left no space for what today we call religious pluralism.

A prompt application was certainly not in the mind of Theodosius himself. The decree of 380 was meant as a programme, as a base for ideological unity he wanted to attain, but with prudence. As late as 389 he tried to avoid clashes with the pagan circles in Rome and in Alexandria. And he needed the Goths, who, since their gradual conversion had started in the 340s on the Balkans, adhered to Arianism (which had then and there been predominant, see Chapter 4, pp. 87–8). But Ambrose was more impatient than the Emperor he admired. Under his urgent influence, Theodosius in 392 issued a law that forbade all pagan cults. But he did not cast an interdict on the – as it was called – 'Sect of the Jews', and he left them the freedom to make decisions in matters of their own religion, ordering a strong line against anti-Jewish excesses by Christians.[78]

Theodosius' anti-pagan legislation annoyed the senatorial aristocracy of Rome, which gave its support to a usurper, who took power over the west after Valentinianus II had been murdered (392). When, in 394, Theodosius defeated this rival in a battle, it was like a repetition of the battle Constantine had won at the Milvian Bridge in 312 (see Chapter 2, pp. 36–7): once again a

Christian emperor had triumphed over a political and military opponent who had sought help in the old Roman religion. It can, therefore, be said that by the year 394 Theodosius and Ambrose, in good company, had established the political and theological victory of orthodox Christianity over the Roman world.

A transformation of the relationship between Church and State

Though Ambrose stated that the emperors should not interfere in matters of faith and doctrine and should leave decisions to the bishops, it nevertheless had been Gratianus and Theodosius who in 380 had opted for the Nicene faith as the correct and exclusive form of Catholic Christianity. Ambrose could not but rejoice in this decision, and he certainly did so. When in the period prior to this decree he had been asked to instruct Gratianus about the relevant theological issues, he said that the Emperor obviously had been enlightened with knowledge of the faith by God himself. Why then should he still have taken great pains to give the Emperor the right insights? Or was it just a 'subtle flattery'?[79] Which difference is there with Eusebius, who had so abundantly praised Constantine for his piety and theological leadership? This brings us to the question if, after all these years of dogmatic tensions between large parts of the Church and the emperors, something had really been won.

On this question, the opinions diverge. Some see the penance for the massacre of Thessalonica as the compliance of a repentant sinner with the ruling discipline of expiation, which the Church required in the case of mortal sins. As a convinced Christian, Theodosius would just have acknowledged that these moral standards were also valid for him. By no means his act of submission could be considered as 'a victory of the Church over the emperor or as a landmark in the relationship between State and Church'.[80] Others consider Ambrose's requirement of public penance as 'something fundamentally new', because a minister of the Church did not bow before a sovereign whose support for an orthodox Christianity he could not but welcome. Even an emperor, who was 'good' in the view of the Church, could not claim to have a special indulgence nor to be above the law that applies to every faithful member.[81]

It seems quite right to endorse the second view for two reasons. First, though penance for a mortal sin suited the rules of pastoral discipline, the fact that the supreme political authority and main protector of Christianity was publicly submitted to it signified an application of the thesis that the emperor is *in* and *not above* the Church; it was certainly felt by everyone as a sign of the independence of the Church and the upper clergy. Second, this requirement, which a bishop presented to an emperor, does not stand alone, but is another sign not only of the personal courage of Ambrose but also of an increased self-consciousness of the church leadership vis-à-vis the emperor. The refusal to celebrate the Eucharist as long as Theodosius had not fulfilled his obligation in the same way as any church member can be seen as justifiable. But the fact that Ambrose threatened to withhold the sacrament in two other cases – the Victoria altar and the demolished synagogue – is no doubt a misuse of his sacerdotal competence to enforce a measure in the sole interest of the Church. Setton is right in saying that Ambrose

> was doubtless motivated by a desire to establish the superiority of *sacerdotium* [church ministry] over *imperium*, not from any personal delight he might take in wielding the greater power, but from the sincere conviction that only thus could the independence of the Church be insured. His tactics were much less commendable than his courage.[82]

It must be clear that Ambrose did not advocate a separation between Church and State – far from that! He did not deny the emperor's right to assure that the state and all its subjects would follow the correct religion, he only denied him the right to decide or to manipulate the contents of that religion. In this respect, the Church leadership should be autonomous. His opposition against an emperor who wanted to interfere in religious matters as well as his inflexibility towards an emperor who, orthodox as he was, had offended the moral standards, enriched the Church with a consciousness of independence, which it had been lacking since the days of Constantine or had only aspired to with hesitation and caution. Again we can agree with Setton: 'Christian humility towards the Emperor had undergone a remarkable transformation during the fifty years that separated Eusebius of Caesarea from Ambrose of Milan.'[83] The historical and contextual importance of Ambrose is that he succeeded in reducing the bill of tractability, which Eusebius' influence had run up so much. For Eusebius had cut off the possibility of theological and ecclesiastical criticism of the emperor since he forwarded the idea of a direct line of inspiration from the *Logos* to the emperor, whom he extolled as reflecting His universal sovereignty and teacher role. Ambrose inserted between Christ and the emperor the responsible authority of the bishops, without diminishing the emperor's duties in the field of public religion. By this he staked off the domain of doctrine and discipline of the Church as something not dependent on imperial interests and arbitrariness. This meant progress in contextualisation inasmuch as, within the given strong alliance between the Christian religion and the Roman Empire, the balance of power now shifted to a greater self-consciousness of the Church.

Togetherness of Christianity and the Roman world

In one respect, however, Ambrose did not break with an idea that Eusebius had cherished: the link between the Roman Empire and world civilisation. Whereas Eusebius had thought of this rather in terms of the right knowledge and worship of God, as taught by the *Logos* through his servants (including the Christian emperor), Ambrose conceived of civilisation more as shaped by

Christianity, which with imperial support had defined itself as an orthodox Catholic Church. We learnt that against the senatorial wish to restore the Victoria altar, the old symbol and guarantee of Rome's supremacy, Ambrose argued that Rome should keep pace with the progress of history, i.e., with the Christianisation of the Empire. This was the new form through which Rome could spread over the world the blessings of its civilisation. In the past, pagan thinkers had often expressed the idea that Rome was marked out to bring a golden age over the world and that in periods of forsaking its moral and religious standards only a revival of old values and practices could renew the Empire to its glorious vocation of old. Now Ambrose picked up this idea of the 'Eternal Rome', replacing the call for reviving old traditions by a call for conversion to Christianity, which in his time would renew the historical vocation of Roman world dominion. In Ambrose's view, the true Rome merges with the Church as the Church merges with the Roman Empire. Uncivilised and barbaric Goths may be Arians, but good Romans are Catholic Christians.[84]

This way of involving the role of Christianity in the Empire's destiny and vice versa also had an influence on the terms that Ambrose used for Christ. He spoke of him as Saviour and Lord. More than that, he preferred to call him 'King of Glory', and to present his way through the crucifixion up to the Ascension as a triumphal course. 'The cross of Christ is our victory', he would say, 'and the glory of the cross we have put on'.[85] Imperial style and habits were entering the Church!

In spite of his valuable contributions to a modification of the position of the Church in relation to the Christianised state, Ambrose's views might narrow our views of the status of the Christian religion at the end of the fourth century. We should not overlook that there was Christianity also outside the borders of the Roman Empire, nor that inside the Roman world there was a Christian countermovement against church life that had become settled, comfortable and had grown worldly. To these equally important phenomena we will turn in the last chapter.

6 External and internal repercussions

Introduction: repercussions of the imperial and Romanised Church

Up to now, the framework of the Roman Empire and its cultural and political forces have been the context we have concentrated on to discover the patterns of the passive and active contextualisation of Christianity to the changes of the fourth century. Dominant factors were the official recognition of the Christian religion by the Roman Empire and the increasing interferences of the imperial court in the matters of the Church. We saw how the latter gradually provoked resistance and the emergence of self-consciousness among the Church leadership. We also studied the impact of the close connection with the State and with the classical culture on Christian theological thought. It is now time to look at the repercussion of this close connection of Christianity with one specific political and cultural entity – however 'universal' and widespread it was in the world of the time – on Christian communities and their contextualisation outside the Roman territories. After that, we have to examine some repercussions of that close connection on spiritual life inside the Roman world and the official Church, viz., on the flourishing of monastic life and on the Christian life and worship of common people. These three subjects will form the successive sections of this final chapter.

Christianity beyond the Roman borders

The close relationship between Church and State in the Roman Empire had one precedent, the Kingdom of Armenia. Later, two other neighbouring countries were to adopt Christianity as state religion: Armenia's Caucasian neighbour Georgia and Ethiopia. Hostile to the spread of Christianity were the Persian kingdom, Rome's continuous arch-enemy, and – for some decades – the Goths who settled along the Empire's northern borders in the Balkans. The Christians in Persia suffered most from the alliance of Christianity with the Roman State. Gothic tribes gradually adopted it, albeit in the Arian expression that was prevailing in the middle of the century. In most of these missionary successes, the conversion of the king and his nobles was the beginning of the Christianisation of the whole population, but this conversion had always been preceded by initiatives of courageous individuals.

The south: Ethiopia

The fourth century shows the beginnings of a Christian nation in Ethiopia. As far as we know, two young men from Phoenician Tyre, named Edesius and Frumentius, introduced Christianity into this area. Accompanying their teacher on a journey of exploration along the Red Sea, they were captured and sold to the Ethiopian king, whose residence then was Axum.[1] They rose to positions of trust, probably because they were men of letters, which gave them great prestige. Frumentius became the King's Secretary. After they had obtained freedom, they travelled north to Egypt, visited Athanasius in Alexandria and advised him to undertake missionary activities in Ethiopia. This must have happened during the undisturbed decade of Athanasius' episcopate, 346–56.[2] Athanasius thought he could do no better than to entrust Frumentius himself with this mission and to send him back to Ethiopia in episcopal dignity.

This official mission inaugurated a period of fluctuating attitudes of the kings towards the new religion. By the end of the fifth century, the Ethiopian people had definitely adopted Christianity. But already in the second half of the fourth century, the creation of an alphabet opened the way for the use of the national language for a Bible translation and an indigenous liturgy. Frumentius was a faithful follower of the Nicene faith; if not, Athanasius would never have consecrated him. Thus, the Ethiopian Church was Nicene right from the beginning. It seems that Constantius, after having expelled Athanasius from the Alexandrian see in 356, tried to bring the Ethiopian Christians to an alignment with the 'Arian', i.e., *homoean* confession, which he wished to be generally adopted.[3] But this attempt failed.

The east: Persia

For centuries, the Persian Kingdom was the only strong nation with which the Roman Empire found itself confronted. In 226,[4] the powerful dynasty of the Sassanides founded the New Persian Empire and for the greater part of the fourth century (309–79), the Romans had to do with Shapuhr II, pretentiously hailed 'King of Kings'. Shapuhr was an implacable enemy of the Roman Empire. In the year 297, Galerius, by then Diocletian's Caesar in the east,[5] had succeeded in pushing the Persian dominance eastwards beyond the river Tigris. As a result, Upper Mesopotamia had come under Roman authority. But in 363, Julian lost a battle against the Persians and half of this newly won territory reverted to the hands of the Persian king. The new frontier line ran between the cities of Edessa and Nisibis (Turkish Urfa and Nusaybin, both near the actual Syrian border): Edessa remained Roman and Nisibis, 250 kilometres away, came under Persian power. Both cities were centres of Syriac-speaking Christianity.

In Edessa stood the oldest-known Christian church building. Translations of the New Testament into Syriac were achieved here. The name of the apostle Thomas was connected with Edessa. Nisibis housed a theological centre for the Persian Church. Due to the loss of this region to the Persians in 363, the school had to be transferred to Edessa for safety reasons. This theological school was a combination of a Christian university and a church seminary. Its chief characteristic was that for its theological work it did not seek support in the thinking and the concepts of the Graeco-Roman culture but in the Semitic cultural sphere. Research and education were addressed to the needs of the local church. The language was Syriac, which is a Semitic language. Thus, the School of Nisibis/Edessa contributed to the formation of a national culture that would prove to be of lasting and profound influence. It gave specific features to what is called East Syrian Christianity.[6]

A great teacher at the school, whom circumstances forced to move with the institute from Nisibis to Edessa, was Ephrem Syrus (306–73). He wrote exegetical works on the Bible and theological poems, for instance, several hymns on the Christian feasts.[7] His doctrinal works dealt with the Arian and Neo-Arian (*anhomoean*) Christology,[8] which he combatted. His works prove that Syriac Christianity did not cut itself off from the main theological debate in the imperial church. From that side, there was interest in Ephrem's writings, as can be seen in the fact that they have been translated into Greek as well as into Armenian.

In spite of these signs of a flourishing East Syrian Christianity, the Christians of Persia suffered much because of their faith. Like the Roman emperors, the Persian King of Kings also wanted all his subjects to adhere to one state religion, Mazdeism.[9] When the Roman Empire, following Constantine's example, embraced the Christian religion and gradually made it the national religion, the Persian Christians were automatically suspect as fifth columnists of the arch-enemy. From 339 onwards, Shapuhr II launched a bitter persecution of the Christians, who were a minority but a considerable one. Their communities were for the largest part situated in the basin of the rivers Euphrates and Tigris, but also on the plateau of modern Iran. They had an episcopal centre in Seleucia on the Tigris (now Baghdad), the capital city of the King of Kings. Shapuhr's persecution continued until his death in 379. Three successive Bishops of Seleucia were tortured to death, and for forty years the see remained unoccupied (348–88). The repression was particularly severe against the clergy and the monks, viz., the spiritual leaders of the faithful. Contacts with Christians in the west were forbidden and, consequently, dangerous. Nevertheless, the West Syrian Church of Antioch tried to help their fellow Christians under Persian rule as much as they could. It was only towards the end of the century that the hostility of the Persian King against the Christians quieted down.

As a result of this peace, the Persian Christians were able to assemble in

Seleucia for a council in the year 410, which restored the organisation of the Church and adopted the creeds of Nicaea and Constantinople.[10] By this decision, Syrian Christianity of the east joined the theological position of the ecumenical church. All modern descendants of Syriac Christianity subscribe to the Nicene-Constantinopolitan Creed as the true ecumenical confession of Christendom. They maintained a special bond with the see of Antioch, which they saw as a neutral authority. Moreover, the Antiochene way of theological thinking was congenial with theirs.[11]

The north-east: Armenia and Georgia

Adjacent to the Roman Empire (Cappadocia) as well as to the Persian kingdom, Armenia was a bone of contention between these two powers: at one time, it was under Roman protection, at another, the region passed under Persian domination. Armenia had its 'apostle' in the person of Gregory the Illuminator (240–332), a Christian from Cappadocia. He came to Armenia and converted King Tiridates. The metropolitan Bishop of Cappadocian Caesarea consecrated Gregory bishop for the nascent Armenian Church. This church accepted married bishops with the result that Gregory became the head of a dynasty of archbishops. Soon after 300, the King's conversion being followed by the aristocracy and then by the whole population, Armenia became the very first nation in history that had Christianity as its state religion. Preceding the Roman Empire in this respect, they have always been proud of that.[12]

During the fourth century, the Christian faith got deeply rooted in the hearts and minds of the Armenian people. This was especially due to Gregory's great-grandson Nerses, Archbishop from 364 to 374. Under his episcopate, a national synod took place at the royal residence Ashtishat. Here too, the vehicle of the spreading and rooting of the Christian faith was the national language: an alphabet was created and Scripture, liturgies as well as biblical commentaries and other writings of the Greek Fathers, were translated into Armenian. No doubt the use of the native language was a great help for the Armenians to appropriate the Christian religion: when their land came under Persian influence, they succeeded in resisting any assimilation to Persian culture and religion.

Neighbouring Georgia also knew the fate of transfer from Roman to Persian rule: in 297 it became a Roman territory; in 363 the Romans lost it to Persia. Here the 'apostle' was a remarkable woman, Nina, a slave girl from Cappadocia, who brought the Christian faith to the royal house and the royal house to the faith (*c.* 330). Christianity rose to the level of state religion and, here again, the use of the native language was of great importance.

The north: Small Goths and Visigoths

In the course of the fourth century, Gothic tribes began to invade Europe in successive waves. The first were the Visigoths. Their earliest home was modern Ukraine, from where they were driven westwards by the Huns of central Asia. The first groups settled along the lower reaches of the Danube. Because of the ongoing incursions of the warlike Huns, these Goths asked for an area on the southern bank of the Danube, since this broad river formed the easily defendable frontier of the Roman Empire. Whereas one chief was opposed to embracing the Christian religion, since this would be a betrayal of the ancestral religion and the adoption of the religion of the Romans, another chief, Fritigern, thought it wise to change over to Christianity in order to obtain protection from Valens. This emperor indeed allowed the Visigoths to settle on the southern bank of the Danube (modern Bulgaria). In return, the Emperor expected some benefit from the settlement of Goths, who would help to keep the Huns out of Roman territory. He therefore granted them the status of 'Ally of Rome' (376).

But then the Goths felt so strongly that they provoked an armed conflict with the Roman army, in which they were victorious. In the battle at Adrianople, Valens fell (378). Although Theodosius, called in by Gratianus, defeated the disloyal Goths, he well understood that he would still need their help and soon rendered them their status of Roman Allies (382). From now on, Goths were admitted into the Roman armies and administration.[13] But Theodosius was unable to assimilate the newly Christianised Goths to the form of Catholic Christianity he had proclaimed state religion two years before. Valens, who favoured Arianism, i.e., the *homoean* conception of Christ's sonship of God, had initiated Fritigern and his tribesmen into Christianity by calling in the assistance of the so-called Small Goths.

Once more, Cappadocia was the cradle of the Christianisation of a non-Roman people. Already in 264 a vanguard of wandering Goths had invaded Asia Minor where they kidnapped a number of Cappadocian Christians, taking them along as slaves into the Danubian area. Among them was a couple whose daughter, married to a Goth, gave birth to a boy who received a Gothic name, Ulphilas, but a Christian education. Basil of Caesarea knows about another Cappadocian called Eutyches, who went across the Danube to bring the Gospel to the Goths. This first penetration of Christianity among the Goths provoked several persecutions, of which the brutalities committed in 348, forced Ulphilas and others to take refuge in the Roman part of the Balkans.[14] He had been there before, as a delegate of the nascent Gothic Church to a meeting in Constantinople; there he attracted the attention of Bishop Eusebius of Nicomedia, who consecrated him missionary bishop for his people.

Ulphilas (311–83) was an intelligent and energetic missionary. He possessed a good knowledge of Greek and Latin besides his native language. He created an alphabet for the Gothic speech and translated the Bible, with the remarkable exception of the Books of Kings, which he feared would encourage the Gothic appetite for capturing land! He was determined to dissociate religion from battle and conquest and, therefore, translated 'Saviour' by 'Healer' and not by 'Lord', which would sound as warlord. For 'co-religionist' he found no better word than 'tribesman', and for 'charity' just 'friendship', which embraced the notion of fidelity but lacked the biblical notion of undeserved mercy. The Germans, to whom the Goths belonged, had no sense of personal guilt. They embraced the Christian faith as deliverance from their traditional fear of the meaningless blows of blind powers, far more than from the regret of personal sins. Thus Ulphilas took full account of the conceptions among his people, using them as vehicles for the key words of the Christian faith.[15]

When Ulphilas visited Constantinople and, later, when he sought refuge south of the Danube, 'Arianism' was the prevailing confession (see Chapter 4, pp. 87–8). It was only natural that he introduced this form of Christianity among the Goths, with whom he was living in the safe area granted to them. This group of refugees was living on stock farming and was without import- ance for Roman military and economic objectives. But this colony of so-called 'Small Goths' became important as a missionary link between the Roman imperial church and the more powerful Visigoths, at the time Valens allowed their immigration. We saw above that this emperor called in the assistance of the 'Small Goths' as soon as it had become clear that Chief Fritigern and his men were prepared to change religion and be Christianised. Ulphilas was then still alive. We possess a confession from Ulphilas' hand, which clearly reflects the moderate 'Arian' position of the 340s and 350s: the Father is called the only Ungenerate; the Son 'only-begotten' and 'our Lord and God, artisan and designer of the entire creation', but 'subject and obedient to the Father', who is also his God; the Holy Spirit on the contrary 'neither God nor Lord, but the faithful servant of Christ'.[16] In Ulphilas' conception of the Trinity, the relation between the three persons is one of subordination. Ulphilas also took part in the synod of 360 in Constantinople, where Con- stantius celebrated the triumph over all Nicene opposition in east and west, which he had achieved the year before.[17]

Through the great influence of Ulphilas and the 'Small Goths', the Visigoths adhered to the *homoean* theology, which the adherents of the Nicene Creed always defamed as 'Arianism'. As we said, Theodosius was not in a position to persuade the Goths to align with the Roman state religion and adopt Nicene orthodoxy, a failure that chagrined his friend and adviser Ambrose (see Chapter 5, p. 151). The *homoean* faith remained the Christianity of the Goths and of later German invaders, to whom they passed the Christian religion.[18]

Some concluding remarks

We have examined how in the course of the fourth century Christianity penetrated into four regions on the fringes of the eastern Roman Empire, following a wide arc from Ethiopia in the south to the Goths in the north, passing through Persia and the Caucasian kingdoms. Some common features are noteworthy.

The first and most striking fact is the linking-up with *local language and culture*. Except for Syriac, which was a written language and had been adopted as a Christian means of expression at an early date, the missionary pioneers elsewhere met with unwritten languages and had first to create an adequate alphabet before they could set themselves to the translation of the Bible, exegetical works and liturgical texts. By doing this, these pioneers, be it in Ethiopia, Armenia, Georgia or among the settling Goths, contributed to the formation and development of a national culture, which in each area would prove enduring to this day. The use of the national language and a growing connection of the Church with the life of the nation have very much become a characteristic of eastern Christianity.[19]

The contextualisation of Christianity within the Roman world in the fourth century was determined by the two needs of (1) handling the Christianised imperial power and its interference in church leadership and theology; and (2) integrating most of the classical cultural and intellectual heritage now that the Christian world-view had almost become dominant. Over and against this linking-up with the Graeco-Roman civilisation, the Christians beyond the borders found themselves faced with the task of expressing the faith in their own language and, consequently, in different cultural speech. Those living in the Persian kingdom were, moreover, hampered by the conviction of their faith brothers in the Roman Empire that the Roman emperor had been charged by God to spread Christianity all over the world and to act as the Christians' protector everywhere.[20] We have noticed that Eusebius of Caesarea had promoted the idea of Constantine as the universal monarch on Earth, in the image of the universal rule of the unique *Logos*. His theological thesis was that the sole monarch of creation required a single monarch on Earth, in order that the monotheistic faith (of Christianity) should triumph over polytheism and that one order of civilisation would eclipse the diversity of nations and their religions. Although more critical about the relationship between the imperial power and the Church, Eusebius' antipode Ambrose did not have a different opinion on the connection of true religion and Roman dominion and civilisation: in his eyes, Christian mission went together with integration into the Roman world order. The nascent Christian communities outside the Empire meant a correction of this mentality, and they form a necessary complement to the one-sided contextualisation that was going on in the Roman world.

Second, the establishment of Christianity in Ethiopia as well as the Christianisation of whole populations as happened in Armenia, Georgia and with the Visigoths, was doubtless the result of the conversion of the respective kings and nobles. But this should not make us overlook the *initiatives* that in each case were taken *by courageous individuals*: they were the ones who understood how to use opportunities and how to transmit the faith in which they had grown up to the masters they were forced to serve. We recall the examples of Edesius and Frumentius, of Nina, and of Ulphilas' grandparents and mother, all taken as slaves to alien lands. Ulphilas himself and Gregory the Illuminator were free men, but every bit as much individual 'apostles' to yet unconverted national communities. The risky undertakings and the readiness of these individuals to witness are the true beginnings of the introduction of Christianity in Ethiopia, the Caucasian countries and among the Goths.

The third remark concerns the role of Cappadocia as cradle of missionary endeavours. The 'apostles' of Armenia and Georgia, Gregory the Illuminator and Nina, as well as Ulphilas' grandparents and the missionary Eutyches, all came from this province which had such a rich and stimulating Christian life.

The prime of ascetic and monastic life

Inside the Roman Empire, a first repercussion of the preferential treatment by the State was the retreat of radical believers from common religious life. This phenomenon of turning away from a religious life that was becoming safe and comfortable originated in the forty years of de-facto tolerance from 261 till *c.* 300. In Egypt and Syria, individuals went in search of the utmost isolation and harsh challenges, and they found these in the desert, where they lived as hermits. They were motivated by the wish to safeguard their ethical, especially ascetic commitment and by a drive to confront the realm of the demons with the forces of Christ and of their own perseverance. When Christianity became more and more fashionable, the numbers of ascetics increased in all eastern provinces, soon followed by the west. Monks were living apart as hermits or – before long also – in communities. In the second half of the century, church leaders understood the importance of the ascetic movement for the revival of the Church.

From asceticism to monasticism

Asceticism belonged to Christianity from very early times and it was highly estimated. In the sports of Greek Antiquity, *askesis* just meant 'training', 'exercise'. Applied to religious and philosophical life, it meant 'denial of pleasures' considered as a hindrance for mental concentration on 'higher', intellectual or spiritual goods. Such denial of pleasures generally concerned:

- Food and drink: an ascetic abstains from appetising dishes like meat and wine, and only takes the necessary minimum to keep himself alive.
- Marriage and sexual intercourse: the ascetic is strictly celibate. This field of abstention is the origin of the names 'monk' and 'nun': monk is derived from the Greek *monachos* (single person), and nun from the Coptic *nonnè* (untouched woman).
- Luxury and property: an ascetic person lives in an utterly sober way and gives up his material and social certainties, including the family bonds. The combination of the last two abstentions can lead to a wandering life or to retirement into the desert: the 'hermit' or 'anchorite' derived his name from the Greek words *erèmos* (desert) and *anachorèsis* (retirement).

Fasting, celibacy and poverty are the basic forms of asceticism. Early Christianity developed in a context in which ascetic ideals were propagated for several distinct reasons. There was the philosophical call for discipline as a reaction against a go-as-you-please lifestyle of lustful sensations and temperamental emotions. This appeal was rooted in a dualistic anthropology that put the value of the soul above the appetites of the body. The philosophical ideal was that of *apatheia*, freedom from emotions and reasonable moderation in all respects. Another motivation was found in the Gnostic systems, which saw the whole world as an accidental mixture of spirit and matter, destined to be separated again: asceticism was the only appropriate way for those enlightened by 'Knowledge' to cope with one's own mixture of opposing elements. Christianity could hardly avoid linking up with the moral earnestness of these ascetic ideals, but it had its own motives: (1) the imitation of the apostles who, when following Jesus' call, left everything behind (Luke 14:26, 33 and 18:28–30); (2) the community of goods, allegedly practised in the mother church of Jerusalem (Acts 4: 32–7); (3) the assumption that the time appointed by God for the return of Christ has grown very short, so that it is recommendable not to be possessed by feelings for a partner, by joy or sorrow, or by concerns for worldly property (1 Cor. 7:29–31). The last argument is rather eschatological (the remaining time of the world is short) than dualistic (corporeal and material goods are to be despised because of their nature). These authentic primitive Christian motives, however, did not fail to mingle with the properly dualistic arguments of the surrounding world – the early Church did not want to fall short of the surrounding moral earnestness, in which it saw a kind of an ally.

At the beginning of the third century, several Christian authors still held the view that asceticism was a natural obligation for every Christian. But from then the inflow of candidates for baptism as well as the distinction between ordinary believers and intellectually and spiritually more advanced Christians[21] were responsible for a mitigation by the bishops of the equation of 'faithful' and 'ascetic'. Asceticism became a matter of free choice, which means of only a part of Christ's flock. This development stimulated a search for new ways by those who wanted to live radically for the faith. Ascetics no longer felt at home in the growing Christian communities that were characterised by the concessions to moral laxity made by bishops for pastoral and pedagogical reasons.[22] The first steps of withdrawal from the ordinary community with its decreasing ascetic standards were made in Egypt.

Hermits and monasteries

It should first be noted that the English word 'monastery' is commonly used for a group of unmarried men living a community life, as well as for the building in which they live this more or less isolated life. But originally the Greek *monastèrion* meant the cell of a monk and the word *monachos* a man who lives in solitude. Thus we find the term in Athanasius' *Life of Antony*. A *monachos* is not only a celibate, but he also lives at a shorter or greater distance from the inhabited world. This second characteristic gave him the names of 'hermit', desert-dweller, or 'anchorite', who withdraws from the world. The original label for a community of ascetics was a Greek word meaning 'sheepfold', which in the ancient Near East was a walled-in space. In Latin the surrounding wall gave rise to the word 'cloister', which nowadays rather means the quadrangular space for meditation and silence.[23]

The beginnings of the retirement of those who wanted to keep their asceticism up to the mark did not coincide with the growing worldliness of church life as a result of its privileging by the state. These beginnings took place earlier, namely, in the second half of the third century and they were rather caused by the de-facto tolerance, lasting about forty years (261–303) and by the moral laxity, which went hand in hand with the increase of conversions. The famous Coptic hermit Antony (whose life was written by Athanasius shortly after Antony's death in 356) began to withdraw from the civilised world in *c.* 286. Thus, the secularisation of the Church as a result of the Christianisation of the Roman Empire was not the first cause of the *anachoretic* movement, though it is of course true that secularisation pushed the movement to great proportions.

These ascetics sought the desert not only for spiritual concentration on a life with God alone but also to fight in the name of Christ the demons that were supposed to populate deserted areas and to hold these in their power.[24] Antony was not the first to find a dwelling place for himself on the edge of the inhabited and cultivated land, which in Egypt is marked by the mountains bordering the fertile Nile valley; his predecessors already used to live in the tombs that were located there. But he was the very first to venture into the deep desert, exposing himself in complete solitude to the wild beasts and to the phantasms by which the Devil sought to frighten and to chase him. This made him famous; his example was followed by a growing number, and Athanasius' biography helped a great deal to spread the ideal of solitary life, devoted only to God, both in the east and in the west.[25] Athanasius drew on circulating stories about Antony, but his aim was not just to record and spread these local traditions. In presenting the moral and mental imperturbability of the famous Desert Father, Athanasius explained that his resistance against the Devil's assaults and temptations was, in the last resort, due to Christ, since by bearing human flesh the Lord has endowed the human body with victorious power. By relating the achievements of the ascetic to the assumption of the human flesh by the divine son, Athanasius sought to claim Antony for the sake of his views on salvation, which differed from those of the Arians.[26]

In the largely Christianised area of southern Gaul, where no desert is found, the hermits settled down on rough, uninhabited islands off the Mediterranean coast. The hermits of Egypt, followed by those of Palestine and Syria, established colonies in which they were living apart together. Each hermit had his own cell, but these were at a short distance from each other (for instance, situated in caves in the same valley[27]), so that the hermits could assemble for Sunday service and common talks. But such colonies were no monasteries in the proper sense, i.e., they had no community life. The creation of a form of communal life for monks and nuns was the achievement of another Egyptian, Pachomius (*c.* 290–346).

Pachomius is the founder of conventual monasticism.[28] After a start as the disciple of a hermit, he grew concerned about the failing perseverance of individual ascetics, when they were left to their own spiritual discipline. He saw that anchorites who lived in the remote regions were preoccupied with their subsistence much of their time, whereas others were pleased with the admiration from visitors, who were attracted by the singularity of the hermits' lifestyle and by the miracles of healing they reputedly achieved. Thus, as Pachomius found many well-motivated hermits fond of visiting marketplaces or yielding to spiritual pride, he thought that a communal life could remedy the situation. The community was set up as an economic unit. Division of labour would give each member more time for private meditation and for common prayer. Only a very restricted number of monks and, moreover, in rotation, would be necessary to visit the marketplaces for making purchases and selling the community's products of handicraft; contacts of the monks with ordinary people and with the other sex could be limited. An important function was that of the doorkeeper to whom visitors and postulants had to report. In times of insecurity and famine, many a man or woman preferred the protection and nourishment – however plain this was! – they would receive in the convent. Therefore, the doorkeeper had the responsible task of screening the candidates. Pachomius, who is said to have served in the army before his conversion, made a *rule* including all these, and other, regulations. He also introduced a probationary period for newcomers, the *noviciate*. Following the example of the primitive community of Jerusalem, the members had all things in common and no private property was allowed. This original creation of Pachomius is the first rule for monastic life and it was to be followed by other rules, both in the eastern and in the western Church. In a period of twenty-five years, a network of no fewer than twenty-five monasteries under central supervision came into being; among these was a convent for women.

The hermits found another way of initiating candidates into their way of life: applicants had to pass some time with one or more experienced 'fathers', imitating their examples and confessing to them all their longings for the relatives and good things they had left behind. The main purpose of this discipleship was to learn how to distinguish good from evil spirits and edifying from seductive thoughts. The wisdom of these Desert Fathers has been compiled in several collections of sayings: the best known is the *Gerontikon*, which contains over 900 points of advice and tales that circulated on the name of this or that Old Father.[29]

Syria was another birthplace of both anchorites and monastic communities. Their origin was quite parallel to the ones in Egypt, but independent from there. In comparison with Egypt, Syrian asceticism showed a tendency to austere asceticism and extreme self-chastisement: here the hermit's life was far more popular. A reason for this may be that in Egypt it was easier to lead a life in isolation than in Syria because of the proximity of towns and villages. Some very radical Syrian hermits submitted to an unsheltered life, to the eating of grass, to the wearing of heavy chains, or they locked themselves up in a narrow cave or shed. The Spanish nun Etheria, who made a pilgrimage to the Near East late in the fourth century, reports that she found a high density of monasteries in Syrian Mesopotamia.[30] From Syria the new and radical forms of Christian asceticism spread to Asia Minor, where they provoked great enthusiasm in the Cappadocian Fathers.

Monasticism also penetrated Palestine, a region that would soon be filled with monasteries and *lauras*.[31] Influences came from Egypt and from Syria. On her journey from Egypt to Palestine through the Sinai peninsula, Etheria found monasteries almost everywhere. Another impulse came from Italy, when upper-class women settled at the holy places with the intention of opening city convents of a type that already existed in Rome. In 372, a rich woman, Melania 'the Elder', founded a monastery on the Mount of Olives near Jerusalem. She, and others who followed, were intellectually supported by western scholars such as Jerome (342–420), who left Rome and settled at Bethlehem in 386, having spent five years as a hermit in the Syrian desert beforehand.

The fourth century thus shows a general, more or less natural, transition from the early asceticism of the hermits to the more regulated life of monks living as a community, though the latter was by no means replacing the first all along. The two forms of the colony of hermits and the structured community of monks or nuns continued to exist side by side. No less remarkable is the rapid spread of the monastic ideal in both east and west. It also spread under people of different social classes. It has long been thought that the first generations of monks, until the end of the fourth century, were uncivilised and poorly educated peasants, as only they would have been able to cope with the rough circumstances of the desert and to nourish primitive representations of an almost physical struggle with demons and their machinations. But recent research may convince us that people such as Antony were lettered and well up in the Origenist way of Christian thought. Antony shared with the great Alexandrian master not only the background of an education in Platonic philosophy, but also Origen's views on the essentials of Christian theology.[32] However, the colonies and monasteries would also receive many drop-outs of society: men on the run from police or tax collectors. Fourth-century monasticism was indeed a cross-section of all levels of society. It was a new way of living Christian religious radicalism in days when being a Christian had become a safe and comfortable choice. Significantly, the monks of that age called their hardship 'a daily martyrdom'.

Monks and the Church

Monasticism started as an attempt to evade ordinary social intercourse, including Church community. The ascetics had the device: 'avoid women and bishops'! Both were seen as seducers – the woman because of her sexual attraction, the bishop because he was a mere administrator and a person of social prestige. Monastic circles considered it a betrayal of true asceticism when a monk agreed to become bishop, since this office was now so much linked up with worldly affairs. But there were notable exceptions.

In Gaul, a certain Martin was serving in the army when he met a naked beggar and cut off half his cloak to clothe him. He received a vision through which Christ called him to baptism and a religious life. Martin left the army, visited several Christian leaders such as Hilary of Poitiers, the western opponent of Constantius' policy (see Chapter 4, pp. 102–3), and then founded the first monastery in Gaul. He met criticism from monastic circles when he was appointed Bishop of Tours in 372 and accepted. But his biographer emphasises that as a bishop Martin did not abandon his usual ascetic lifestyle and that he encouraged the spread of monasticism.[33] The monasteries helped a lot to evangelise the countryside of central Gaul, which had remained untouched by Christianity as yet.

Athanasius was the first to understand the enormous importance of the monks and their spiritual zeal for the Church. As the biographer of Antony, he emphasised the great sacrifices of his hero during his many years of retirement in the desert, but also his involvement – in spite of his desire for isolation – in the events that struck the church of Alexandria: the persecution of the year 311 and the tough debate with the early Arians, who seem to have tried to win Antony for their cause.[34] Athanasius reports Antony's respect for the clergy,[35] and, on the other hand, the fact that he admonished the head of a monastery not to be tied to this function and rather to accept the call for the episcopacy for – Athanasius writes – there are several bishops who fast, don't drink wine and have no wife, whereas one cannot say that every monk remains faithful to his vows![36]

But the greatest promoter of the integration of monastic life and spirituality into church life was without doubt Basil of Caesarea. We already brought out the spiritual aspects of his theology in connection with his stand in the doctrinal questions that were solved at the synod of Constantinople, 381 (see Chapter 5, pp. 128–30). Basil did the most to integrate the monastery into church life. Since monks were advanced in spiritual life and knowledge, their communities were natural centres of theological reflection. We saw that Basil called this profound research into the faith *dogma*, contrasting it to *kerygma*, i.e., the public confession of the essentials to which everyone had to adhere. Basil saw the monastery also as a centre and example of practical mercifulness towards the poor and the sick. He founded several hostels and hospitals and organised forms of care that should lead to lasting relief. In his eyes, the monastic community was the Church in the proper sense and quality; it should, therefore, be a real source of inspiration and spiritual renewal for the secularised church of the masses. He wanted monasteries to be near towns or villages. It is no wonder that Basil did not hold with hermits living a pious life in isolation for their own spiritual benefit: perfect service of God had to be achieved in community life, guided by a superior. Basil perfected the achievement of Pachomius by drawing up rules for monastic life. He did so in the years before his appointment as Bishop of Caesarea. As bishop, he cared very much for the founding of monasteries and entrusted them with both educational and charitable tasks.

The rule he put forward has become the basis of the Rule that is still followed by religious in eastern Christianity. The rule prescribes the hours of prayer and of manual labour. It enjoins on the monks chastity and renounce-ment of property, but also the care for the poor. This was the way a great and influential church leader met with two pressing needs of his days: spiritual and social. The biblical incentive that led his mind and actions was the image of the first community of Christians in Jerusalem as it is described in Acts.[37]

Liturgical life and Christian commitment

In spite of their isolated life and critical distance from the institutional church, monks got, at the end of the fourth century, more and more involved in the life of the Church. This happened not only because some of them accepted episcopacy and because monastic communities gave fine examples of Christian charity and earnestness in a time of growing religious slackening; they also impressed the stamp of their daily devotions on the liturgical life of the congregation as a whole. The breeding place of this new and developed form of worship was Jerusalem. The previously Jewish and then pagan city was made entirely Christian by Constantine and his mother Helena, who honoured the sacred places of Jesus's ministry through splendid buildings which stimulated a rich liturgical life. From here, models spread in all direc-tions, both east and west. These models were related to three fields: daily hours of prayer, the ecclesiastical year and Christian initiation. The latter was a subject of special concern to bishops since the masses were now flowing into the Church. In spite of this, North Africa and Spain were the theatre of movements of protest against the secularisation of Christianity.

Jerusalem as liturgical breeding ground for the whole Church

After the Emperor Hadrian had quelled the second Jewish insurrection in the year 135, the Jews were denied admittance to Jerusalem. Hadrian transformed the Holy City into a pagan town under the Roman name of *Aelia Capitolina*. Temples were erected: a sanctuary for Venus, the goddess of female beauty, sex and procreation, for instance, covered the hill of Golgotha. Aelia housed, to be sure, a small Christian community, but during the second and third centuries it did not produce any leader or theological author of any importance. This changed when Constantine rose to power in the east.

His mother, the Empress Helena, visited Aelia as early as 326. On her instigation, churches were built on the Mount of Olives, where local tradition showed a cave as the place of Jesus's final instructions to his disciples and from the top of which he had ascended to heaven, as well as at Bethlehem, the town of the Saviour's nativity. By Constantine's orders, pagan sanctuaries were demolished and when the temple of Venus was excavated, a piece of wood was found and declared to be the original cross of Christ. Constantine then ordered the construction of a large and magnificent complex of church build-ings, covering both the places of the crucifixion and the resurrection of Christ. This complex is today called the Church of the Holy Sepulchre, but in the fourth century one distinguished between the *Anastasis*, a domed church above Christ's sepulchre, the *Sanctuary of the Cross*, situated on the site of Golgotha (where the wood that had been found was kept for veneration[38]) and the *Martyrium* or *Major Church*, opposite to the *Anastasis* on the other end of a large court. The construction work took several years and the dedication took place in 335, with splendid pomp and circumstance. Constantine had this religious event, which so clearly marked out the changes he had brought about, coincide with the festivities for his own thirty regnal years and with the presence of many eastern bishops who were assembling at Tyre for the synod that had to decide on the position of Athanasius.[39] The alliance between Church and Empire could hardly be made more visible than in the very places where the life of the divine *Logos* on Earth had reached its culmination!

Other places, such as the Upper Room where Jesus had held his Last Supper with his disciples and where they had been waiting for the descent of the Holy Spirit, and Bethany, the dwelling place of Lazarus, Mary and Martha (John 11), were enriched with Christian sanctuaries as well.

Incited by the illustrious example of the Empress Mother Helena and attracted by the monumental buildings, a new phenomenon came into being: pilgrimages to the Holy Land. In the year 333, an unknown man from Bordeaux made a journey to Jerusalem and back, making mention of the stations he visited on his way and describing the holy places of Jerusalem. We have mentioned above (p. 163) the example of Jerome, who left Rome for Bethlehem in the company of several ladies from the capital. The most fam-ous example from our period is that of the Spanish nun Etheria, who traversed nearly the whole empire from north-west Spain (or south-west Gaul) to Egypt, Palestine and Mesopotamia and left to us a detailed account of all her trips, the churchpeople she had met and, in particular, of the holy sites in and around Jerusalem and all the liturgical moments that were customary at the end of the fourth century.[40] Thanks to her curiosity – which she herself admits in her writing! – we know a great deal of the services on Sundays, during the ordinary weeks, as well as during Lent and the Holy Week. The pilgrims who had assisted at these various ceremonies brought their impressions back home and, thus, the liturgical model of the Jerusalem church spread and was followed in other areas.

We may speak of a remarkable response of the Jerusalem Church to the new and surprising data of the imperial interest in the places sanctioned by Christ's ministry on Earth and of the flocking of pilgrims from everywhere. We learn from Etheria's report, for instance, that catechesis was given in Greek and in Syriac and, when necessary, in Latin.[41] But the most obvious use of the new possibilities was the joining of the main moments of Christ's ministry with distinct, corresponding localities. This custom favoured a direct and emotionally affecting remembrance of the acts and words of the Saviour, as well as liveliness, since the congregation was often en route from one location to another, as was especially the case during the Holy Week. In her introduction to the pilgrimage of Etheria,[42] Hélène Pétré calls the Palestinian worship 'a historical reconstruction, a commemoration of the episodes of the Sacred History', a new feature prevailing over the original custom of celebrating incarnation and redemption in one feast, as one all-embracing mystery of salvation.[43] Upon every component of the liturgy Etheria remarks that the lessons, hymns and prayers that were pronounced, were 'exactly suitable to the day and to the place'. The commemoration of the events of the Holy Week was pushed so far as to celebrate the raising of Lazarus at Bethany where he had lived and died, to perform again Jesus's entry into Jerusalem with children swinging palms and all, and to lament his flagellation by Roman soldiers near the leftover pillar outside Pilate's palace. Etheria has, so to say, checked every liturgical moment with the Bible in her hand, and it is clear that this way of resuscitating well-known scriptural texts deeply moved her, as – one may suppose – it did many other participants. The direct confrontation with the very places of biblical history effected the persuasion of the truth of the Christian faith in all its moments, as did the tombs of martyrs and saints, and the miracles that often happened there.[44] For pilgrims coming from far away, it was doubtless a unique experience.

The excavation and ornamentation of concrete historical sites was the privilege of Jerusalem and its surroundings. This made possible a spreading of the commemoration of the great moments of the Passion story, from Jesus's going up to Jerusalem to his ascension and the descent of the Holy Spirit (which were celebrated together on Whitsunday).[45] Outside Palestine, of course, these visits were not possible. But the partitioning of the Gospel story over a longer liturgical period and the commemoration of its distinctive moments was a model that found its way to many parts of the Church.

Highlights of the liturgical year; initiation into the Church

When discussing the building activities of Constantine and his mother Helena, we mentioned Bethlehem. In her diary, Etheria tells her sisters at some length about the festivals that took place both at Bethlehem and Jerusalem to celebrate Christ's coming on Earth.[46] That such celebrations were part of the liturgical year seems quite natural to us, but in the fourth century it was still rather new. During the first three centuries, indeed, the Church had shown no interest at all in having one fixed date for commemorating Jesus's birth. As we said above, the whole work of salvation was celebrated in one annual cycle of which Easter was the pivot. Feast days for martyrs always fell on the day of their execution, never on that of their birth; it was the ultimate act of obedience and witness to God's kingdom that was commemorated and this feeling was applied to Christ himself as well.[47]

However, in the course of the third century, reflection on the origin and nature of the *Logos*/Son, whom the Father had sent into the world, had started developing and, in connection with this doctrinal interest, the desire for a specific celebration of the incarnation came about. This manifested itself first in Egypt, although not as a commemoration of Jesus's birth at Bethlehem, but of his baptism in the river Jordan. A Gnostic group – Gnostics thought human procreation far too carnal and unworthy for a divine being! – preferred the moment when the heavens were opened, the Spirit of God descended like a dove on Jesus and a voice proclaimed him as 'My beloved Son' (Matt. 3:16–17) for celebrating the appearance (in Greek: *Epiphany*) of the divine Son. The date they chose was 6 January (including the night before), probably since this date was that of a pagan god, Osiris, and the water of the Nile was supposed to have a miraculous healing power that particular night. Christians wanted to testify, in opposition to this belief, that Christ is the true heavenly healer, who all at once appeared on Earth in the moment of baptism in another river, the Jordan. The main Church took over this date and, as they saw Jesus's birth as the very moment of the entrance of God's son into the world, combined birth and baptism. Other 'appearances' were associated: Jesus's first sign by which he manifested his glory, changing water into wine at a marriage (John 2:11) and his manifestation to the heathens, represented by the Wise Men from the east, who had understood an uncommon star as the sign of the birth of a new king (Matt. 2:1–2).[48] The night from 5 to 6 January got reserved for commemorating the birth of Christ, the day of 6 January for his baptism (and the other manifestations).

From Egypt, the feast of the Nativity spread to neighbouring Palestine and Syria. In the middle of the century, Ephrem Syrus (see above, p. 154) wrote a hymn in which the different elements of Epiphany were combined:

> The whole creation proclaims it.
> The Wise Men proclaim it.
> The star proclaims it:
> Behold, the Son of the King is there!
> The heaven opens,
> The waters of the Jordan foam,
> The dove appears:
> This is my beloved Son!

Ephrem saw 6 January as the loftiest of all Christian feasts. And when Etheria visited Jerusalem it was not only in use, but indeed celebrated with great pomp. She tells that it started with a night service at Bethlehem, after which a procession walked to Jerusalem, to the Church of the Holy Sepulchre where all assembled at 7 o'clock. She continues:

> Now it would be superfluous to describe the adornment either of the church, or of the Anastasis, or of the Cross, or in Bethlehem that day; you see there nothing but gold and gems and silk. For if you look at the veils, they are made wholly of silk striped with gold, and if you look at the curtains, they too are made wholly of silk striped with gold. The church vessels too, of every kind, gold and jewelled, are brought out on that day [. . .] and what shall I say of the decoration of the fabric itself, which Constantine, at his mother's instigation, decorated with gold, mosaic, and costly marbles, as far as the resources of his kingdom allowed him [. . .][49]

The feast of the Epiphany covers eight consecutive days (an *octave*), clergy, monks and laypeople moving from the Holy Sepulchre to the sanctuaries on the Mount of Olives, to Bethlehem again, and back to Jerusalem. Etheria wrote:

> Thus, then is the feast celebrated with all this joyfulness and festal array throughout the eight days in all the holy places which I have mentioned above. And in Bethlehem also throughout the entire eight days the feast is celebrated with similar festal array and joyfulness daily by the priests and by all the clergy there, and by the monks who are appointed in that place.[50]

In the fourth century, however, another date was brought into vogue, the well-known 25 December. This happened in Rome, and there are two probable reasons for it. The first is of doctrinal nature: the church of Rome, which supported the dogmatic formula of Nicaea and Athanasius' resistance against deviating definitions (see Chapter 4, pp. 84–5, 88), may have found a reason for dissociating the commemoration of Christ's incarnation from that of his baptism, viz., to make it clear that he was not God's son from the moment of the descent of the Spirit on him, but by nature and thus from the very beginning.[51] At the same time, the pagan population of Rome was still much attached to the veneration of the *Invincible Sun*. An important element of the popular religion of Mithras was the cult of the sun, the force of which appeared when (in the northern hemisphere) the days were beginning to lengthen again, i.e., on 25 December. In the third century, the city of Rome organised festal games in honour of the victory of the sun over darkness and people lit fires in order to 'help' the sun's rising. In this context, Christians wanted to put their feast of the 'Light for revelation to the Gentiles' (Luke 2:32) over and against the pagan cult of the sun, for 'the true Light that enlightens every man, coming into the world (John 1:9). The symbolism of 'light' suited very well the worldwide significance of the enlightening Word of God made flesh. Ambrose of Milan would oppose the Christian feast to the pagan cult by stating: 'Christ is *our new* sun!' This trend matched the religious policy of Constantine: he, indeed, was the one who gave 25 December the official status of feast day of the Nativity.

Constantine's own way to Christianity had passed (as we saw above, Chapter 2, p. 35) through the veneration of the sun. This cult was in a way monotheistic:[52] there is one sun sending light and life to all. In becoming a Christian, Constantine never abandoned the symbolism of the sun for, as he called it, the 'Supreme divinity': it was a way to combine a popular and not outdated or objectionable, pagan religion with one central article of the Christian faith, monotheism. In the Roman world, one day of the week was already reserved for the veneration of the sun, the Sunday. Long before Constantine, Christians had taken over this name for the day of Christ's resurrection, originally called 'the Lord's day'.[53] By this naming, they gave a Christian meaning to the weekly day of the sun.

Such a confluence pleased Constantine and he did not wait long to proclaim the Christianised Sunday the statutory weekly holiday (321).[54] We may, therefore, suppose that it was also with his full consent, if not at his instigation, that in Rome (and the west) the commemoration of the birth of Christ was moved to the date that was pre-eminently the day of the great annual feast of the sun, 25 December. The habitual popular fire-lighting could go on and now be seen as celebrating the light that had come into the world in the person of Christ.[55] The celebration of Christmas[56] on the original day of the Invincible Sun must have been officially introduced in Rome before the year 336, i.e., still under Constantine's reign.

Rome may also have known the eastern feast day of 6 January. In the second half of the fourth century, a mutual influencing took place with as a result that in about 400, both parts of the Empire had exchanged their feasts of the Nativity. The east, where this feast had originated, proved reluctant to accept the new date of 25 December: Constantinople introduced it in 379;[57] Antioch, after much resistance, in 386; whereas Egypt and Palestine refused it until far into the fifth and sixth century.[58] So both dates could transfer particular biblical meanings to one another (and adopt other gospel elements), since neither of them was the true birthday of Jesus. They have been chosen for symbolic reasons, in particular in order to eclipse traditional pagan motives by 'stealing' their symbolism.

The other highlight of the liturgical year was, of course, the Holy Week and Easter. This week was preceded by the period of Lent and, like Epiphany, followed by an octave. In Jerusalem, Etheria observed that, as distinct from her homeland, Lent was spread over eight weeks, because there was no fasting on Saturdays and the biblical number of forty days should be completed anyway.[59] Besides the fasting, the degree of which was left to everyone's own choice,[60] Lent was in particular reserved for the initiation of new church members. Etheria indicates them by the Greek word *cathecumini*, which means 'those being instructed', and she devotes a whole section of her diary to the initiation rite, 'lest you, my reverend sisters, should think that these things are done without good reason'.[61] The day before the Lenten course, the names of the candidates are written down and the bishop makes inquiries about the lifestyle of each, asking those who present them: 'Does this person lead a good life? Is he obedient to his parents, is he not given to wine, nor deceitful?' and about other possible vices, 'which are more serious in man'.[62] These enquiries show in a precise way which ethical standards the Church was trying to uphold among its members: before the catechesis could start, the bishop wished to be sure about the conduct of the neophyte and the degree of moral discipline that could be expected from them.

The catechising took seven weeks, every morning from 6 to 9 o'clock. Lectures were given on the Bible, the resurrection and 'all things concerning the faith'. Repeated exorcisms were accompanying the lectures with the aim of chasing evil spirits from the catechumens and strengthening their hope of salvation. Then the text of the creed was revealed to the candidates, who were expected to learn it by heart and repeat it two weeks later. This procedure was called 'the acceptance and rendering of the Symbol'. During the last weeks, the candidates, who were now called 'those being enlightened',[63] were taught the meaning of the creed, as Etheria says, first its literal and then its spiritual sense.[64] But the meaning of baptism itself used to be explained only after the rite had been accomplished, in the so-called 'mystagogical catecheses', given during the eight days following Easter.

Some fifty years before Etheria made her pilgrimage, Cyril was Bishop of Jerusalem and he has left us some examples of this *mystagogical catechesis*.[65] Etheria mentions this part of the rite of initiation as well: during those eight days – she writes – the bishop 'explains all things that are done in baptism' and she adds that no catechumen is allowed to hear the mysteries, only those who have been baptised, now or before, since those faithful, who like to revive their commitment, are welcome too.[66]

What then was said to the newly baptised? Cyril of Jerusalem's catechises show a clear distinction between instructions before and after the moment of baptism. There is no allusion to infant baptism: he is addressing adults. In the 'procatechesis' he is already evoking a sphere of initiation into an unexperienced privilege. When the catechumens have been inscribed, the bishop solemnly says that they are already at the entrance hall of the King's House. God's calling depends on their honesty of purpose. Cyril impresses upon his pupils that it is a serious matter to join the faith community: 'I will behold each man's earnestness, each woman's reverence'. If the purpose is not good, 'although the water (of baptism) will receive you, the Spirit will not accept you', he warns. At the end of the five weeks of catechising, he states that 'you are now standing on the frontiers' and adjures them not to tell anything of what they have been taught to a stranger, nor even to new catechumens.[67]

The subject of the catechetical lectures, properly speaking, was, of course, the intimation of the creed and the commenting on it.[68] Once again, Cyril adjures the candidates not to bring in the streets the things into which they are being initiated, for everyone is allowed to hear the gospel, but the glory of it is reserved to the true followers of Christ.[69]

Having been baptised, the neophytes were given 'the more perfect instruction'. This was done by taking a retrospective view of the steps of the baptismal rite. These steps were: renouncing to 'Satan and all his works, all his pomp and all his service'. Pagan practices such as 'the watching of (the flight of) birds, divination, omens, or amulets, or charms written on leaves, sorceries or other evil arts' are given as examples of services to the Devil.[70] While saying this, the candidate was looking to the west, the side of darkness and death; then turning to the east, the side of light and resurrection, he or she had to say: 'I believe in the Father and in the Son and in the Holy Ghost and in one Baptism of repentance'. This commitment was taken on in the porch of the church. Then, entering the church, they put off their garments as an image of 'putting off the old nature with its practices' (Col. 3:9) and 'imitating Christ, who hung naked on the Cross'. Each candidate was led to the baptismal basin, 'like Christ was carried from the Cross to the Sepulchre', to descend into the water three times, confessing the three salvific names of Father, Son and Holy Spirit. The ascending from the water following the three immersions assimilated the candidates to Christ, who had been in his sepulchre for three days.[71] Now they had 'put on Christ' (Gal. 3:27) and prepared to receive the emblem of the Holy Spirit by a separate act of anointing. As the proper meaning of 'Christ' is 'The Anointed One', those baptised now rightly were bearing the name of Christians.[72]

Theodore of Mopsuestia has also left us a series of catechetical lectures, which are a source not only for the knowledge of liturgical practices in the Antiochene area, but also of his theology of the sacraments.[73] He stresses that baptism and eucharist perform to the believer what once happened to Christ. He has become the first fruit of mankind and the first to receive in his humanity the change from corruption and mortality to incorruptibility. And now 'we believe that through these symbols, as through unspeakable signs, we possess sometime beforehand the realities themselves.'[74] Theodore means that the sacraments communicate this new nature, but as ground of a hope, i.e., potentially. As 'signs' or 'symbols' they are comparable to food that is suitable to the present state of the average Christian, i.e., to a believer who lacks perfection. Therefore, he insists that weakness should not deter us from the use of the sacraments, for 'if we do good works [. . .] and truly repent [. . .] we will obtain the gift of remissions of sins'.[75] Theodore attached much importance to a life of practical Christian action.

From all this valuable information about the process of initiation in the second half of the fourth century we may draw three conclusions:

1   Our texts show in an impressive way how in the context of their time bishops had to deal with a new situation and to face the danger of rash entries into the Church. In their view, admission had to remain a serious and true initiation and they were obviously convinced that the practice of maintaining secrecy for fear of profanation had to be continued. Whereas the profanation earlier had come from pagan hostility against Christianity, there was now a danger of many inconsiderate entries, since the masses were attracted to the Church because of its glorious position and all the benefits it was receiving from the Roman State.

2   A numerous personnel of clergy and monks assured the chain of liturgical services during the week and at the annual festivals. Ascetics, who first had sought isolation, were now becoming an urban phenomenon and in Jerusalem they set their stamp on the daily hours of prayer, consisting of Scripture readings and supplications. Through this impressive religious framing of people's everyday life, the pomp of the ceremonies and the array of the buildings, the Christian religion was something that addressed the whole person, soul and body. All senses were captured when one was marching in long processions from one church to another, standing in full view of the relics of a saint, listening to the gripping rhetoric of sermons and lectures, undergoing the telling symbolism of exorcism, total immersion, anointments, etc. This appeal both to the senses and the soul, combined with the total annexation of one's world for Christianity must have given the feeling that being Christian was a glorious and safe thing.

3   The faith that old and new Christians were asked to confess was the faith of the Church, expressed in local creeds and – more and more – in conciliar definitions. But bishops like Cyril and Theodore, Basil and Ambrose introduced their catechumens into it in such a way that they presented the common faith also as a pound, entrusted to the individual in order that he would make the most of it. Great emphasis was laid upon instruction and knowledge, seen as indispensable for the sanctification of individual life.

However, not only bishops were concerned about the growing laxity as a consequence of the majority position of the Church and its privileges. There were other reactions in the form of endeavours to bring back the former radicalism of Christian commitment: Donatism in North Africa and Priscillianism in Spain. These two movements in the western Church merit our attention in order to complete the picture of the fourth century.

Two protest movements

Donatism

After the end of the persecutions and Constantine's seizing of power in the west, the Christians of North Africa had split into two rival church groups: Catholic and Donatist. Constantine had put the Catholics in the right, but the Donatists did not give up. Having tried in vain to force them back into the official church, Constantine let matters in Africa take their own course when his attention was drawn to conquering the east and settling the more dangerous disputes there.[76] Thus left in peace, the Donatist movement could develop and it spread so much that in 336 Donatus, their charismatic leader, could preside over a synod of 270 bishops of his persuasion. The hotbeds of the schism were Carthage, the capital city, and the Numidian high plains. Why did they have so much success?

First, their conception of what the Church should be linked up well with the African radicalism of the preceding century. Convinced and consequent Christians can only be a minority in this world and their sufferings are a proof of their obedience. To the Donatists it seemed to make little difference whether the Roman Emperor was a heathen or a Christian, since Constantine, too, had begun to oppress them. They lowered the radical requirements from all church members to the clergy and held that none of their priests had ever committed a mortal sin nor had been ordained by a lapsed bishop.[77] Consequently, they argued that a sacrament dispensed by an unworthy priest could have no validity. This regarded baptism, eucharist and ordination alike. But they did not lower the requirements for common churchpeople to such an extent that they accepted a hierarchy of commitment between ordinary believers and monks like it was common in other regions and among the African Catholics.[78]

Second, the Donatists had their constituency mainly among the original population, like the Berbers. North Africa was populated by a high number of Roman colonists, who formed the economic and cultural upper class.[79] The population of the Numidian villages was only slightly Romanised, but the Catholic Church had never made an effort to evangelise the Berbers in their own language. So they felt disadvantaged, not only linguistically but also economically, since Roman colonists were often landowners, who exploited the poor villagers as cheap seasonal workers. The Donatists were the first to communicate the Gospel to the Berbers. They also endowed them with their own saints, because their clergy tolerated the veneration of Donatist martyrs at local sanctuaries. The Donatists succeeded in 'inculturating' Christianity among a large marginalised population. As Frend says, 'Donatism was principally a Numidian and agrarian movement', in which 'divergence of religious belief coincided with divergence of environment and economic interest.' Though a 'heretical form of Christianity [it] struck deepest roots where native linguistic and cultural traditions were most vigorous.'[80] In recent times the judgement of Donatism has shifted from a negative verdict of a heretical and contending church group to the rather positive appreciation of a form of Christianity giving a sense of proper value to people for whose interests the Church of the Roman elite was closing its eyes.[81]

In 347/8 the Emperor Constans showed a renewed interest in the African schism. Even the Donatist leadership had asked for a settlement of the affair by the political authorities. But the Roman interference led to oppression and to a forced union with the Catholics. Donatus himself was expelled. But the spirit of resistance endured, notably in southern Numidia. And here some bishops made an alliance with the violent *Circumcelliones* in the hope to be defended against the Roman police forces. The background of the appearance of these Circumcellions is an economic recession during the 340s. More and more the wandering seasonal workers remained unemployed and were in the debt of landowners. They came to form gangs, which raided unpopular landowners and administrators on their way, thus remedying the social and economic injustice of which they were victims. They used to gather and hide their loot at *cellae*, i.e., remote chapels and tombs of martyrs, and thus received their name meaning 'those around the *cellae*'. The confluence of the schismatics with this movement of social protest procured the Donatists an instrument of violent resistance against the Roman forces and the Catholics and the Circumcellions a religious basis to justify their actions.

In the long run, this alliance with violence proved to be a disadvantage to the Donatists, because it led to internal discord between those who glorified the fight against the Roman State and those who wanted to make peace. But for some forty years (348–91) the Donatists were able to consolidate their church, though they never made disciples outside North Africa. Until the reign of Julian (361–3), the Catholics rejoiced in the support of Roman power, but precisely this earned them the odium of comfortable state-supported Christianity. According to Frend, the essential 'differences between Donatist and Catholic turned on the relations between Church and society, between Christianity and the Roman Empire'. In this contrast 'the Donatists retained the antithesis preached by Tertullian and Cyprian'.[82] Lack of great leaders on the Catholic side, moral laxity and the ongoing economic misery were responsible for a massive adherence to the Donatist Church, because of its better moral standards and its being deeper rooted among the socially disadvantaged. Another charismatic leader, Parmenian (d. 391), succeeded Donatus (d. 355). And when Julian withdrew all state measures which were in favour of any Christian party and ordered the return of all exiled bishops,[83] the Donatists profited still more from the situation and took revenge on the Catholics, who were now without state protection. The Donatists had not forgotten the many years of oppression and, thus, Julian's reign did not bring an improvement in the relation between the two rival churches; 'a barrier of fear, hatred and superstition separated Donatist and Catholic.'[84] The Donatists paralleled themselves with Matthias who was elected to take over the place and ministry that Judas had forfeited by his treason.[85]

The Donatists even produced an important and original theological thinker in this heyday of theirs, Tyconius (d. *c.* 390). Donatists were scarcely involved in the trinitarian and Christological issues which were exciting the rest of the Church in those years; all the more they were concerned about the true nature of the Church. Having agreed for a long time with the principal thoughts of Donatus and Parmenian, Tyconius finally abandoned one of the central pretensions of Donatism, viz., to be the community of true believers, and this 'heresy' led to excommunication from his own group. Tyconius doubted if it was really possible to unite all true children of God in one church body. This ideal was deeply rooted in the African minds, shaped as it was by Tertullian and Cyprian.[86] But could the borderline between the just and the wicked ever coincide with the frontiers between two distinct visible and organised church communities? This was Tyconius' question to his own community. If in this world the Kingdom of God and the Devil's dominion still confront each other, and both avail themselves of humans because their hearts are alive to both, then the presence of false brethren inside the Church of God is unavoidable. Such a presence is indeed useful, because it helps the true servants of God to stand out even better. Tyconius also refused the consequence that, if the true Church was only Donatist and there were no Donatists outside Africa, there could be no 'good' churches elsewhere.[87]

After his excommunication by the Donatist Church, Tyconius did not find the way back to the Catholics, in spite of the fact that they had for a long time been familiar with the idea of a Church counting both firm and weak members. He probably held to the Donatist view that the Church is holy in its members, and not as an institution. He also expected that the ecumenical church would shine from Africa.

Priscillianism

Another movement of protest against the worldliness of the Church originated in Spain. And, once again, the background was the concern that baptism did not seem to entail real and radical obligations. In this case, the concern did not bother the minds of the bishops (as we have seen in the east) but those of rich and educated laypeople. When they were baptised, they added to the regular engagements the vow of complete surrender to Christ and of renunciation of the world, which meant taking on poverty, fasting and chastity. They considered the basic forms of asceticism (see above, p. 159) to be compulsory for every baptised Christian. They called themselves 'Men of Christ' and wished their life to be an image of the crucified Lord.

Priscillian was their charismatic leader. Groups of like-minded believers formed inside the congregations and Priscillian's requirements also attracted educated women and members of the clergy. It is easy to imagine that prominent bishops saw such a movement with envious eyes and tried to stop it. Basically, it was the fear of the established Church ministry of an uncontrolled charismatic whirlwind. In 380 the bishops succeeded in having Priscillianism condemned by a local synod.

Like the Donatists, the Priscillianists regarded themselves as a legal form of Christianity and when the higher clergy tried to involve public authority, Priscillian, too, appealed to the Emperor. In order to increase the chances of a general condemnation of the Priscillianists, the Spanish bishops, supported by some colleagues in Gaul, charged them with the heresies of Manicheism and magic. They were certainly not Manichees, although their almost dualistic opposition to the world may have given such an impression. Anyhow, Priscillian and some followers were taken to court at Treves, where he himself and six prominent partisans were condemned to death and executed (385). The execution of a death penalty for a religious offence (if there was any!) could never have taken place without the involvement and the consent of the Emperor. The western territories, Britain, Gaul and Spain, were at that moment in the power of a usurper, Maximus.[88] The esteemed monk-bishop Martin of Tours tried to prevent this execution, but in vain. Ambrose of Milan uttered vehement protestations. But the use of secular power to suppress oppositional and heretical persuasions was a welcome and attractive attainment within imperial Christianity, from which neither critical movements like Donatism and Priscillianism, nor independent and self-conscious churchmen like Ambrose could wholly break away.

Both phenomena, the 'natural' reliance upon the State and the longing for a church handling and settling its own matters independently, are the result of the stumbling, as well as the vigorous contextualisation of Christian thought and life in the fourth century. And so we end this study with the disputed but impressive leader figure of Bishop Ambrose, whose death in 397 we have chosen as the closing moment of the fourth century.

Epilogue

We close this book without giving such conclusions as would recapitulate the manifold aspects of the course of Christianity throughout the turbulent fourth century. We rather invite readers to draw their own conclusions when they have taken the trouble to follow the political and cultural complications into which early Christianity got involved and to project themselves into its viewpoints and dilemmas. In general, the conclusions of scholars regarding the transformation process of Christianity in that century move along a scale, going from severe criticism in terms of 'Christianity's Fall' or 'Degeneration' as a result of its alliance with political power, on the one end, to a positive appreciation of its capacity to adapt to unexperienced situations and to the challenge to take joint responsibility for the religious and moral standards of the Roman commonwealth, on the other. Many nuances are possible between these extremes. We hope to have given the necessary factual information as well as a sufficiently refined analysis of the various developments, to enable the reader to sum up that Great Turn which for ages brought Christianity to a privileged situation in an ever-extending part of the globe.

We made *contextualisation* the guideline of this study. This key word had two meanings. On the one hand, it was meant to describe the *changing context* of Christianity in the period from 295 to 397. These years saw events that directly affected the destiny of the Christians in the Roman Empire, viz., the instalment of the tetrarchy, which was the signal for the great persecution, and the stabilisation of the relations between Church and State under Ambrose and Theodosius, who were a pair of friends. However, there were also Christians beyond the Roman borders and they, too, felt the repercussions of what happened to the Church in the Empire, politically and dogmatically. Christianity in Ethiopia, Persia and Armenia would eventually deviate from standardised imperial Catholicism in liturgical practices and in some doctrinal respects, just as for the time being the Christianised Goths did, who would not abandon their persuasion which was of the 'Arian' sort. Those deviations were to become visible only in the next century, but one may say that the beginnings of these developments resided in the close alliance between Christianity and Roman Empire attained in the last two decades of the fourth century. It was indeed due to the events of 380 and 381, viz., the elevation of Catholic Christianity to state religion and the adoption of the creed of Nicaea-Constantinople, that the majority of the Christians were united into the body of the Roman imperial Church.

On the other hand, our key word was meant to *discover the responses* of Christianity to this new context. We wanted to know how the communities and leaders of different regions and traditions reacted to the hitherto inexperienced possibilities, challenges and temptations that were so suddenly put before them. We may say that almost all along the line Christians were surprised by the fact that the emperor and his powerful state apparatus was now on their side. The expression of this feeling in terms of a theology of history, linking the role of victorious Constantine to the all-embracing work of God's *Logos* in human history, is the achievement of Eusebius of Caesarea, who influenced the spirits for several decades. According to Aland: 'The image Eusebius drew up of Constantine had a determining influence on the views of the fourth century, and through that image he [Constantine] continued to be influential.'[1] Eusebius was so enthusiastic about the guide role of this God-given, pious emperor for the benefit of the Church, that he subscribed to a confession, viz., the one that was proposed to the Council of Nicaea, even though it did not correspond with his own beliefs nor with the confession of his home community. His gladness over the unity was too great to oppose for reasons of theological conscience. An obsession with unity was prevalent, and the Empire and the Church found each other in that effort. Their enthusiasm and mutual demand for help contributed to the rise of a new, Christianised emperor cult – not with statues and sacrifices as under the pagan rulers, but in hailing the emperor as instrument of God and, consequently, with a mind full of awe that could easily verge on docility. This state of mind could then be manipulated by such coercive rulers as Constantius turned out to be.

But there was among church leaders a growing awareness of the limits that needed to be set to the interference by the emperor. Both the tyrannical policy of Constantius and the official indifference of Julian proved to be helping factors. All along the Arian crisis we have been looking for traces of independence of thought and of legitimate self-consciousness on the side of the Church that were sufficient to determine its own theological and ethical priorities. We were interested to see in how far theologians in influential posts were trying to preserve the main characteristics of the Christian tradition and of biblical values, however much 'contextualising' there might have been in adopting prevailing philosophical language and forms of thought. Impulses to rethink the meaning and implications of customary epithets for God, Christ and the Spirit, and of terms for human salvation were at the same time impulses to oppose unsuitable, irritating formulations. Those impulses came from two principal considerations, centred on *salvation in Christ* and on *ethical traits* both in God and in the way humans come up to his character and requirements. We will make some remarks on both impulses.

A central question behind the different and divisive viewpoints on the relation between God and Christ and, as a consequence, inciting opposing parties to push through their opinion, was the very nature of human salvation effected by the person of God's Word by means of his humanity. Who exactly was the most proper person or subject in Jesus, and which way of humans' returning to God and of renewal and sanctification of life is being offered, respectively guaranteed through him?

It could be the *ascetic* way, i.e., the way of exercising obedience to God's will, with eventual adoptive childhood as recompense. In accordance with this view, Jesus could very well be seen as 'the pioneer and perfecter of our faith, who for the joy that was set before him endured the cross, despising the shame, and is seated at the right hand of the throne of God' (Heb. 12:2). In other words, Jesus as the one who walks in front on the path of true faith, which is to endure sufferings, to despise worldly goods and to be recompensed for that in God's kingdom. Such a saviour necessarily has his place, in the cosmological order of beings, *on our side*. He would be capable of training his will and obedience, and of receiving promotion to a divine rank. Even his most intimate subject must be of *alterable kind*. This was the position of old and new Arians (in the strict sense of Arius' teachings).

It could as well be the *communicative* way, i.e., the way of receiving an 'inflow' of properly divine attributes and forces that would liberate humans from their own inclination to sin and death and would elevate them above their weaknesses to a godlike life. This process could be thought of as a result of the assumption by the Word of a human individual who at the same time, being a member of the human race, was acting in a collective way, upon his brothers and sisters by nature. In this view, man's physical and ethical renewal is based upon the communication of divine gifts and has rather the character of regeneration. This was the salvation concept of Athanasius, which would fall short if the subject of the incarnation had not been fully God, to the same degree as his kinship with humankind had to be totally real. Athanasius' approach was basically shared by the Cappadocians, who, however, were in a more penetrating and subtle manner concerned about the safeguarding of the proper characteristics, within the Trinity, of the Word who became flesh for us, and of the Spirit who is imparted on us.

Reflections and positions of this kind strengthened Athanasius and Basil in the east, and Hilary and Ambrose in the west, in their fierce opposition against the imperial policy which intended to impose the official and common faith definitions that would leave the salvation background indecisive. The insistence upon ecclesiastical standards led Ambrose to confront more than one emperor. The self-consciousness he displayed in a way stopped the process of sacralisation of the Christian emperor, brought about by Eusebius half a century earlier. Ambrose came to the remarkable and different statement that the emperor was not master over but son of the Church! On the other hand, he looked up at his high position which obliged him to use his power for the spread and triumph of the true religion. As a minister of the Church, Ambrose considered it his mission to remind the emperor of this responsibility as well as of his duty to be a fine example for his subjects.

The general sphere of ethics was still determined by the philosophical ideals of *contemplation* and of *harmony*. Following the tradition of Platonism, it was often seen as the proper destiny of humans to elevate their minds above the material and visible things and to contemplate the higher invisible and spiritual 'Goods'. Stoicism had taught that man should live in harmony with Nature and with his inner self, undisturbed by lower passions. The fundamental assumption was that those 'goods' or nature were intrinsically good. Since they had been identified with 'god', the character of this god was static and devoid of emotions. Consequently, impassibility had become an essential trait in God and a goal for all serious men to strive to. All great Christian theologians of the fourth century, from Eusebius and Athanasius to the Gregorys and Ambrose, were indebted to these Hellenistic ideas and tried more or less consciously to absorb them.

However, they neither could nor would leave out the specific notions and implications of biblical and Christian tradition. Here the first trait in the conception of God was not impassibility but love and mercy with the fallen world. It was not enough to define God as absolute goodness, which does not envy being to others, or as synonym for universal harmony. God, as the Christians knew him, had had to face a counterforce – Satan, human indifference and sin – provoking his determination not to abandon his beloved creatures to the forces of corruption and destruction. This brought a factor of emotion and 'passion' into the inherited concept of a totally impassible God. When God's 'impassibility' was interpreted as insensibility for any influence or pressure from outside his own being, then love and mercifulness could be seen as the principal motives for his actions. Christ then was the one in whom God could assume sufferings and passion while remaining at the same time above human passions. On the human side, the ideals of harmony and imperturbability were superseded by the equally emotional standards of neighbourly love and humility. We recall the institutional forms of love for the neighbour, in particular the poor and sick neighbour, which Basil created alongside his rules for monastic life. Monasticism was a new, equally contextual form of Christian commitment in a time when being a Christian was becoming a matter of course and even profitable. The monks were putting before their ordinary fellow believers the original ethical values in a radical form. They reminded the secularising Church of its vocation to be of a different order and quality than the kingdoms of the world, however much it was also called to assume joint responsibility in solidarity with those kingdoms and their societies.

We think that our analysis of the events of the fourth century has convincingly shown that at the beginning of the Arian struggle there was no truly common and accepted doctrine in spite of the fact that by the end of it the Church had been legalised and possessed a fixed and essentially undiscussed doctrinal statement about the nature and relations of the three divine persons. Even Nicaea with its creed did not comprise or constitute *orthodoxy*. It received its status of standard of orthodox belief only afterwards, by retroactive effect. Orthodoxy was the outcome of a complicated process of debate and of refinement of conceptual language – complicated not only because of the difficult character of the subject matter (the oneness of three worshipful divine agents of salvation!) but also because of the ongoing interference by the state authorities. The most ecumenical creed of Christianity, the creed of Nicaea-Constantinople, is a *result of the intertwining currents of political interests, cultural influences and theological conscience*. Should it therefore be disliked and put aside? Should we deplore the impurity caused by this complexity and by the presence of 'error on both sides'?[2] Or would it be better to recognise that confessions and even ecumenical creeds always show the traces and spearheads of the concrete context in which they originate, echoing even conflict and stumbling? And that, in spite of their historical and consequently relative and one-sided character, they may appear to hide a surplus of meaning reaching to times and contexts for which they were originally not drafted? In principle, this is equally the case with the confessions which originated in antiquity and with recent confessions like the Barmen Declaration (1934), the Confession of Alexandria (1976) or the Belhar Confession (1982). Reproducing and rethinking the ways that led to an ever tentative and contextually conditioned expression of Christian faith can help us today to attain necessary refinements and fresh perspectives.

Notes

Introduction

1 This does not imply that Christians were the majority of the population of the Roman Empire. It is difficult to estimate their exact percentage, but it certainly was higher in the eastern than in the western part.

2 Armenia was successively an independent kingdom, a Persian and a Roman province. In 387 it was divided up between these two empires.

3 The main reason for forging the term 'contextualisation' was that in the Ecumenical Movement the need had been felt to distinguish between the kernels of Christian faith and the western theological establishment, because the latter had no eyes for central issues such as the expression of faith in non-western culture and the struggle for social justice. See L.A. Hoedemaker (ed.), *Theologiseren in Context*, Heerlen – Kampen 1997, Part IV 'Reflexions on Contextuality', pp. 261–318.

4 See, for instance, Norman R. Ericson, 'Implications from the New Testament for Contextualization', in David J. Hesselgrave (ed.), *Theology and Mission*, Grand Rapids, Mich. (1978), pp. 71–85, who calls the New Testament 'a prime example of contextualization' and discovers in it dynamic 'patterns . . . which give us direction as to the nature of acceptable contextualization.' In other words, the New Testament is not only a document of a historical process of contextualisation in modern sense, but also provides us with normative criteria for its present-day application.

5 Fritz Frei, 'Kontextuelle Theologie', in G. Collet (ed.), *Theologien der Dritten Welt*, Immensee (1990), pp. 142–161.

6 By 'North Africa' we understand the Roman provinces which covered the territory of modern Algeria, Tunisia and the western part of Libya. East Libya formed one cultural and ecclesiastical entity with Egypt and this area does not belong to '(North) Africa' in the sense in which this appellation is used here. We will deal with the phenomenon of Donatism in Chapters 2 and 6.

7 Karl-Heinz Ohlig, *Fundamentalchristologie. Im Spannungsfeld von Christentum und Kultur*, Munich (1986) has convincingly demonstrated this in the field of early Christian Christology (Part II).

8 See W.H.C. Frend, *The Donatist Church: A Movement of Protest in Roman North Africa*, Oxford (1952).

9 Shoki Coe, 'Contextualizing Theology', in Gerald H. Anderson and Thomas F. Stransky (eds), *Mission Trends No. 3: Third World Theologies*, New York-Grand Rapids (1976), pp. 19–24.

10 The notion of *Missio Dei* was issued in 1952 and means that the human missionary enterprise should spring from the idea of God, who sent himself by making a covenant with his people, by bringing his only Son into the world and by

communicating his Holy Spirit. All human missions are just a consequence of, and a participation in, this primordial divine movement towards the world.

11 Norbert Brox, 'Zur christlichen Mission in der Spätantike', in Karl Kertelge (ed.), *Mission im Neuen Testament* (Quaestiones Disputatae 93), Freiburg i.Br. (1982), pp. 190–237. See also Einar Molland, 'Besaß die Alte Kirche ein Missionsprogramm?', in Heinzgünter Frohnes and Uwe W. Knorr, *Kirchengeschichte als Missionsgeschichte I*, Munich (1974), pp. 51–67. Molland answers in the negative the question if the early Church had a missionary programme, but agrees with Harnack's sentence that the early Church 'was missionary by virtue of its existence and through its holy properties and regulations, much more than through the service of professional missionaries'.

12 The first examples are Tertullian of Carthage and Hippolyte of Rome, both writing *c.* 200. See J. Roldanus, 'Heilsrepräsentierung im konkreten, geschichtlichen Umfeld: Verschiedenheiten in der Deutung Tertullians', in Ed Noort (ed.), *Theologie zwischen Ost und West* Vol. I, Groningen (2000), pp. 51–65; 'Danielvisionen als Interpretament zeitgenössischer Ereignisse: Hippolyt und Hieronymus', Vol. II (2001), pp. 35–45.

13 Brox has pointed to the at least literary tendency to see the missionary command of Matthew 28:19, 'Make disciples of all nations', fulfilled in the multi-ethnic character of the Roman Empire (212).

14 I. Tödt (ed.), *Theologie im Konfliktfeld Südafrika: Dialog mit Manas Buthelezi*, Stuttgart/Munich (1976).

1 Earlier contextualisation

1 The guidelines on how to deal with persons accused of being Christians had been given by the Emperor Trajan (98–117) in answer to questions put before him by one of his provincial governors in Asia Minor, Pliny. The instructions did not contain active tracing of all Christians, but approved of sacrifice as an instrument to test the correctness of the accusation and, in case of refusal, to proceed with punishment.

2 See Ramsay MacMullen, *Christianizing the Roman Empire (A.D. 100–400)*, London and New Haven, Conn. (1984), p. 40 n. 38: 'There existed [. . .] no formal social life in the world of the Apologists that was entirely secular.' The Christian apologists commented on the situation from *c.* 150 until the days of Constantine.

3 *Diogn.* 5; Tert., *Apol.* 37, 8; 42, 3.

4 *Apol.* 38, 3. This may be heard as an echo of the earlier self-definition by Christians as being a new, universal people, into which the two main religious categories, Jews and Gentiles, were converging.

5 Tert., *Apol.* 42, 2–3.

6 Tert., *Apol.* 42, 4–8.

7 Or., *Cels.* VIII, 73–4.

8 See above, n. 3. 'Third' because they had appeared after the Jews and the Greeks (pagans), recruiting from both and realising, by the faith in Christ, a reconciled unity of humankind.

9 Just., *Dial.* 119, 5. According to K.L. Schmidt, Justin was probably the first to interpret by the concepts of 'new people' and 'third race' the 'political and social existence of the Christians'; Karl Ludwig Schmidt, *Die Polis in Kirche und Welt* (1940) Zürich, p. 51.

10 See Schmidt, p. 64.

11 Or., *Cels.* VIII, 75; 80. Tatian had said that there is as much legislation as there are urban communities (*OrGr.* 28, 1).

12 *Diogn.* 5, 9–10.

13 *Cels.* IV, 45, 65.
14 Against other opinions Schmidt rightly judged that Origen had a relatively positive attitude towards the earthly state (p. 79 of the work quoted in n.9).
15 *Cels.* II, 30. Origen saw in the *Pax Romana* a fulfilment of Ps. 72:7, 'In his days [viz., of the king] may righteousness flourish, and peace abound.'
16 'Christ is also among the barbarians' (*De Corona* 12:4. Cf. *Iud* 8:9). Or *Cels.* VIII 68.
17 2 Thess. 2:7: 'For the mystery of lawlessness is already at work; only he who *restrains* it will do so until he is out of the way. And then the lawless one will be revealed, and the Lord Jesus will slay him.' Cf. *ResCar.* 24, 17–18: 'Who else can be meant thereby [viz., by the restrainer] than the Roman State?'
18 1 Tim. 2:1–2: 'supplications, prayers, intercessions and thanksgivings be made for all men, for kings and all who are in high positions, that we may lead a quiet and peaceable life.'
19 *Apol.* 31–2:1. The early Christians had joined the Jews in the idea that Roman dominion was the last empire before the Kingdom of God would erupt into History and end it. For some, like Tertullian, this expectation conferred on the Empire a positive value, however, he might protest against all the official prejudices against the Christians; for others, like his contemporary Hippolyte of Rome (d. 235), it would not.

   Hippolyte rather represents the apocalyptic vision that the last empire before God's final intervention is the worst. He thought the universal character of Augustus' empire to be rather a satanic mimicry of the Kingdom of Christ, erected at the moment of the Incarnation in order to compete with God's designs. The gathering of nations and races under Roman rule must be a false one, a diabolic competition and not a useful preparation (see the articles referred to in note 12 of the Introduction).
20 This passage opens with: 'Be subject for the Lord's sake to every human institution, whether it be to the emperor as supreme, or to governors as sent by him to punish those who do wrong and to praise those who do right.' The functions for the service of justice are the same as in Rom. 13:3–4, but 1 Pet. does not refer to a divine origin of the Authorities.
21 1 Tim. 2:1–2; see above, note 18.
22 *Apol.* 30, 1–3. Tertullian does not intend to say that by becoming emperor, he is no longer human. Even in his power, he depends on God as the Bestower of life, i.e., as Creator. Comp. 33:3: 'Let it be enough for him, to be called "emperor": this title is sublime and it is God who grants it. Anyone who calls him "god" denies his emperorship: he can't be emperor, unless he is a human.'
23 *Apol.* 30, 4–6.
24 *Cels.* VIII, 73.
25 The government's task is concentrated on the administration of justice, whereas no criterium is given for a 'just war'. Origen simply states that Christians do not join the military in physical warfare: their prayers are of good, maybe even of better help! (*Cels.* VIII 73–4). In the time of Tertullian, Hippolyte and Origen, it was a normal rule of Christian discipline not to take a military job (there was no conscription in the Roman Empire). In their writings we find indications that it was sometimes difficult to uphold this discipline. Among the rich literature about the early Christians and war, violence and militia, I refer to: Roland H. Bainton, 'The Early Church and the War', *Harvard Theological Review* 39 (1946): 189–212, and J. Roldanus, 'De vroege kerk en de militaire dienst – een interpretatieroute', *Kerk en Theologie* 33 (1982): 182–202.
26 Catechumenate was not just an instruction in the Christian faith, but in the first place a period of testing the candidate's lifestyle and steadfastness. The Church wanted to prevent the backsliding of those who had received baptism.

27 Hippolyte, *Apostolic Tradition*, 16.
28 ClAl, *Paed.* (*passim*).
29 By this exclusion from the eucharistic community the Church did not pretend to anticipate on the judgement that God will pronounce on the apostate on the Last Day. The severeness was a matter of Church discipline during this life only.
30 See J. Roldanus, 'No Easy Reconciliation. St Cyprian on conditions for re-integration of the lapsed', *Journal of Theology for Southern Africa* 92, (1995): 23–31.
31 ibid. See particularly the section 'Guidelines for a New Situation', 25–7.
32 *CathEc.* 5. For Cyprian this authority given to all the apostles was an argument not to recognise the primacy of one specific bishop, viz., of Rome, over the others.
33 The famous Greek philosopher Socrates, who had accepted his death penalty rather than denying his teachings, was highly estimated by early Christian writers; see W. Rordorf, 'Socrates in de christelijke literatuur van de eerste eeu-wen', in H.S. Benjamins, G.D.J. Dingemans et al. (eds), *Evangelie en beschaving. Studies bij het afscheid van Hans Roldanus*, Zoetermeer (1995), pp. 69–92.
34 *Paidagogus* is the title of one of his works, dealing with Christian life and manners. It is the second work in a trilogy, which starts with an *Exhortation to the Greeks*.
35 *Hom. in Nm* XXIII 2.
36 *Hom. in Ezk* VI 6.
37 According to Gnosticism, only those who possess a germ of divine nature, enveloped in their 'flesh', will be saved by the awakening of 'knowledge', which is at the same time knowledge of God and of one's deep self. Those who do not have such a part of God can therefore never receive this saving knowledge.
38 Origen was only eighteen years old when, after a persecution that had forced Clement to leave Alexandria in 202, he was appointed his successor as head of the Catechetical School. This was a kind of open academy, receiving the cultivated classes and in contact with the University of Alexandria in order to present the Christian faith as a serious and trustworthy view of world and man. Leaving the instruction of 'beginners' to a fellow worker, Origen soon started to concentrate his teaching activities on the 'advanced' and philosophically trained seekers of Truth and Wisdom. In this function, Origen was not a member of the local clergy and therefore not allowed to preach. Due to a conflict about this with his bishop, Origen left Alexandria in 231 and moved to Caesarea in Palestine, where he continued his teaching, becoming an often-consulted adviser in theological debates.
39 F. Ledegang, *Origenes – een experimenteel theoloog uit de derde eeuw*, Kampen (1995).
40 Eduardo Hoornaert, *The Memory of the Christian People*, Tunbridge Wells (1989), Chapter VIII. Hoornaert speaks of a 'cultural oppression' or even 'cultural *war*' (his own italics) on the country people by the city of Alexandria and its strong Greek population and culture.
41 The great pioneer in this field was Justin Martyr (d. *c.* 155). From the apostolic times onwards, there has been a maybe not rectilinear but at least consistent line of meeting with the Hellenistic culture as a challenging missionary task (Ohlig, *Fundamentalchristologie*, 54).
42 It appears incorrect to suppose a deep contrast between Alexandrian intellectual town-dwellers and Coptic unlearnt farmers, craftsmen and traders (ibid., 145). Ohlig says: 'In Egypt, notably in Alexandria, the leading stratum was marked by Greek blood and Greek training; however the population of the hinterland also made close acquaintance with Greek culture'.
43 E. Mühlenberg has characterised the central message of Christianity in Late Antiquity as 'God – victor of demons'. *Epochen der Kirchengeschichte*, Heidelberg/Wiesbaden (1991).

44 Dom Gregory Dix, *Jew and Greek: A Study in the Primitive Church*, London (1953), esp. Chapter 1 'The conflict of the Syriac and Greek cultures'. Ohlig, *Fundamentalchristologie*, II/1 'The new situation: the increasing dominance of Hellenistic-Christian elements in communities and theology' (135–59).

2 Crisis and recognition

1 From 217 to 284 the Roman Empire had no fewer than twenty-five emperors!
2 Heiko A. Oberman, Adolf Martin Ritter (ed.) *Kirchen und Theologiegeschichte in Quellen I: Alte Kirche*, Neukirchen-Vluyn (1977), p. 113.
3 Jesus had taught that true worship is now only 'in spirit and truth' (John 4:23).
4 There had been an incident, when the presence of Christian officers was supposed to have disturbed the finding of an oracle by the examination of intestines.
5 Constantius certainly hindered the gathering of the Christians in their buildings, but most probably did not touch persons and lives. Constantine, when succeeding his father in 306, immediately restored freedom of assembly in his part of the empire. There is an indication that in Gaul no bishop had been in danger of apostasy (see Heinz Kraft, *Kaiser Konstantins Religiöse Entwicklung*, Tubingen [1955], p. 3 n. 1). This would mean that Constantius only executed the first part of the first decree.
6 The details are not important for our subject.
7 The tetrarchy still existed in 317 as a pure form, then serving in the game of pinching adjacent provinces from the other *Augustus* by transient alliances with his *Caesar*. This was the way Constantine started driving Licinius further eastwards.
8 *Augustus* literally means 'the blessed or exalted One'. The interpretation of the contemporary political events by Christian writers as 'theology of history' will be dealt with in the next chapter.
9 Maxentius, ruling over Italy and North Africa, had declared war on Constantine, estimating that his own army was superior. Maximinus Daia had annexed Asia Minor to his (south-eastern) territories and had even crossed over to take the Balkans, held by Licinius.
10 Already retired in 305, Diocletian died in 311, deeply frustrated by seeing his reform collapse.
11 Text in Lact. *MortP*. 34. My italics.
12 In Lact. *MortP*. 48. My italics.
13 'As so often, Constantine's religious prejudices neatly coincided with his political interest.' Timothy D. Barnes, *Constantine and Eusebius*, Cambridge, Mass. and London (1981), p. 75. One of Licinius' measures was to forbid all assemblies of bishops.
14 Barnes, p. 43.
15 As son of one of the *Caesars*, Constantine was an heir presumptive to the rank of a *Caesar* (and later of *Augustus*). He was taken to the court probably in the year 292 and escaped to his father's headquarters at York (Britain), when Diocletian handed over his reign to Galerius (305).
16 Kraft (p. 15) calls the 'god' of this philosophical conception 'rather a scheme than a person': the highest essence above and behind the gods of polytheism, who represent but particular, limited aspects of the one divine being. Such a divinity is abstract and has no personal character.
    It is to be noted that in classical Greek religion gods and humans were sharing one and the same ontological base, but that since the second century 'religious' philosophy tended to elevate the godhead into a sphere of transcendence.
17 Jan N. Bremmer, 'Het bekeringsvisioen van Constantijn de Grote', in H.S. Benjamins (ed.), *Evangelie en beschaving. Studies bij het afscheid van Hans Roldanus*,

Zoetermeer (1995), pp. 63–4. Bremmer rightly argues that this story could not have circulated without Constantine's consent.

18 Christian symbols appear on coins only from 319. The effigy of the *Sol* was maintained until 325.

19 The pagan sacrifices were forbidden only in 324.

20 Eus. *HE* 10, 5–6. Comment in Kraft, *Religiöse Entwickelung*, pp. 160–3.

21 Lact. *MortP*. 44.5–6; Eus. *VitCons*. 1.28–30. An ample discussion of the value of both records is given by Jan N. Bremmer, 'Bekeringsvisioen.' (See above n. 17).

22 With Bremmer, p. 66 and Barnes, p. 14. Bremmer has another convincing argument: according to Eusebius' story, Constantine had introduced the *Christogram* upon the standard of the army, passing over the *Staurogram* which Lactantius describes. As a matter of fact, the *Christogram* was first seen on a helmet of Constantine in 315 (p. 65).

23 Kraft, p. 56: 'It is highly probable that Constantine embraced Christianity via a religion in which great significance is attached to the sun; for he has constantly kept to insights from that religion, which were not contradictory to Christianity.'

24 Augustus first adopted this title in the year 12. It literally means bridge-builder, viz., between gods and men. As such, the emperor was the head of Graeco-Roman paganism.

25 Text of the letters in Eus. *HE* 10, 5 and 6 (Kraft, pp. 160–3).

26 In a legal text dealing with the conversion of Jews to Christianity the converts are described as 'those who devote themselves to the holy cults and want to be Christians'. Mark the order!

27 The word 'diocese' was by then used for an administrative, not an ecclesiastical unity. The provinces mentioned in the text coincide with the coastal areas of modern Tunisia, Algeria and Libya.

28 It was in Africa, not in Rome, that the first Christian literature in Latin appeared.

29 Kraft, p. 28. This contrast is represented by the tendencies visible in Tertullian, on the one hand, and Cyprian, on the other.

30 For the consecration three bishops were required. In the case of Caecilian the participation of only one 'traditor' would have spoiled the ceremony.

31 The classic study of the history of *The Donatist Church* has been written by W.F.C. Frend (1952).

32 They probably preferred bishops from Gaul, because there could hardly be any lapsed among them, since Constantine's father had not extended the persecution orders to persons (see p. 30).

33 Each bishop was allowed to take with him two priests and three servants!

34 The Council of Arles also made decisions with regard to the degree of loyalty of Christians in public service and in the army, now that 'the Church had peace', viz., with the State. See for the discussion of the meaning of the canons in question: J. Roldanus, 'De vroege kerk en de militaire dienst – een interpretatieroute', *Kerk en Theologie* 33 (1982/3): 182–202.

35 Letter to Celsus, Vicar of Africa, in Kraft, p. 194.

36 According to Kraft, Constantine discovered the importance of the Church as community, not only as a cult institution, pp. 57–61 and 85–6.

37 Whereas the *Staurogram* only had the shape of the cross, the *Christogram* showed the first letters of the name Christ.

38 There were exceptions, for instance, when after 324 Constantinople (Constantine city) was built as the new imperial capital: for that reason it had to reflect the public architecture of old Rome and so some pagan temples also were erected, alongside Christian churches.

39 The reason may have been that bishops were supposed to be incorruptible and only interested in doing justice and not in interminable juridical duels.

40 Some legal texts seem to have sanctioned the crucifixion of slaves and freedmen, i.e., that this form of death penalty was for some time still applicable to the lowest social class! As a deterrent? But in those days a pagan author wrote that Constantine had abolished the crucifixion and the breaking of bones (see John 19: 31–3).

41 Whereas the Church was forbidding divorce, the State continued to have regulations in this respect.

42 The *Letter to Diognetus* (see Chapter 1, p. 13) mentions as a remarkable and distinctive trait of Christian conduct that they don't expose little children (*Diogn.* 5).

43 The reader is reminded of the relatively higher percentage of Christians in the east and of Licinius' religious ambivalence which had favoured some degree of persecution. No wonder that the Christians of the east welcomed Constantine ardently.

44 So in a *Speech to the Assembly of the Saints* (viz., before a Christian audience), which he held *c.* 320. See Barnes, pp. 74–6.

45 Letter from the Emperor Constantine to Alexander of Alexandria and Arius, H.-G. Opitz, *Urkunden zur Geschichte des Arianischen Streites* 17 (see Kraft, *Religiöse Entwicklung*, Brief 16). The letter was written in October, after Constantine had taken power over the east.

46 Kraft, *Religiöse Entwicklung*, 55. 74–8. This attitude did not keep him from murdering family members who could be suspected of claiming his power.

47 According to Hans-Georg Beck, *Das byzantinische Jahrtausend*, Munich (1978), p. 92, Constantine 'had to bite the bullet of Orthodoxy, to make Orthodoxy his political task [. . .] Constantine did bite. He did it reluctantly and listlessly [. . .] but at the same time he found a fresh legitimisation in his self-confidence and his claim to authority with respect to the sphere of religion, the more so as it was the Church itself which pushed him to take steps, demanding them from him.'

48 We will return to the Donatist criticism in Chapter 6, pp. 174–6.

3 The Church Fathers assess the change

1 Two of them, Lactantius and Eusebius, have been quoted in the preceding chapter because of the record they gave of the religious experience Constantine had the night before the decisive battle that would bring him to power over the whole west.

2 There were many 'Caesarea's in the Roman Empire; the name means 'imperial city'. The Palestinian Caesarea, on the Mediterranean coast, was in New Testament times the residence of the Roman governor. It is related to the missionary travels of Peter (Acts 10) and Paul (Acts 23). After 230 it became Origen's workplace.

3 Latin titles: *De Ira Dei* and *De Mortibus Persecutorum*.

4 The works in question bear the titles *Against Hierocles* and *General Elementary Introduction*. The latter survives in only four books (of ten) which deal with Old Testament prophecies concerning Christ.

5 Justin Martyr already asked the question of how far God had prepared the coming of his Word in Jesus both in Israel and in the Greek search for wisdom. The *Preparation for the Gospel* was followed by the *Proof of the Gospel*, an exposition of Old Testament prophecies and figures which were fulfilled in Christ and Christian times. This work reflects Eusebius' interest in demonstrating the Ministry of Christ as the fulfilment of the Old Testament and its true interpretation over against Jewish exegesis.

6 At the dedication of the Church of the Holy Sepulchre in Jerusalem, built by order of Constantine, Eusebius delivered a speech in which he reiterated several

basic thoughts from the *Theophany* (Timothy D. Barnes, *Constantine and Eusebius* (1981), p. 187. See also Chapter 6, pp. 165–7).

7 This is the opinion of recent scholarship, for instance, of Barnes, p. 164; H. Kraft in his Introduction to the German translation of *HE: Eusebius von Caesarea. Kirchengeschichte*, Munich (1989) and S. Calderone, 'Il pensiero politico di Eusebio di Cesarea', in G. Bonamente and A. Nestori (eds), *I Cristiani e l'Impero nel IV secolo*, Macerata (1988), pp. 45–54. We follow this view against G. Ruhbach, 'Die politische Theologie Eusebs von Caesarea', in his *Die Kirche angesichts der Konstantinischen Wende*, Darmstadt (1976), pp. 236–58. Ruhbach sees Eusebius as someone who has 'always remained an apologist', having 'enlarged the traditional apologetics with the field of History', and 'embodied the schematic and rationalistic theology of the (earlier) apologetics' (pp. 252, 254). Apologetics is supposed to be the denominator, even of the historical work. Older scholarship also saw Eusebius primarily as an apologist: H. Berkhof even stated that 'Eusebius was an apologist and not a theologian' (*Die Theologie des Eusebius von Caesarea* [Diss. Leiden], Amsterdam (1939), p. 162).

According to Barnes, Eusebius' thought is dominated by three characteristics, which are 'a continual emphasis on the Bible, an intellectual framework which derives from Origen, and celebration of the success of Christianity in the Roman world' (p. 105). Calderone thinks it the proper invention of Eusebius that he extended to his own time the Old Testament conception of God making alliance with his people through a leader, and made it a scenario for Constantine and the Roman commonwealth of peoples. Both Barnes and Calderone see biblical theology as the key by means of which Eusebius wanted to interpret the history of the Church in the world from apostolic times to his own days.

8 Book 8 is an adaptation and enlargement of a former picture of the sufferings and the heroism of *Palestinian Martyrs*. This work, which exists separately, is selective in that it tells the stories of those martyrs about whom he knew personally, including some Egyptians who were martyred in Palestine.

9 In the preceding chapter we have referred to the vision and the dream of Constantine on the eve of the battle at the Milvian Bridge. In the *HE* Eusebius knows nothing of the kind and only tells that Constantine marched on Rome 'after he had invoked the help of God, who is in Heaven, and Jesus Christ, His Word, the Redeemer of all' (9 9). *HE* is of great value since it conserved the text of many letters and declarations of the first three centuries. Here, for instance, we read the texts of Galerius' Edict of Tolerance and of the Declaration of Milan.

10 In my *Le Christ et l'homme dans la théologie d'Athanase d'Alexandrie*, Leiden (1977²), pp. 374–9, I have adopted the dating in the Treves exile. Others have tried to find a point of contact in the outburst of the Arian controversy in Alexandria. On this ground J.C.M. van Winden, 'On the Date of Athanasius' Apologetical Treatises', *Vigiliae Christianae* 29 (1975): 291–5, pleads for an early date. His arguments have not proved convincing. Later research has brought arguments in favour of a moment between 330 and 335, i.e., at the time when Athanasius already was occupying the episcopal see of Alexandria but before he was deposed and sent into exile; see for a recent account on this question: M. Slusser, 'Athanasius, *Contra Gentes* and *De Incarnatione*: Place and Date of Composition', *Journal of Theological Studies* ns. 37 (1986): 114–17. Barnes, *Athanasius and Constantius*, Cambridge, Mass. and London (1993), joins the position that Athanasius wrote *Gent-Inc* 'with Eusebius' *Theophany* in mind to argue a similar general thesis from a different theological viewpoint'. As he dates the *Theophany c.* 325, he supposes the immediately following years to be the time in which Athanasius 'responded'. I will state in this chapter that Athanasius indeed intended to present the incarnation from a different soteriological viewpoint (see pp. 65–7).

11 Barnes, p. 58.
12 Hans von Campenhausen, *Lateinische Kirchenväter*, 74. Barnes, p. 75, points to the fact that Constantine, in his *Speech to the Assembly of the Saints*, 'also appeals to two authors whom Lactantius had invoked in the *Divine Institutes*'.
13 There is no proof of his being menaced physically; *c.* 310 Lactantius was back in the region of Nicomedia.
14 Von Campenhausen, p. 66.
15 Gert Haendler, *Von Tertullian bis zu Ambrosius. Die Kirch im Abendland vom Ende des 2. bis zum Ende des 4. Jahrhunderts*, Berlin (1986), p. 79. (Gert Haendler, Kurt Meier und Joachim Rogge (eds), *Kirchengeschichte in Einzeldarstellungen* I/3).
16 See above Chapter 1.
17 Lactantius, *De Mortibus Persecutorum*, ed. and transl. by J.L. Creed, Oxford (1984), p. xxxi.
18 F.L. Cross and E.A. Livingstone, *The Oxford Dictionary of the Christian Church*, Oxford (1974) (repr. 1978), p. 792. According to Barnes 'the work has a violent and aggressive tone, with no attempt to disguise its author's bias, his profound admiration for Constantine, his deep loathing of Constantine's political adversaries.' (Barnes, p. 13).
19 In his Introduction to the edition and translation of *MortP.*, Creed sees Old Testament influence in 'this delight at the discomfiture of enemies' and he refers to passages such as Exod. 15, Judg. 5, Jer. 51 (xxxix).
20 *Lateinische Kirchenväter*, 73.
21 Since Lactantius is of North African origin, it is natural to look to that region for possible roots of such willingness to enter into an alliance with the State. It may be found in Tertullian who, against the common emphasis on his antithetic attitude towards Roman authorities and cultural behaviour, perhaps fostered a more positive hope of a future cooperation of the Christians with the State. He indeed did never criticise the institutions, but merely their momentary corruption by idolatrous ideology and officers. The Christians, being the best subjects any good emperor could wish, were the ideal help to purify the institutions. However, the acknowledgement by the emperor that he was not divine but merely human (although charged by God to be 'the second ruler', after and under him!) was the *conditio sine qua non* for such an ideological assistance from Christian side. See for this revealing interpretation of Tertullian: Richard Klein, *Tertullian und das Römische Reich*, Heidelberg (1968). Klein quotes Tertullian's impatient exclamation in *Orat.* 5:1 'We would like to rule more readily, instead of only serve!' See also my article on Tertullian, referred to in n. 12 of the Introduction.
22 Barnes, *Constantine*, p. 140.
23 ibid., p. 186.
24 In 231 Origen moved from Alexandria to Palestine in connection with a conflict with his bishop there; see Chapter 1, p. 21 and n. 38.
25 *Cels.* VIII, 68. See the Introduction by H. Kraft to the German translation of the *HE*: *Eusebius von Caesarea, Kirchengeschichte*, Darmstadt (1997), p. 26.
26 J. Rebecca Lyman, *Christology and Cosmology: Models of Divine Activity in Origen, Eusebius and Athanasius*, Oxford (1993), p. 99.
27 ibid., 90.
28 'The apologetic, optimistic theology of Justin and Origen was foundational to his [viz., Eusebius'] work' (ibid. 83/4).
29 Lyman's conclusion about Eusebius is that he 'presents an optimistic and universal account of divine power and human progress founded on the historical evidence of Jesus' life and the triumph of the church' (p. 123).
30 Lyman stresses the contextual importance of this emphasis on human free will over against the various forms of fatalistic thought in Graeco-Roman society (pp. 98, 104, 123).

31 Lyman, pp. 83, 88.
32 'As a Christian historian, he defended the efficacy of human decision and the possibility of discerning the pattern of divine will in past events' (ibid., p. 84).
33 Kraft, 'Introduction', pp. 27, 29–30.
34 Barnes, p. 142.
35 *HE* 8,1 (my italics).
36 Lyman, *Christology*, p. 104.
37 Kraft, p. 72: 'When writing the prologue of *HE* (c. 312) the utmost he could conceive of was a naturally tolerant state, which as state was pagan.'
38 Barnes, p. 179.
39 Barnes, p. 166.
40 *HE* 10 4, 60. The quotation is taken from a speech which Eusebius held at Tyre. He referred to 'supreme men in power' since at that moment there were still two Christian emperors on the political scene, Constantine and Licinius, and the latter had not yet revealed his animosity (see Chapter 2, p. 33, and for the occasion of the speech n. 44).
41 *LausCons.* 16. Origen had said the same in *Cels.* II 30.
42 Barnes, p. 186.
43 *HE* X 4.6. See also Ruhbach, 'Politische Theologie', p. 241.
44 Ruhbach, p. 247: Eusebius 'esteems that thanks to Constantine he himself has arrived at a turning point of world history and he sometimes gives the impression that he was experiencing the eschatological time of Rejoicing.' Barnes' judgement is somewhat different when he says: 'now, Eusebius writes, the world is drawing to its close, and Christians must always be prepared for the advent of their Lord' (*Constantine*, p. 185).
45 Ruhbach, 'Politische Theologie', p. 247. Again on p. 252: 'His image of Constantine is almost exclusively determined by his perspective of the history of salvation, in spite of all apparent connection with the religious policy of the emperor'. But in between Ruhbach writes that 'exactly because he understands the activities of Constantine exclusively in the sense of Salvation history, he can unreservedly applaud the emperor's attitude towards the Church. And with regard to his efforts to maintain unity in both the Empire and the Church, Eusebius' position was in close contact with the emperor's policy' (p. 251). This boils down to the admission that there was a convergence of Eusebius' views with Constantine's policy.
46 Berkhof, *Theologie des Eusebius*, p. 59. Berkhof also pointed to the fact that when repeating large parts of his *Theophany* in the second part of *LausCons.*, Eusebius often replaced the saving role of Christ by that of Constantine, his imitator: 'The messianic significance of this emperor clearly stands out here.'
47 There was no criticism from the side of the Church of the fact that Constantine, like so many despots, murdered several members of his family and even his son Crispus, fearing that they might drive him from the throne. Bloodshed was the last of the three mortal sins to which the Church would apply the system of repairing by indulgence (see Chapter 1, p. 16).
48 *LausCons.*, V, 1.
49 *VitCons.* IV, 24. It should be remembered that the Greek word *episkopos*, which had become the technical designation for a defined ministry of the Church, could still have the original meaning of 'overseer' or 'supervisor'. It is by this meaning that Constantine may have expressed that, by virtue of his being appointed by God to an office of supervision, the bishop's title was due to him as well. See J. Straub, 'Kaiser Konstantin als επισκοπος των εκτος', in G. Ruhbach (ed.), *Die Kirche angesichts der Konstantinischen Wende*, Darmstadt (1976), p. 187.
50 See Chapter 2, pp. 41–2.
51 In the Reformation period, Luther would make such a distinction between two

spheres in which the Christian is living and under which he must obey to conflicting obligations. (Luther developed this twofold character of Christian life in his famous treatise on *The Christian's Freedom*). But Luther had to do with political authorities which normally were Christian and acted in awareness of their God-given ministry. Eusebius' spiritual forefather Origen also made a distinction in his exegesis of Rom. 13:1: 'Let every person [in Greek: soul] be subject to the governing authorities. For there is no authority except from God'. Pointing to Paul's use of the word 'soul' (distinguishable from 'spirit' which is the highest element in man and the proper place for religion), Origen stated that God charges the political authorities to impose discipline on the ambivalent, emotional and unstable human element 'soul', but never to have a say in religious life. If the state coerces idolatry, the Christian must abide by Peter's word 'We must obey God rather than men' (Acts 5:29). In order to corroborate this distinction Origen also pointed to Acts 15:28–9, saying that the Apostles' Council issued only religious instructions, leaving civil lawsuits to the ministers of justice. It should always be kept in mind to what large extent theological statements on Church–State relations, and particularly on the delimiting of their respective competencies, are influenced by the factual attitude of – in the first instance – the political power.

52 See below, Chapter 6, pp. 153–4.
53 *LausCons*. I, 3. II, 1.
54 'He who by the royal virtues in his soul has been made a copy of the above Kingdom, he is in his aspect formed according to the archetype of the Great King' (i.e., of God) – *LausCons*. V.
55 ibid. VII, 12.
56 Lyman, p. 123.
57 'What he [Constantine] wanted, was that Christianity would be the empire's religion, but which kind of Christianity was of no importance, provided that unity and peace be maintained', Leslie W. Barnard, 'Athanase et les empereurs Constantin et Constance', in C. Kannengiesser (ed.), *Politique et théologie chez Athanase d'Alexandrie*, Paris (1974), p. 136.
58 'The sole monarch on earth – and Eusebius sees no other before him than Constantine – is corresponding to the sole divine Monarch in heaven [. . .] The overall conception, which connects Empire, Peace, Monotheism and Monarchy with one another, is a unity created by Christians', E. Peterson, 'Der Monotheismus als politisches Problem', in E. Peterson, *Theologische Traktate*, Munich (1951), p. 93.
59 K. Aland, 'Der Abbau des Herrscherkultes im Zeitalter Konstantins', in K. Aland, *Kirchengeschichtliche Entwürfe*, Gütersloh (1960), pp. 240–56. He speaks of 'an unbroken continuation of the entire complex of the emperor-cult'.
60 'The high praise with which Eusebius spoke of the first Christian emperor determined the Byzantine interpretation of the emperor's place in the Christian (world-)scheme down the ages.' Barnard, 'Athanase et les empereurs', p. 128.
61 H. Berkhof, *De Kerk en de Keizer*, Amsterdam (1946), pp. 63–79.
62 Peterson, 'Monotheismus'. Peterson wrote this article in 1935, when 'political theology' meant something quite different from what it meant in the late 1960s. In the German context of the 1930s 'political theology' was the common denominator for theologies which were built upon the assumption that revolutionary events in the political sphere are epistemological principles. In point of fact this meant that 'Nazism and Christianity, Third Reich and Church were mutually conditioning, explaining, elucidating and accounting for each other' (Klaus Scholder, *Die Kirchen und das Dritte Reich*, Vol. 1, Frankfurt-Berlin, [1986] p. 546). Peterson recommended to the churches political reserve. To him, Eusebius was a warning example of a theology which prostitutes itself to a

political ideology and in the end proved without future (see Ruhbach, pp. 236–7). It is no wonder that Berkhof, who studied in Berlin in the late 1930s and came into contact with the Confessing Church, also saw the danger of ideology in Eusebius' thought, since it was – in his view – mere 'apology' instead of proper theology. Eusebius, who established a close relation between his theology of progressive fulfilment in history and contemporary political events, was highly relevant in the confrontation between the Confessing Church and the so-called German Christians. The research went on after the Second World War.

63 Introduction to *HE*, pp. 71–4.
64 Eusebius would partly be corrected by Ambrose – see Chapter 5, pp. 142, 150.
65 Barnard, 'Athanase et les empereurs', p. 137. For text and translation, see Athanasius, *Contra Gentes and De Incarnatione*, ed. R.W. Thomson, Oxford (1971). For the date, see above n. 10.
66 *Gent.* 39.
67 *Gent.* 38.
68 Barnard does not do so, probably because there is no question of a chief.
69 This image recalls the parable in Matt. 21:33–45, the householder being replaced by a king.
70 *Gent.* 29; 30ff. and 35ff.
71 *Inc.* 1.
72 *Inc.* 3.
73 *Inc.* 11.
74 *Inc.* 8.
75 *Inc.* 11, 13, 15.
76 *Inc.* 14.
77 See my *Le Christ et l'homme*, Chapter 1. Eusebius' position is described by Lyman as follows: 'The incarnation of the *Logos* has restored communion – that is, knowledge and power – with God, and has thus restored true power and freedom to humanity' (pp. 104–5).
78 In the past century we have seen both: the 'German Christians' saw the national awakening, led by the Nazis, as a direct manifestation of God's will and purpose with the German people, to such a degree that they adapted biblical theology to the standards of 'Aryan' and 'Nordic' popular sentiments. Protestant leaders in East European Socialist 'People's Republics' said that the drastic introduction of a social order based on Marxism-Leninism, was also an act by which God helped the Church to diagnose the sins of its past, and to better distinguish its call to serve its people. The Romanian Orthodox Church developed a 'Social Apostolate' and the Hungarian Reformed Church a 'Diaconical Theology'. According to these theologies, Socialism was no divine Revelation but a hard practice of rediscovering the true meaning of Revelation.

4 Defining Christ's relation to God

1 After 350 Constantius first had to get rid of the usurper who had eliminated Constans, before he established his power over the whole empire (353).
2 That is, when Licinius was the eastern emperor and even before he started to allow the oppression of the Christians (see Chapter 2, p. 33).
3 *The Making of Orthodoxy*, ed. by Rowan Williams, is the title of a volume of essays in honour of Henry Chadwick (Cambridge and New York 1989). The article by Richard Hanson, 'The achievement of orthodoxy in the fourth century AD', of which I will make ample use, is particularly fruitful for our subject (pp. 142–56).
4 Barnes, *Constantine and Eusebius*, 210.
5 Constantinople was to remain the capital of the Roman Empire, however much its territory shrunk in the course of the ages, till the Ottoman Turks captured it

in 1453. Then it was given the present name, of Istanbul. Scholars use the names 'Byzantium' and 'Byzantine Empire' for the long period from *c.* 600 onwards, i.e., after the definitive loss of the western territories and the substitution of Latin by Greek as official language.

6   The Emperor wrote that the questions at stake were of a philosophical nature. They did not affect the central doctrines of the divine law. Like the philosophers, Christians could disagree on details, but to those outside they should manifest brotherly love. If not, they would make themselves guilty of blasphemy and schism! Text of the letter in Eusebius, *VitCons.* 3, 60–2. See also Barnes, pp. 212–13.

7   It seems that Paul used for this identity the term *homoousios* (of one being). Rejected in connection with Paul's dynamism, this term would be used in the credal definition adopted by the Council of Nicaea and later become the target of all its opponents (see below, pp. 88 and 71).

8   Gen. 1:26–7. In verse 26 the Bible even reads 'in *our* image'. See on this theme Henri Crouzel, *Théologie de l'image de Dieu chez Origène*, Paris (1956).

9   See above, Chapter 1, pp. 20–1 and J. Rebecca Lyman, *Christology and Cosmology*, Oxford and New York (1993), Chapter 2 'Origen: Goodness and Freedom'.

10   Such texts are for instance: Matt. 11:27, 26:36–9, Mark 13:32, Luke 22:42, John 3:35, 5:30, 12:27–8, Acts 2:36, Phil. 2:5–11; Heb. 3:1–2. There are many others of the same kind. Athanasius gives a list of all the Arian prooftexts in *OrCAr.* 3, and discusses them at length.

11   R.C. Gregg and D.E. Groh, *Early Arianism: A View of Salvation*, London (1981). The second part of the title speaks unequivocally for their key of understanding! Their main thesis reads: 'So firmly entrenched in all of our minds has been the picture of Arius as a logician and dialectician that our tendency has been to underrate and overlook his concern for biblical exactitude' (p. 3).

12   Hanson, 'Achievement', p. 145.

13   Gregg and Groh state that Arius 'protested against any formula that would bring the divine essence into contact with the human suffering' (*Early Arianism*, p. 4). Hanson says 'the Arians believed that the only way to achieve a rational theology of a suffering God was to postulate the existence of a high God who was impassible and a lesser God who experienced the suffering for him' ('Achievement', p. 145).

14   F. Ricken, 'Nikaia als Krisis des altchristlichen Platonismus', in *Theologie und Philosophie* 44 (1969): 336.

15   Arius said: 'Christ is god, not in a full sense but by participation [. . .] for he is not the true and only *Logos* of the Father, but by a name only he is called *Logos* and Wisdom and by grace is called Son and Power' (Athan., *OrCAr.* 1:9). He also said that the Son is only incorrectly called God's 'Logos and Wisdom', since it was by his inherent *Logos* and Wisdom that God created (first) the Son and (then) all the rest (Ricken, 'Nikaia', p. 333).

16   Gregg and Groh, p. 22. They quote *OrCAr.* 1:5: 'God, foreknowing Christ to be good, proleptically gave him this glory, which he had afterward as man of virtue; so that from his works, which God foreknew, he made such a one as him now to be begotten.' This means that in his heavenly pre-existence Christ was already in possession of the glory, which he still was to deserve by his earthly path as obedient servant of God. Arius equated the biblical words 'son' and 'servant-boy', making sonship dependent on truly fulfilled service.

17   He probably based this upon Mark 14:36: 'Abba, Father, all things are possible to thee; remove this cup from me; yet not what I will, but what thou wilt' (See Gregg and Groh, pp. 26–7).

18   ibid., pp. 29–30.

19   Athanasius was to find other targets, but these are connected with his different

theology of creation and salvation, as will be shown below. See also Gregg and Groh, p. 8: 'In the case of both Arianism and orthodoxy in the early fourth century, their general biblical hermeneutic exactly corresponds to their soteriological programs.'

20 The Arians also referred to 1 Cor. 15:24, where it reads: 'Then comes the end, when he [Christ] delivers the kingdom to God the Father, after destroying every rule, authority and power.' This would not mean the end of the existence of the *Logos*/Christ, not any more than of anyone of the adoptive sons of God, by virtue of their participation to the divine power; but it indicates the end of all his services to God the Father.

21 Gregg and Groh, p. 19. Alexander stated his ideas in a letter to his colleague Alexander of Thessalonica, which is the main source of his position (Opitz, *Urkunden zur Geschichte des Arianischen Streites 318–328*, p. 14).

22 Arius concludes his letter in this way: 'We are being persecuted, since we say: "The Son has a beginning, but God is without beginning". We are being persecuted for that. And also since we say that he has been made out of non-being. We say that, because he is neither a part of God nor made from any other substance. We are being persecuted for that [. . .] I pray, remember our tribulations, you my fellow-Lucianist, you truly Eusebius [man of piety]. (Opitz, *Urkunde* 1).

23 Rivalry between Alexandria and Nicomedia, soon substituted by Constantinople, was to play an important part in the doctrinal struggles of the fourth and fifth centuries.

24 Lyman, *Cosmology*, pp. 117–23.

25 Lyman, pp. 111–15. According to Barnes, in Eusebius 'the Son is a second God, with a different substance and essence from the Father. He is the Word, the second cause, the servant and subordinate of the Father' (*Constantine*, p. 186).

26 *Cosmology*, p. 107.

27 Barnes, *Constantine*, p. 186.

28 Africa, Spain (Hosius himself), Gaul, Italy and Pannonia (Austria and Hungary).

29 The seventh and last of this kind of ecumenical council was held in 787, also at Nicaea. The Byzantine Orthodox Church does not recognise any later council as 'ecumenical'; the Roman Catholic Church continued to hold general assemblies calling them 'ecumenical councils', the most recent of which was the Second Vatican Council (1962–5). All subsequent councils have been convoked and led by the Roman pope.

30 Lyman: 'his explanation of *homoousios* followed his own pre-Nicene account of the Father as the direct cause of the Son, rather than allowing any sense of identity of essence between them' (p. 97).

31 Text and comparison are, with slight variations, taken from William A. Curtis, *A History of Creeds and Confessions of Faith*, Edinburgh (1911), p. 70.

32 The word *substantia* was more familiar to the Latins.

33 Constantine's Letter to the Church of Alexandria, in H.-G. Opitz, *Urkunden zur geschichte des Arianischen Streites 318–328*, Berlin and Leipzig (1935), Urk 25, p. 4. See Kraft, *Konstantins religiöse Enwicklung*, p. 218.

34 'So wurde das Glaubensproblem auf die Ebene der persönlichen Angelegenheiten verschoben; Konstantin ließ sich auf diesen Weg locken' (Ortiz de Urbina, p. 141).

35 See Chapter 6, p. 166.

36 See Chapter 3, p. 65.

37 The name of this successor is not mentioned. Barnes supposes that it was the Meletian counter-bishop, already in function in Alexandria (Timothy D. Barnes, *Athanasius and Constantius: Theology and Politics in the Constantinian Empire*, Cambridge, Mass. and London 1993, p. 23). Besides Arius the Meletians were also received into communion by the Tyre synod.

38 Under Constantius they would work themselves up to the position of court bishops and would play a role in the church politics of the 350s; see Chapter 4, p. 98.

39 The bishops of Alexandria were indeed called 'pappas' ('father'), a title later claimed exclusively for the Bishop of Rome.

40 Barnes, *Athanasius*, pp. 24–5.

41 Barnes, *Constantine*, p. 225.

42 Arius died in Constantinople in 336. The ominous circumstance of his end (on a public toilet just before entering a church) became a blot on his reputation and was exploited as sign of a divine verdict. Twenty years later Athanasius thought it worthwhile to describe the details in a letter to one of his partisans.

43 Since his followers met the intruder Gregory with violence, Athanasius risked to be arrested by the imperial administration. He left Alexandria in April 339 and went to Rome.

44 Marcellus was already bishop of Ancyra (present Ankara) by the year 314. He attended the Council of Nicaea and was a fervent anti-Arian. Because of his consequent opposition against Arius, which he manifested at Tyre (335), a synod in Constantinople in the next year deposed him. Like Athanasius, Constantine sent him into exile, from where he was allowed to return in accordance with the amnesty, proclaimed by the late emperor's sons. Upon his return there were riots.

45 Meanwhile Constantine II had disappeared from the scene; see the introduction to this chapter.

46 The composition of the work in the early 340s is disputed, many scholars putting it rather in the middle of the 350s. I am inclined to an early date (see my *Le Christ et l'homme*, pp. 386–9) and so is Barnes, *Athanasius and Constantius*, p. 53.

47 Two books *Contra Marcellum*, one of his last works, since he died in 339. It was on the basis of this examination that the Antioch synod in 338/9 condemned and deposed Marcellus.

48 They were bishops of a provincial capital. In the western Church the function of 'metropolitan' was later called 'archbishop'.

49 Lyman, pp. 125–6.

50 In Egypt the authority of Antony, the much respected 'father of the desert monks', was solicited by both the Arians and Athanasius.

51 At the 'Dedication Council' at Antioch (341) the bishops in favour of Arius' Christological approach said that they were not his followers 'for how, as bishops, could we follow a priest?' But they had admitted him to communion, rather than followed him, 'after appointing ourselves examiners and assessors of his creed' (Barnes, *Athanasius*, p. 57).

52 Named after Eusebius of Nicomedia, more politician than his namesake of Caesarea. Court-intriguer Eusebius died 342.

53 Maurice Wiles, 'Eunomius: Hair-Splitting Dialectician or Defender of the Accessibility of Salvation?', in Rowan Williams (ed.), *The Making of Orthodoxy*, Cambridge (1989), p. 159.

54 Today Serdica is Bulgaria's capital Sophia. In those days it was a border town between the two territories.

55 The west had to wait for a man like Hilary of Poitiers, who thanks to his exile to the east learnt to understand Greek theological thought.

56 Thümmel, *Kirche des Ostens*, p. 69.

57 Sirmium was an imperial residence in the northern Balkans. Today its name is Sremska Mitrovica, west of Belgrade.

58 Athanasius, *On the Decisions of the Nicene Council*, composed in 351.

59 John 10:30 and 38.

60 1 Cor. 15, 24 – one of Marcellus' favourite prooftexts.

61 Thümmel, pp. 66–7.

62 The debate concentrated on the relation of Christ to God. The position and nature of the Holy Spirit only came into the debate in the late 350s – see Chapter 5, pp. 121–61.

63 'Athanasius used *homoousios* cautiously, and only in the context of the Nicene creed' (Lyman, p. 149); same conclusion in Thümmel, p. 65.

64 For Eusebius, see Chapter 4, pp. 78–9 and for Marcellus, p. 89.

65 *OrCAr.* 3, 60.

66 Lyman, p. 148.

67 R. Hanson: 'Athanasius above all recognised that if we take the NT seriously, we must conclude that Christ is not a safeguard against God the Father involving himself with human affairs, but a guarantee that he has done so' (p. 155).

68 Raymund Schwager, *Der wunderbare Tausch: Zur Geschichte und Deutung der Erlösungslehre*, Munich: 1986, notices in Athanasius an 'unmistakable prioritising of the physical above the free acting [. . .] above the outcome of the will' (pp. 59, 68).

69 Lyman, p. 133.

70 *Inc.* 3 and 11. See Chapter 3, pp. 66–7.

71 I have analysed this specific Athanasian anthropology in my *Le Christ et l'homme*, Chapters 3 and 4.

72 This expression, invented by Martin Luther, has been adopted by Raymund Schwager as general title for his study of the doctrine of Redemption, in which Chapter 3 deals with Athanasius under the title 'Curse and Mortality – Sacrifice and Immortality'. See above n. 68.

73 *OrCAr.* 1,45; 2,70.

74 *OrCAr.* 3, 38.40.

75 *OrCAr.* 3, 25. See for the implications of this idea of 'connection' Johannes Roldanus, 'Die Vita Antonii als Spiegel der Theologie des Athanasius', *Theologie und Philosophie* 58 (1983): 205–10.

76 *OrCAr.* 3, 33. The biblical quotation is from Gal. 3:13. Lyman remarkably characterises Athanasius' theology by the coherent couple of words 'Transcendence and Transformation' (Chapter 4).

77 *Inc.* 54. *OrCAr.* 3, 33. Schwager explains this 'logofication' as 'a full permeation of the human flesh by the divine *Logos*' (p. 71). In order to strengthen his argument Athanasius has forged here the term 'logofied'.

78 *OrCAr.* 2, 61. 2, 69 and 3, 53 express the same view of human kinship with the flesh of the Word.

79 And he said, 'Father, remove this cup from me; yet not what I will, but what thou wilt' (Mark 14:33–6); see p. 76, n. 17.

80 Christ says about the final tribulations: 'of that day or that hour no one knows, not even the angels in heaven, *nor the Son*, but only the Father' (Mark 13:32) and Luke tells that 'Jesus increased in wisdom and in God's favour (Luke 2:52).

81 Like Matt. 11:27, 28:18; John 3:35, etc. Athanasius enumerates all Arian prooftexts in *OrCAr.* 3, 26, before discussing their correct meaning at length in 27–57.

82 *OrCAr.* 3, 29.

83 Lyman, p. 156.

84 *OrCAr.* 3, 33: 'We all are vivified in Christ, after having been "born anew of water and the Spirit"'.

85 *OrCAr.* 1, 50. The last words are taken from John 1:16.

86 Composed in 359. *The Letters of Saint Athanasius concerning the Holy Spirit*, trans. and edited by C.R.B. Shapland, London (1951).

87 *The Festal Epistles of S. Athanasius, Bishop of Alexandria*, trans. from Syriac, edited by Henri Burgess, London and Oxford (1854). A. Robertson (ed.), *Select Writings and Letters of Athanasius, Bishop of Alexandria* (Nicene and Post-Nicene Fathers of the Church, 2nd ser. 4), repr. Edinburgh (1987), pp. 506–53. Four letters

preserved in Coptic are translated by D. Brakke, *Athanasius and the Politics of Ascetism*, Oxford (1995), Appendix F.

Athanasius followed the Alexandrian custom of annually sending a pastoral letter to his flock at the beginning of Lent. He sometimes missed a year because of his exiles.

88 Lyman, *Christology*, p. 159.

89 Lyman, pp. 127–8. She quotes R. Williams, *Arius: Heresy and Tradition*, London (1987), and C. Kannengiesser, 'Athanasius of Alexandria and the Foundation of Traditional Christology', *Theological Studies* 34 (1973): 103–13. In her own words: 'a new religious context' and a 'theological controversy [. . .] led him to emphasize certain Christian themes at the expense of others.' In our opinion it is the context of both contexts which gives this emphasis, viz., on the communication of divine life to humans and of their transformation by the Christocentric event, the value of an innovation.

90 Brakke has shown that 'Athanasius was shaping an ethos for the new imperial Christianity that would cohere with his particular brand of trinitarian theology and episcopal organization' and thereby produced more than one 'transformation of the Alexandrian spiritual tradition' (*Politics of Ascetism*, 267/68). By 'ethos' he means the ascetic attitude, and by 'organization' the establishment of 'a unified and dominant Church in Egypt' (p. 271).

91 Ricken says: 'what Athanasius takes the trouble to express in the Greek thoughtforms is the soteriological message of the New Testament und not the Middle-Platonist issue of Transcendence and Cosmos' ('Nikaia als Krisis', p. 339).

92 Ricken: the apologists and Alexandrians before Athanasius had 'adopted the cosmological interpretation of Being from Middle-Platonism and, as a result, there was the constant danger that the thought-scheme they had drawn up to explain the Kerygma would deploy its inherent dynamics and disfigure the Christian message of Salvation' (pp. 325–6).

93 Roldanus, *Le Christ et l'homme*, p. 370.

94 'Curiously, Platonic contemplation remained central in Athanasius' soteriology, albeit transformed by its use in an incarnate setting: by Christ's dwelling in the flesh, sin might be perfectly expelled from the flesh, and we might have a free mind' (Lyman, p. 142).

95 Athanasius first had to defend himself before Constantius against the charge that he had contacted the usurper Magnentius, who had eliminated Constans in 350 but was defeated by Constantius in 353. See for Athanasius' attitude towards the Emperor, Leslie W. Barnard, 'Athanase et les empereurs Constantin et Constance', in Charles Kannengiesser (ed.), *Politique et Théologie chez Athanase d'Alexandrie*, Paris (1974), pp. 127–43, and Karl Friedrich Hagel, 'Die Lehre des Athanasius von Kirche und Kaisertum', in Gerhard Ruhbach (ed.), *Die Kirche angesichts der Konstantinischen Wende* Darmstadt (1976), pp. 259–78.

96 Barnes, *Athanasius and Constantius*, p. 113.

97 Barnes, *Athanasius*, p. 132. An example of this attitude is the hope he fostered in 335 that Constantine would overrule the decision of the Council of Tyre to remove him from his see.

98 Lyman, p. 159. The same author says: 'the power of salvation lay not in the progress of history, but in the incarnational event which created islands of redeemed humanity in the fallen word' (p. 146).

99 This expression inspired Derwas J. Chitty to give his study of the Egyptian and Palestinian monachism in the Christian (Roman) Empire the title *The Desert a City*, Oxford ([1966] 1977). The origin is found in *VitAnt*. 14 where it reads: 'He [Antony] persuaded many into solitary life. And so, from then on, monasteries [cells for hermits] came into being even in the mountain area and the desert

became like a city of monks who had abandoned their goods and subscribed to the life of the heavenly city'. In this sentence the playing on two words derived from *polis* produces the suggestive picture of a colonisation of the desert, i.e., the habitat of the devils, by people who by their conduct are citizens of heaven. Cf. my *Le Christ et l'homme*, pp. 326–7. Though *VitAnt.* was composed by Athanasius only after Antony's death in 356, his contacts with the world of the monks were of earlier date. See further Chapter 6, pp. 160–3.

100 George had already been appointed to replace the condemned Athanasius in 349. His consecration took place in 352, his entry in Alexandria, under military protection, only in 356. Rioting against him forced him to leave the city in 358. He came back in November 361 to be lynched on Christmas Eve.

101 Barnes, *Athanasius*, p. 112. About 351, Athanasius wrote *On the Decisions of the Nicene Council* (cf. n. 58).

102 Before making his statement, Liberius had summoned Athanasius to Rome in order to verify his stance. But Athanasius refused to come, either because in the critical situation after 'Sirmium' he did not risk to leave Alexandria, or simply because it was not in his nature to accept to be summoned by someone of equal rank!

103 It was Paulinus, Bishop of Treves, where Athanasius had been in exile some fifteen years ago. C.F.A. Borchardt ('Hilary of Poitiers' Role in the Arian Struggle' [Thesis Leiden], The Hague 1966, p. 21), thinks that Paulinus was prepared to condemn Marcellus and Photinus, but not Athanasius. Borchardt thinks it improbable that Hilary, the later leader of the western opposition against Constantius, attended the synod.

104 Respectively modern Osijek (Croatia) and Belgrade.

105 Borchardt, p. 23. Barnes, *Athanasius*, pp. 115–18.

106 Milan, the imperial residence of the west, thus became an Arian stronghold and Auxentius' successor, Ambrose, whom the churchpeople claimed as bishop in 374, had to face a difficult situation; see Chapter 5, pp. 145–6.

107 G. Haendler, *Von Tertullian bis zu Ambrosius*, estimates that Liberius may not have thought it worthwhile to remain isolated for the sake of Athanasius, who in 356 had fled from Alexandria and seemed out of the picture, whereas other eastern theologians worked on new definitions. This valuation would make Liberius 'a wise and settling church leader' (p. 99). For Roman Catholics the valuation of Liberius' move is crucial because of the painful circumstance that a pope (as they see him) broke with the defender of an orthodox dogma. Anyhow, the treatment of Liberius proves Constantius' brutal determination to break down all opposition.

108 Thus Athanasius and Hilary; see Haendler, p. 93.

109 *Historia Arianorum* 44, 6–8 (*Athanasius' Werke*, ed. H.-G. Opitz, II/1, p. 208). Quotation in Barnes, *Athanasius*, p. 175.

110 See above, n. 100.

111 *Defense before Constantius* and *History of the Arians for the Monks*. All the works Athanasius wrote during this third exile are presented and discussed by Barnes in Chapter XIV 'Apologia, Polemic and Theology' in his *Athanasius and Constantius*. Sad to say that he excludes the *Life of Saint Antony*, which most scholars think to have been composed *c.* 357, but which Barnes considers spurious.

112 As usual at the expense of the Emperor; only the bishops of Britain and Gaul declined to be a charge on the public, intending to save their independence. The Seleucia in question is the one on the south coast of Asia Minor.

113 Barnes, *Athanasius*, pp. 145–9.

114 ibid.

115 ibid.

116 See above, Chapter 3, p. 87 and n. 53.

117 Thümmel, p. 72.
118 *Athanasius*, p. 137. Barnes is categorical: 'It should not even be assumed (as it traditionally has been) that the views of Aëtius and Eunomius really were fundamentally similar to those of Arius'. See also Hans Lietzmann, *Geschichte der alten Kirche*, III Berlin (1953), p. 218.
119 Maurice Wiles, 'Eunomius: Hair-Splitting Dialectician or Defender of the Accessibility of Salvation?', in Rowan Williams (ed.), *The Making of Orthodoxy*, p. 159.
120 Thümmel, p. 72.
121 ibid., p. 220.
122 Cyril was dismissed twice: in 358 and in 360, and once again under the pro-Arian Emperor Valens, a fate he shared with Athanasius (see below Chapter 5, p. 117). Cyril will also draw our attention in Chapter 6, p. 171 with regard to spiritual life.
123 Modern Kayseri in Turkey, not to be confused with Palestinian Caesarea, once Eusebius' see.
124 Borchardt, *Hilary of Poitiers' Role*, p. 187. Borchardt's study gives a fine outline of Hilary's thought and political activities.
125 ibid., p. 188.
126 See Robert L. Wilken, *John Chrysostom and the Jews*, Berkeley, Calif. and London (1983), Chapter V.
127 Athanasius' *Tomus ad Antiochenos* was a letter addressed to Antioch, where the different tendencies had resulted in a split of the community into several factions. Although it did not resolve the delicate local situation, it is recognised that the solution proposed by Alexandria gave a model for reconciliation in every place where parties tried to come together.
128 Since the year 339 Athanasius had taken the stance that his theological positions were identical with the faith the Church had confessed ever since. Scholars have pronounced entirely different judgements on Athanasius' character: from a saint who defended orthodoxy to 'a politician through and through', 'someone like a modern gangster, organizing an ecclesiastical mafia' (Barnes). Athanasius most certainly was intransigent and did not shrink from either deliberate political action or partial publicity. It is perhaps the fairest judgement to point at the striking correspondence between his radical tenacity and the likewise radical terms in which he exposed God's salvation through the incarnated Son.
129 Socrates, *Ecclesiastical History* V Proem (MPG 67, 565). In his work Socrates describes the period from 305 to 439 (the year of his death).
130 Barnes, *Athanasius*, pp.168–9, criticises 'the dominant model in recent scholarship of the relationship between the Christian church and the Roman state in the fourth century', because it has been developed by German scholars who lived the typical German situation before the First World War, when sovereigns were heads of territorial (mostly Protestant) churches. Through this model terms such as 'Imperial Church' (*Reichskirche*) and 'Synodal authority in the Emperor's hands' (*kaiserliche Synodalgewalt*) had been introduced into early Church scholarship. These terms frequently occur in several articles in G. Ruhbach (ed.), *Die Kirche angesichts der Konstantinischen Wende*. Over against this view Barnes makes an effort to see in perspective the real influence which the emperor took upon the synods during the years 324–61. Barnes does not seem very convincing: first of all, because he takes Constantine's dealings with the synods as 'normal practise'. But Constantine' sons applied the example set by their father with less scruples, as Constantius' church politics clearly show. Second, even when we look at the list Barnes makes of those cases in which Constantine directly meddled with synods between 325 (Nicaea) and 335 (Tyre), the measure of his

involvement in matters of church doctrine and leadership is only too obvious to be relativised in the way Barnes is doing.

131 E. Wolf, 'Zur Entstehung der kaiserlichen Synodalgewalt, zu ihrer theologischen Begründung und kirchlichen Rezeption', in G. Ruhbach (ed.), *Konstantinische Wende*, p. 178: 'in spite of all the separation of powers is primarily a condition and a modality of their mutual symphony. It could, however, explode the symphony as well.' In the same volume, Orthodox scholar A. Kartaschow, defines the new alliance of Church and Empire as a sympathising encounter in which each side had its own motives: those of the state were purely utilitarian, since it had to be clear that the state can never define the divine truth. Kartaschow also says that none of the great fathers of the fourth century, including Athanasius and Hilary, ever thought of a rupture when they claimed for the Church its own 'priority of teaching' and from the emperor 'a humble layman's obedience' (ibid., pp. 160–1).
132 Barnes, *Athanasius*, p. 174.
133 See above, n. 129.
134 Barnes, *Athanasius*, p. 170.
135 ibid.
136 ibid., pp. 172–3.
137 See F. Dvornik, *Byzantium and the Roman Primacy*, New York (1979), Chapters 1 and 2.
138 For instance, the triumph of the Roman view and practice in the question of the rebaptism of heretics, to which we have referred in Chapter 2, p. 39.
139 M. Goemans OFM, *Het Algemeen Concilie in de vierde eeuw*, Nijmegen-Utrecht (1945).
140 'Whoever considers the juridical supremacy of the Roman bishop the characteristic of the papacy, can surely point out Damasus as the first pope' (G. Haendler, *Von Tertullian*, p. 113). See also Chapter 5, pp. 122–3 and p. 143.
141 Exceptions were, as we saw, Marcellus of Ancyra and his disciple Photinus of Sirmium, who both were unanimously condemned by eastern synods.
142 Thümmel judges: Anyhow, a substantial conception of ousia seems to have been customary for our period. It is significant that the notions of 'ousia' and 'homoousios' in the decades after Nicaea have been avoided on all sides (*Kirche des Ostens*, 60/1). The Latin theologians were less hesitant than the Greeks to attribute to God a kind of 'material' substantiality.
143 We saw how Basil of Ancyra tried to have the words 'in every respect' added to 'similar to the Father', but without success.
144 See p. 90.
145 By Asia Minor I notably refer to its central provinces of Galatia, with Basil of Ancyra, and of Cappadocia, with the three prominent theologians who will be discussed in the next chapter.
146 Thümmel, p. 53.

5 Christianity matures

1 Roman administration had divided the empire territory into four *prefectures*: the *East*, *Illyria*, *Italy* and the *Gauls*, each covering three or four *dioceses* (this term did not yet have the later ecclesiastical meaning of bishopric, but was purely administrative). The Italian prefecture extended northward up to the Danube and included southward the Mediterranean isles as well as modern Algeria, Tunisia and Libya. The prefecture of the Gauls embraced the territories west of the Rhine and the Alps, the Iberian peninsula and modern Morocco.
2 Being exposed to the incursions of the German tribes, the Empire of the west split up in the course of the fifth century and only parts of it (Italy, North

Africa) were temporarily reunited with the eastern empire under the reign of Justinian (527–65). It is noteworthy that the dividing line of 395 has, in the course of time, become the frontier between western, Roman Catholic, and Eastern Orthodox Christianity. This line cuts across the Balkans from north to south, and the creation of one modern state for all South Slav peoples (Yugoslavia, 1920) has not wiped out the historic contrast between an eastern and a western Christian culture, as the bloody conflicts of the 1990s and the dismemberment of former Yugoslavia into independent states have shown.

3   The first partisans of this doctrine of the Holy Ghost, to whom Bishop Serapion of Thmuis (Lower Egypt) drew Athanasius' attention in 359, declared the Spirit to be one of the numerous 'serving spirits' or angels that carry out God's work. In his first answer to Serapion, Athanasius forged the word *pneumatomachein*, i.e., to fight against the Holy Spirit. From this new verb was derived the collective term 'Pneumatomachians', literally 'Assailants of the Spirit'. It is no wonder that old and new Arians (like Eunomius), by attributing divine nature to the Father alone, denied divinity to the Spirit, as they did to the Son. The name 'Pneumatomachians' refers more specifically to those who, though confessing the divinity of the Son, refused to acknowledge an equal status of the Spirit. Apparently they found it difficult to see the Spirit as a person in the same way as the Father and the Son had a personality. The Spirit seemed rather an impersonal power, executing what the two want. Moreover, the Nicene Creed had only the words 'and in the Holy Spirit', without any definition of its nature and functions. One of their arguments was that the Spirit could not be derived from the Father's essence, since the Son is the 'only-begotten'. In the disputes of the epoch they are also called 'Macedonians' after their first leader Macedonius who was bishop of Constantinople from 342–60 (then dismissed as a result of Constantius' 'Arianising' pressure).

4   See Chapter 2, pp. 38–40 and 4, pp. 79–84.

5   This was one of the dioceses of the *prefecture of the East*, which was also called *Oriens*. This prefecture embraced an arc of territories, stretching from modern Bulgaria to Egypt, including the isle of Cyprus; it comprised three metropoles: Constantinople, Antioch and Alexandria.

6   This aspect did not concern the relation of the Son with the Father. Apollinarius always boasted that he was fully congenial with Athanasius.

7   For the moment the followers of Apollinarius were won by means of an ambiguous section in the declaration of the Alexandrian synod, dealing with their specific Christological views: ambiguous, because it could ease their opponents, without forcing themselves to an open disagreement (see Chapter 5, p. 121).

8   The reader will remember that 'Eunomian' stands for dissimilarity – or rather a mere moral resemblance – of the *Logos* with God the Father, whereas 'Marcellian' denotes a confusion of the Son's identity with the Father's. At this time, the ideas of Marcellus (d. *c.* 374) were rather associated with his pupil Photinus of Sirmium, who had been deposed in 351 (see Chapter 4, p. 97).

9   The first three books of his exposition of the faith, *De Fide ad Gratianum*, probably date from the year 380; two others from 387.

10   Their edict issued at Saloniki reads: 'We want all peoples, over which Our moderate clemency is reigning, to adhere to that religion, which has evidently been sown by the divine apostle Peter himself and handed down to the Romans to this day, i.e. that very religion, which is now followed by Pope Damasus and by Peter, the bishop of Alexandria, a man of apostolic sanctity; in order that we believe one Godhead of the Father, the Son and the Holy Spirit, who share similar majesty and holy trinity. We order that those who follow this law shall be called Catholic Christians and that the others, whom we consider out of their senses and foolish, shall suffer the defamation of being heretics. Their gatherings shall not

bear the name of churches. The divine wrath first, and then Our punishment, to which We are authorized by the heavenly judgment, will strike them.'

11 The title was subsequently appropriated by Pope Leo I in the middle of the fifth century and has since become a prerogative of the popes.

12 See Chapter 4, p. 98.

13 It is supposed that already at this synod the text (or a draft) of the Creed which was adopted at Constantinople in 381 was framed; see Reinhard Staats, *Das Glaubensbekenntnis von Nizäa-Konstantinopel*, Darmstadt (1996), p. 81.

14 See above, n. 5.

15 So at Chalcedon; see Chapter 5, p. 141. Nicaea (325) was indicated as the assembly of 'the 318 Fathers'.

16 J.N.D. Kelly, *Early Christian Creeds*, Harlow and New York (1985), p. 329.

17 Because of his Christology, Apollinarius was first condemned in Rome in 377, then by synods in Alexandria (378) and Antioch (379 – see above notes 7 and 13).

18 The literal text enumerates the heresies of the Eunomians or anhomoeans, Arians or Eudoxians, Pneumatomachians who are stigmatised as 'Semi-Arians' (since they are 'Arianising' with regard to the Spirit), the Sabellianist Marcellians and Photinians and the Apollinarists.

19 At the Council of Chalcedon, 451, four eastern patriarchates would be recognised: Constantinople, Alexandria, Antioch and Jerusalem. By then, the west had only one bishop of equal status in the Pope of Rome (after Arles had failed to impose itself as second main centre in the west).

20 At that time, the patriarch of the Egyptian Church bore the title of 'pope', as today does the head of the Coptic Orthodox Church of Egypt.

21 Text of this canon in Ignacio Ortiz de Urbina, *Nizäa und Constantinopel*, Mainz (1964), p. 314. (Dumeige-Bacht, Geschichte der ökumenischen konzilien I). See also Francis Dvornik, *Byzantium and the Roman Primacy*, New York (1979), p. 44.

22 The juridical authority of the patriarchate of Constantinople got firmly established over the (administrative) *dioceses* of Pontus, Asia and Thracia, viz., nearly the whole of modern Turkey (except its south-eastern part which belonged to Antioch) and the eastern half of modern Bulgaria up north to the mouth of the Danube. Nectarius' Roman counterparts were Damasus, in office from 366–84, and Siricius from 384 to 399.

23 Actually, neither Peter nor Paul founded the Christian community of Rome in the first century, but they both suffered martyrdom there, people knew their graves and a martyr cult had developed since the second century. See O. Cullmann, *S. Peter – Disciple. Apostle. Martyr* (1953).

24 Staats, *Glaubensbekenntnis*, pp. 191–2.

25 ibid., pp. 114–20.

26 The reproduction of the original Greek texts is mainly taken from Kelly, *Early Christian Creeds*, pp. 215 and 297. Following Staats I have corrected in the definition of the Holy Spirit the usual 'the Lord' into 'who exerts lordship', as the Greek has the adjective and not the substantive, which is reserved for the 'one Lord Jesus Christ' (*Glaubensbekenntnis*, p. 25).

27 Kelly states that C 'cannot accurately be described as a modified version of N' (*Creeds*, p. 304) and that 'the points of difference between J (Jerusalem) and C are numerous and far-reaching' (p. 314). According to Staats, J has the greatest number of words in common with C, followed by a Roman baptismal creed. He supposes that these different formulas were already put together on the Antiochene synod of 379 and consequently he sees that meeting as paving the way for C (*Glaubensbekenntnis*, p. 170).

28 This point is rightly put forward by Kelly, pp. 323–5. See also Chapter 5, pp. 141–2.

29 See Chapter 4, pp. 84–5 and p. 97. Cf. Kelly, p. 303.
30 The Greek text uses the neutral form of *kurios*, making it an adjective.
31 For Apollinarius' Christology see Kelly, p. 334. For previous condemnations of his Christology, see above n. 17.
32 See Chapter 5, pp. 145–6.
33 Hanson, *Search*, p. 712.
34 ibid., pp. 751–3.
35 Young, *From Nicaea*, p. 102. For the subject as a whole, see Werner Jaeger, *Early Christianity and Greek Paideia*, Cambridge, Mass. (1961); Chapter VII refers to Gregory of Nyssa.
36 Basil wrote nine long sermons on '*The Six Days Work*' (Creation of the universe according to Gen. 1). Ambrose rewrote it as an own work under the same title. In writing a similar work and a special work on the creation of man, Gregory intended to complete the writings of his elder brother and to save them from misunderstandings.
37 The *Oxford Dictionary of the Christian Church* (1974, p. 140) calls him 'statesman-like'. Bishops like Basil and his friends considered themselves of equal rank with provincial governors (so Peter Brown, *Power and Persuasion in Late Antiquity*, Madison [1992], p. 46).
38 The blasphemy against the Holy Spirit which will never be forgiven (Matt. 12:31–2) refers in Athanasius (4*Ser.* 7–23) to the denial of Christ's godhead, in Basil to the depreciation of the divine nature and activities of the Spirit.
39 Hanson, *Search*, p. 699.
40 Hanson: 'on almost every [. . .] critical occasion he ran away' (p. 706).
41 Egypt and the west, strong allies as they were, tried to support another as Bishop of Constantinople; see Chapter 5, p. 120. Saloniki acted as observer for the absent west.
42 Young, *From Nicaea*, p. 114.
43 Hanson, *Search*, p. 710. See also Staats, *Glaubensbekenntnis*, p. 87.
44 See Chapter 5, pp. 120–1. His excellent relations with the imperial court also yielded him the honour of delivering the funeral speeches at the death of the empress and of a princess in the year 385.
45 *Ep.* 38, quoted by Hanson, *Search*, p. 724.
46 ibid., pp. 720–1. Young, *From Nicaea*, pp. 117–18.
47 GrNyss., *Apoll.*, edited by Jaeger III/I, Leiden (1958), 152, 1–6.
48 Young, *From Nicaea*, p. 201.
49 ibid., p. 212: 'The Man assumed paved the way for all man'.
50 GrNaz., *Ep.* 101 (PG 37, 181).
51 For the understanding of this Semitic background, Chapter I of Dom Gregory Dix, *Jew and Greek*, London (1955) (repr.) is very instructive.
52 *DE* IV, 2, 1, quoted by Hanson, *Search*, p. 49.
53 Hanson, pp. 48–9. Another striking quotation, given by Hanson, reads: 'God gives him existence as his first product of all beings, the first born Wisdom [. . .] the perfect creation of the Perfect and wise construction of the Wise, the good issue of the good Father'. In these words the idea of derivation is patent. All the same, Eusebius attributes as much divinity as possible to this first product, because in the same passage he calls the *Logos* 'Mind, Reason Wisdom, Beauty and Goodness in himself'. He does not make a distinction between *ousia* and *hypostasis*, speaking of 'two substances, things and powers' (ibid., p. 57). Nicaea did not make this distinction either.
54 Young, *From Nicaea*, p. 119.
55 See, for the rite of initiation, Chapter 6, p. 171.
56 Young, p. 110.
57 Respectively, the *Oratio Catechetica Magna* and the *Homiliae catecheticae*; *c.* 350

Cyril of Jerusalem had set an example with his twenty-four *Catecheses*, called 'mystagogical', because they were meant to initiate newly baptised members into the mysteries of the faith.

58 Kelly, *Early Creeds*, p. 308.
59 ibid., pp. 329–30: 'Broadly speaking, it was not until the council of Ephesus, in 431, that the pure text of N began to be clearly distinguished from C, although the habit of designating any orthodox formula constructed on Nicene principles as "the Faith of Nicaea" was never eradicated.'
60 ibid.
61 See the *Oxford Dictionary of the Christian Church*, s.v. The Nicene Creed.
62 The same order of importance of what were since called the *Patriarchates* was reiterated at Chalcedon (Canon 28). Rome maintained its refusal.
63 Staats, *Glaubensbekenntnis*, pp. 293–96. He refers to the Faith and Order Paper 140: *Confessing One Faith. Towards an Ecumenical Explication of the Apostolic Faith as Expressed in the Nicene-Constantinopolitan Creed (381)*, Geneva, WCC (1987). See also Dorothea Wendebourg, 'Chalkedon in der ökumenischen Diskussion', *Zeitschrift f. Theologie u. Kirche* 92 (1995): 207–37.
64 Constantine had set the example, deferring his baptism till his deathbed. Prominent civil servants feared that their professional duties could force them to actions that were mortal sins according to Church discipline.
65 During his time in Milan, young Augustine listened to Ambrose's sermons which could satisfy his intellectual search for truth. In 387 Augustine was baptised by Ambrose. Augustine is not discussed in the present book, because his role in the Church and his main literary production date from 397 onwards.
66 G. Haendler, *Von Tertullian bis zu Ambrosius*, p. 104.
67 The selected quotations from Ambrose's correspondence are taken from the translation by Sister Mary Melchior Beyenka, O.P., *Saint Ambrose Letters*, The Catholic University of America, Washington (1967 repr.). The reaction to the emperor's compliance with the request of Symmachus is found in Letter 17, ibid., p. 35.
68 This priest changed his name to Auxentius, which had been the name of Ambrose's Arian precedessor. Under the circumstances it was a programmatic and provocative name!
69 Ambrose referred to Valentinianus' father as being 'a man of ripe old age' and as having been 'baptized though he was unfit for the burden of such a judgment', and said: 'It does not belong to me to judge between bishops'. By these words Ambrose cleverly reminded the actual Emperor that his age was only fifteen and that he had not yet been baptised, and now would take to himself a judgement concerning faith! Ambrose continues: 'But if we examine the context of holy Scripture or of times past, who will deny that in a matter of faith, I say, of faith, bishops usually judge Christian emperors; not emperors, bishops' (*Letter* 21, 53).
70 From the report of the tumultuous events, written afterwards by Ambrose to his sister Marcellina, *Letter* 20, 371 and 367. In an *Address to Auxentius*, 33, he stressed that the Church is faithfully paying taxes on its landed property and would not even resist if the emperor would seize these goods. Against the reproach that he gave money to the poor in order to bribe them for his sake, Ambrose took his stand on the ground that he always remembered the poor since it is written that 'he who is kind to the poor lends to the Lord' (*Prov.* 19, 17).
71 *Address to Auxentius*, p. 36.
72 *Letter* 40, 11.
73 K.M. Setton, *Christian Attitude towards the Emperor in the Fourth Century*, New York (1941), p. 121.
74 This passage reads: 'Son of man, I have made you a watchman for the house of Israel . . . you shall give them warning from me. If I say to the wicked, you shall

surely die, and you give him no warning, nor speak to warn the wicked from his wicked way, in order to save his life, that wicked man shall die in his iniquity; but his blood I will require at your hand' (Ezek. 3:17–18). Ambrose saw himself in a similar position of responsibility for the (eternal) life of Theodosius, because of the cruel iniquity he had done to so many innocent citizens.

75 *Letter* 51, 24–4.
76 Ambrose refers in detail to two moments in King David's life, when he confessed, saying 'I have sinned against the Lord' (2 Sam. 12:13 and 24:10). The sins were the elimination of Uriah in order to take his wife, the beautiful Bathsheba, and the proud numbering of the people. In both cases a prophet was sent to David to make him conscious of his wicked motives. David was forgiven by the Lord, because he was sensitive to these prophetical reprimands.
77 *Letter* 51, 22–4.
78 This does not alter the fact of several anti-Jewish decrees by Theodosius and Valentinianus II: these measures aimed at the prohibition of mixed Christian–Jewish marriages and of Christian slavery in Jewish households.
79 Setton, *Christian Attitude*, p. 118.
80 According to W. Ennslin, 'Staat und Kirche von Konstantin bis Theodosius', in G. Ruhbach, *Die Kirche angesichts der Konstantinischen Wende*, Darmstadt (1976), p. 85.
81 See, for example, K. Aland, 'Kaiser und Kirche von Konstantin bis Byzanz', pp. 72–3.
82 Setton, *Christian attitude*, p. 123. In all this Ambrose was more concerned about the religious dimension than were his contemporaries on the Roman see. Damasus required from the Emperor that the strong hand of the state should assist the Church in bringing into effect the ecclesiastical jurisdiction and measures of organisation. Siricius, his successor, imitated the imperial style of governing when he replaced the usual admonitory manner of speaking by a leadership imposing itself through decrees.
83 ibid., p. 113.
84 Manfred Fuhrmann, 'Die Romidee der Spätantike', in B. Kytzler (ed.), *Rom als Idee*, Darmstadt (1993), pp. 116–17.
85 B. Studer, 'Das Christusbild des Origenes und des Ambrosius', in W.A. Bienert and U. Kühneweg (eds), *Origeniana Septima*, Louvain (1999), pp. 578–9.

6 External and internal repercussions

1 Five hundred kilometres north of Addis Ababa, the actual capital city.
2 See Chapter 4, pp. 88 and 99.
3 See Chapter 4, pp. 99–100.
4 According to others: 224. The New Persian Empire maintained itself until the Arab conquests of the 640s.
5 See Chapter 2, p. 28.
6 Distinguished from West Syrian Christianity, which was concentrated around Antioch and developing inside the Graeco-Roman sphere. A brief survey of Syriac Christianity is given by Wolfgang Hage, *Syriac Christianity in the East*, St. Ephem Ecumenical Research Institute, Kottayam (India) (1988), pp. 1–13. 'Syrian' refers to the area, 'Syriac' to language and religious culture, having spread also outside Syria. On the beginnings of Christianity in Syria, see A.F.J. Klijn, *Edessa de stad van de apostel Thomas*, Baarn (1962).
7 Efrem de Syrier, *Hymnen voor de viering van het kerkelijk jaar*, edited by G. Rouwhorst, Kampen (1991) (Christelijke Bronnen 3).
8 See Chapter 4, pp. 100–1.
9 Mazdeism is the traditional Iranian religion as reformed by Zarathustra (eighth or seventh century BCE). Mazdeism is a strictly dualistic religion, which sees the

world as the theatre of a continuous struggle between the forces of Evil and the Principle of Good.

10 See Chapter 5, pp. 124–6 and 140–2.

11 Only in the course of the fifth century, the East Syrians no longer followed the doctrinal decisions of the Roman imperial church and developed their own Christology. Hage, *Syriac Christianity*, points out that it was their strong need for an own, non-Roman, Christian identity that forced them to break with the imperial church.

12 Constantine's 'conversion' to the Christian religion became manifest in 312 and the eastern part of the empire only noticed this change in 324, after Constantine had eliminated his co-emperor Licinius; see Chapter 2, p. 33. The Armenians hold to 301 as the year of the 'baptism of their people'; so Aram I, *The Armenian Church beyond the 1700th anniversary*, Antelias (Lebanon) 2001, pp. 12–14.

13 See the Introduction to Chapter 5.

14 A report about the death of three martyrs was later sent to their homeland, Cappadocia – a sign of the interest of the local church in its missionary enterprises.

15 G. Haendler, *Die abendländische Kirche im Zeitalter der Völkerwanderung*, Berlin (1983), Kap. 1 (G. Haendler, K. Meier and J. Rogge, *Kirchengeschichte in Einzeldarstellungen* I/5).

16 ibid., p. 31. In his translation of this confession Haendler has also the typical wording that the Son is 'similar to the Father' and the Spirit 'not similar to Christ', which would suggest a clear adoption by Ulphilas of the *homoean* Christology, but Haendler notes that the textual tradition of 'similar' is uncertain. His pneumatology resembles later Pneumatomachianism.

17 At the synods of Seleucia and Rimini, 359; see Chapter 4, pp. 99–100.

18 They were the Ostrogoths, who settled in Italy, and the Vandals, who crossed the Straits of Gibraltar and conquered North Africa. The Visigoths, who were driven on from the Balkan area to southern France and Spain by subsequent waves of invaders, were the last to give up their 'Arianism' for Catholicism (587).

19 In the next centuries Greek would be reduced to the eastern empire of Constantinople/Byzantium, whereas Latin was to become the universal ecclesiastical language in the whole west.

20 Hage, *Syriac Christianity*, p. 7, says it this way: 'The high theological esteem of the Christian Emperor and his Christian Empire implied inevitably the consequence that the Roman Emperor himself, the supreme representative of the Christian Church, was responsible for all the Christians in the world and was the protector of even those living outside his Christian Empire, a claim, which Constantine had already explicitly asserted in the face of the Persian King of Kings.'

21 Especially in the Alexandrian context of Clement and Origen – see Chapter 1, pp. 20–1.

22 See, for the contrast between the ideal of a pure and fully convinced minority church and the pedagogical vision of a majority church leading different categories of Christians to their improvement, Chapter 1, pp. 16–18.

23 In English and in French (cloître); Dutch and German have 'klooster', 'Kloster' for what in English is now called 'monastery' and in French 'monastère'. The latter have thus lost the original element of complete solitude.

24 The synoptic Gospels tell how at the beginning of his ministry Christ by the will of God was led into the desert to confront there the Devil and his false promises and seductions (Matt. 4:1–11; Mark 1:12–13; Luke 4:1–13). For the beginnings of the ascetic movement in the desert, see Philip Rousseau, *Ascetics, Authority, and the Church*, Oxford (1978), Part One: The Desert, and the older but still valuable study by Derwas J. Chitty, *The Desert a City*, repr. Oxford (1977).

25 Composed about the year 357, Athanasius *Life of Antony*, was twice translated into Latin before 373.

26 It seems that the Arians claimed Antony as well for their opinion on Christ and on human salvation, in which voluntary and obedient commitment to God was a central element. For the Arians, see Chapter 4, pp. 74–6; for the role of soteriology in Athanasius' Christology, Chapter 4, pp. 91–3. The claims from both camps on Antony are described by R.C. Gregg and D.E. Groh in Chapter 4 of their *Early Arianism: A View of Salvation*, London (1981).

27 In Palestine such colonies were called a *laura*, which means 'lane'.

28 Philip Rousseau, *Pachomius: The Making of a Community in Fourth-Century Egypt*, Berkeley, Calif. and London (1985).

29 *Gerontikon* means 'book of old men'.

30 *The Pilgrimage of Etheria*, trans. by M.L. McClure and C.L. Feltoe, London (1920). See Chapter 6, pp. 161–77. As far as Syria was concerned, Etheria distinguished between 'minor' and 'major' austere ascetics. A famous Syrian saint was Symeon (390–459), who stayed on the top of a ten-metre-high pillar for thirty years, bowing and praying for hours at a stretch, admired by masses of visitors.

31 See above, note 28. A monograph on Palestinian monasticism is John Binns, *Ascetics and Ambassadors of Christ: The Monasteries of Palestine, 314–631*, Oxford (1994).

32 Samuel Rubenson, *The Letters of St. Antony: Origenist Theology, Monastic Tradition and the Making of a Saint*, Lund (1990), p. 186. By the same author: 'Origen in the Egyptian Monastic Tradition of the Fourth Century', in W.A. Bienert and U. Kühneweg, *Origeniana Septima*, Louvain (1999), pp. 319–37. Rubenson states: 'Egyptian monasticism owed a great deal to the Hellenistic philosophical and religious traditions that spread from Alexandria to the towns of Upper Egypt [. . .] The idea that Egyptian monasticism began among destitute and illiterate Coptic peasants who fled oppression, guided by their simple, fanatical Biblicism, owes more to modern presuppositions than to historical research' (ibid. p. 336). See also J. Roldanus, 'Origène, Antoine et Athanase: leur interconnexion dans la *Vie* et dans les *Lettres*', in E. Livingstone (ed.), *Studia Patristica XXVI: Papers presented at the Eleventh International Conference on Patristic Studies held in Oxford 1991*, Leuven (1993), pp. 389–414.

33 Sulpice Sévère, *Vie de Saint Martin*, trans. and edited by J. Fontaine. Sources Chrétiennes 133 et 134.

34 Athan., *VitAnt.* 46 and 68–70. For the contest for Antony, see above at note 26.

35 ibid., 67.

36 Athanasius, *Letter to Dracontius*, 9. On her pilgrimage Etheria met several bishops who had been monks from childhood (*Pilgrimage* 8. 9. 19. 23).

37 Acts 2:44–7 and 4:32–7.

38 From the second century, Christians had begun to collect parts of the bodies of executed martyrs and to venerate these, preferentially on the spot of their martyrdom. A sanctuary, erected for this purpose on Vatican Hill where the apostle Peter suffered a martyr's death, has become the foundation of the actual St Peter's Church. The tomb of a martyr enhanced the status of a local church and, after the recognition of the importance of Christianity for society and state in the fourth century, also contributed to the glory of the whole city. The possession of the relics of a martyr or saint was much coveted. They were supposed to protect the city against the incursions of robbers and enemies; in private possession against misfortune and illness. The original feelings with regard to physical relics of martyrs and saints were prompted by the Pauline idea that mortal human beings can be vessels of transcendent divine power, viz., of the Holy Spirit. Martyrdom

and a holy life were seen as the proofs of the Spirit's indwelling. The veneration of relics can be seen as a Christianisation of a habit that already existed in classical Antiquity. After the Cross of Jesus had been discovered, parts of it were distributed to a number of important communities all over the empire. But during veneration services, clerics had to see that no worshipper, when kissing the Cross, would secretly bite off a splinter! The popularity of relics increased to such extent that at the end of the century Emperor Theodosius found it necessary to issue a law forbidding the transport and commerce of the bodies (or members) of martyrs, and that bishops had to warn against non-authentic relics, which were put on the market in great quantities.

39 See Chapter 4, p. 83. The synod meeting was interrupted in order to go in a body to Jerusalem.

40 There are two English translations of Etheria's travel story: by M.L. McClure and C.L. Feltoe, London, SPCK (1920), in the *Translations of Christian Literature*, Series III: Liturgical texts and by J.Wilkinson (1971). Etheria wrote her report for the sisters of her convent when on her way back home she stayed at Constantinople. The exact date of her journey is not known: some date it before 394, others after 400. For our goal this may not be very important, since one can presume that the liturgical customs, even when she has learnt them after 400, were already in existence in the nineties of the fourth century. Etheria was away from her convent for three years and for that reason may not have been an abbess but just an ordinary nun. Apart from that she cannot have been 'ordinary' of social rank, because she met with help and respect everywhere, not only from the clergy but also from government officials, so that she could visit whatever she liked. It is even supposed that, since she was a native of northern Spain, she may have been a relative of the Emperor Theodosius. The first and last chapters of the travel story are lost: the actual report begins with Etheria's climbing of Mount Sinai and ends somewhere in the description of the feast of the Dedication of the Church of the Holy Sepulchre (14 September).

41 *Pilgrimage*, VII, 5, p. 94.

42 The French edition, published as Vol. XXI of the series *Sources Chrétiennes* under the title: *Éthérie, Journal de Voyage*, Paris 1948.

43 ibid., pp. 64–5.

44 This was the reason why Christians were shocked by the plans of the non-Christian Emperor Julian to rebuild the Jewish Temple of Jerusalem. If it had come to a realisation this would have questioned the whole conception of progress in God's plans with the world, viz., to bring all humans to the acceptance of Christ and of his teachings (see Chapter 4, p. 104). When by Julian's order the relics of a Christian saint had been removed from Antioch and lightning had struck the local temple of Apollo, Christians saw it as an intervention from Heaven. After Julian's death they built a new *martyrion* for the relics of that saint, leaving the temple of Apollo to lie in ruins: evidence of the veracity of the Christian faith!

45 According to Etheria's description, Whitsunday was the most fatiguing day for the Jerusalem community, because the faithful started their services in the Major Church, then moved to the site of the Upper Room (Pentecost); in the afternoon they gathered first on the top of the Mount of Olives (Ascension), went down to the Cave of Instruction on the slope of the Mount, then came back to the city in a long procession with stations at each of the three buildings of the Church of the Holy Sepulchre, to finish the liturgy at midnight at the Upper Room again. She wrote: 'Thus very great fatigue is endured on that day, for vigil [i.e., the service at daybreak] is kept at the Anastasis from the first cockcrow, and there is no pause from that time onward throughout the whole day, but the whole celebration lasts so long that it is midnight when every one returns home after the dismissal has

taken place at Sion [i.e., the name of the church of the Upper Room' (*Pilgrimage*, VI, 1(d), p. 89).

46 *Pilgrimage*, III, p. 52–6.

47 Origen criticised the commemoration of birthdays as a pagan habit. It was 'Christian' to celebrate a person's passing into the state of complete adoption as children of God.

48 Only the last association with 'Epiphany' has maintained itself in western Christianity. O. Cullmann gives much information about Christmas in the early Church (*Weihnachten in der alten Kirche*, Basel [1947]).

49 *Pilgrimage*, III, 2, pp. 53–4.

50 ibid., p. 55.

51 Athanasius stated that being the Son, Christ, eternally possessed the Spirit, but that at his baptism in the Jordan the Spirit was imparted to the human nature – of Christ and, through him, of all men (*OrCAr.* I, 46–7).

52 'In a way', because the existence of other gods was not denied, as strict monotheism does. The idea of one supreme god is, more properly, called 'henotheism': 'one' god is worthy of being worshipped, without being proclaimed as the 'only' god.

53 Or just 'the first day of the week' – see 1 Cor. 16: 2.

54 Cullmann calls this law 'one of Constantine's most sweeping measures' (*Weihnachten*, p. 23). The Sunday as day of rest and church attendance has indeed become a global institution.

55 The lighting of candles at Christmas is a far consequence of this Christianised pagan habit.

56 The syllable '-mas' in Christmas comes from the Latin *missa*, which originally meant (the moment of) dismissal of the faithful when the service was completed. We find it for the first time in Ambrose as indication of the service as a whole.

57 Under Bishop Gregory of Nazianzum, whose irenical and ecumenical mind we have met in the period around the synod of 381 (Chapter 5, p. 121 and Chapter 2, p. 131).

58 The Armenian Church has never accepted the shift from 6 January to 25 December and has still the former as its day for Christmas.

59 Matt. 4:2. In most regions, where Saturday was also a day of fasting, six weeks and four days sufficed. In Jerusalem one needed eight by five days; the Saturday between Good Friday and Easter brought the total up to forty-one (*Pilgrimage*, IV, p. 57).

60 Of course monks and nuns did more than ordinary people. However, 'no one exacts from any how much he should do, but each does what he can, nor is he praised who has done much, nor is he blamed who has done less; that is the custom here' (*Pilgrimage*, IV, 5, p. 62).

61 ibid., VII, 2, p. 91.

62 ibid., p. 90. It is not clear whether Etheria means by 'man' only 'males', or both sexes. The 'more serious vices' may refer to sexual misbehaviour, which the nun Etheria was too prudish to name.

63 In Greek: *photizomenoi* and in Latin: 'those competing', viz., for baptism.

64 ibid., p. 92.

65 F.L. Cross, *St Cyril of Jerusalem's Lectures on the Christian Sacraments*, London, SPCK (1951). The Catechetical lectures are the only literary remains of this Cyril and were probably given *c.* 350. Cyril adhered to the *homoeusian* persuasion and was twice dismissed from his see by the political leader of the Anhomeans (358 and 360). Later he turned to the Cappadocians and was chased another time by pro-Arian Emperor Valens (see Chapter 4, p. 102 and Chapter 5, p. 117).

66 She mentions that the doors are literally shut before the catechumens 'lest any of them should draw near' (*Pilgrimage*, VII, 5, p. 94).

67 *St. Cyril of Jerusalem's Lectures*, Procatechesis 1. 4. 12.
68 The local creed of Jerusalem became the principal model of NC. See Chapter 5, pp. 124–5, n. 28.
69 *Cat.* VI, 28. Cyril is referring here to Matt. 13:11: 'To you it has been given to know the secrets of the kingdom of heaven, but to them (the listening crowds) it has not been given.' At the time of Etheria's visit to Jerusalem, the bishop used to say: 'During these seven weeks you have been taught all the law of the Scriptures, you have also heard concerning the Faith, and concerning the resurrection of the flesh, and the whole meaning of the Creed, as far as you were able, being yet catechumens. But the teachings of the deeper mystery, that is, of baptism itself, you cannot hear, being as yet catechumens. But, lest you should think that anything is done without good reason, these, when you have been baptised in the Name of God, you shall hear in the Anastasis, during the eight Paschal days, after the dismissal from the church has been made. You, being as yet catechumens, cannot be told the more secret mysteries of God.' (*Pilgrimage*, VII, 4, p. 93).
70 *Mystagogical Catechesis* I, 8.
71 ibid., 2, 2–4.
72 ibid., 3, 1. 5.
73 See above, Chapter 5, p. 134.
74 *Hom. Cat.* xvi, quoted in Young, *From Nicaea*, p. 212.
75 Quoted in Young, *From Nicaea*, p. 212.
76 See above, Chapter 2, p. 40.
77 See Chapter 2, p. 38.
78 It should be noted that the monks in Africa lived rather comfortably on fertile grounds and did not show the same radicalism as the hermits of Egypt and Syria. See W.H.C. Frend, *The Donatist Church*, Oxford (1952), p. 320.
79 The Roman state used to remunerate veterans of the army, for instance, with landed property in North Africa.
80 Frend, *Donatist Church*, pp. 50, 56, 59.
81 H.-R. Weber, 'L'Eglise en danger de mort. Quelques enseignements tirés de l'histoire de l'Eglise en Afrique du Nord', *Flambeau* 29, Yaoundé CLE, 1971, pp. 33–40. In this lecture for missionary workers Weber presented the Donatist counter-church as a 'sign on the wall', showing up how a privileged church may fail to pass frontiers.
82 Frend, *Donatist Church*, pp. 324–5.
83 See Chapter 4, p. 105. Julian expected that through his measures, the Christian parties would ruin each other.
84 Frend, p. 191.
85 ibid., p. 316. The parallel was taken from Acts 1:15–26.
86 See above, Chapter 1, pp. 17–18.
87 Frend, p. 317.
88 We have already met the city of Treves as the residence of western emperors, for instance, Constantine in his early period when he was still a member of the tetrarchy (see Chapter 2, p. 35). Maximus was army commander in Britain and proclaimed emperor against Gratianus in 383. When he tried to lay hands also on Italy (where the minor Valentinianus II was officially in power – see the Introduction to Chapter 5), Theodosius intervened and defeated Maximus, bringing Italy under his own power (388).

Epilogue

1 K. Aland, 'Der Abbau des Herrscherkultes im Zeitalter Konstantins', K. Aland, *Kirchengeschichtliche Entwürfe*, Gütersloh (1960), p. 242.
2 Hanson, pp. 142–56.

Selected bibliography

Adam, Alfred, Lehrbuch der Dogmengeschichte 1 Die Zeit der Alten Kirche. Gütersloh (1965).

Bainton, Roland H., 'The Early Church and the War', *Harvard Theol. Review* 39 (1946): 189–212.

Barnes, Timothy D., *Constantine and Eusebius.* Cambridge, Mass. and London (1981).

—— *Athanasius and Constantius: Theology and Politics in the Constantinian Empire.* Cambridge, Mass. and London (1993).

Berkhof, Hendrik, *Kirche und Kaiser: Eine Untersuchung der Entstehung der byzantinischen und theokratischen Staatsauffassung im vierten Jahrhundert.* Zurich (1947).

Binns, John, *Ascetics and Ambassadors of Christ: The Monasteries of Palestine 314–631.* Oxford (1994).

Brakke, David, *Athanasius and the Politics of Asceticism.* Oxford (1995).

Borchardt, Carl F.A., *Hilary of Poitiers' role in the Arian Struggle.* 's-Gravenhage (1966).

Bremmer, Jan N., 'The Vision of Constantine', in A.P.M.H. Lardinois, M.G.M. van der Poel (eds), *Land of Dreams: Greek and Latin Studies in Honour of A.H.M. Kessels.* Brill (2006), pp. 57–79.

Brox, Norbert, 'Zur christlichen Mission in der Spätantike', in Karl Kertelge (ed.), *Mission im Neuen Testament* (Quaestiones Disputatae 93). Freiburg i. Br. (1982), pp. 190–237.

Campenhausen, H. von, *The Fathers of the Greek Church.* (1963).

Chadwick, Henry, *Early Christian Thought and the Classical Tradition.* Oxford (1966).

—— *The Early Church.* Rev. edn, Harmondsworth (1993).

Chitty, Derwas J., *The Desert a City.* Oxford (1966).

Cochrane, Charles N., *Christianity and Classical Culture: A Study of Thought and Action from Augustus to Augustine.* London and New York (1944).

Coe, Shoki, 'Contextualizing Theology', in Anderson-Stransky (ed.), *Third World Theologies.* New York-Grand Rapids (1976), pp. 19–24.

Coleman-Norton, P.R., *Roman State and Christian Church: A Collection of Legal Documents to A.D. 535*, 3 vols. London (1966).

Daniélou J., and Marrou, H.I., *The Christian Centuries*, Vol. I, *The First Six Hundred Years.* (1964).

Davies, J.G., *The Early Church.* London (1965).

Diesner, H.-J., *Kirche und Staat im spätrömischen reich.* Berlin (1964).

Dinsen, F., *Homoousios: Die Geschichte des Begriffs bis zum Konzil von Konstantinopel (381).* Kiel (1976).

Dunn, Marilyn, *The Emergence of Monasticism*. Oxford (2000).

Ehrman, Bart D. and Jacobs, Andrew S., *Christianity in Late Antiquity 300–450 C.E. A Reader*. New York and Oxford (2004).

Fox, Robin Lane, *Pagans and Christians*. Harmondsworth (1986).

Frend, W.H.C., *The Rise of Christianity*. London (1984).

—— *The Donatist Church*. Oxford (1952).

Gregg, Robert C. and Groh, Dennis E., *Early Arianism: A View of Salvation*. London (1981).

Grillmeier, Alois, *Christ in Christian Tradition*. Vol. I, *From the Apostolic Age to Chalcedon (451)*. London (1975).

Haendler, Gert, *Von Tertullian bis zu Ambrosius. Die Kirche im Abendland vom Ende des 2. bis zum Ende des 4. Jahrhunderts*. Berlin (1986).

—— *Die abendländische Kirche im Zeitalter der Völkerwanderung*. Berlin (1983).

Hanson, R.P.C., *The Search for the Christian Doctrine of God: The Arian Controversy 318–381*. Edinburgh (1988).

Hesselgrave D.J., and Rommen, E., *Contextualization: meanings, methods and models*. Grand Rapids, Mich. (1989).

Jaeger, Werner, *Early Christianity and Greek Paideia*. Cambridge, Mass. (1961).

—— *Gregor von Nyssas Lehre vom Hl. Geist*. Leiden (1966).

Kannengiesser, Charles (ed.), *Politique et Théologie chez Athanase d'Alexandrie. Actes du Colloque de Chantilly 23–25 septembre 1973*. Paris (1974) (Théologie Historique 27).

Kelly, J.N.D., *Early Christian Creeds*, 3rd edn, New York (1985).

—— *Early Christian Doctrines*. London (1958).

Klein, R., *Constantius II und die christliche Kirche*. Darmstadt (1977).

Kraft, Heinz, *Kaiser Konstantins Religiöse Entwicklung*. Tübingen (1955).

Lehmann K. and Pannenberg W. (eds), *Glaubensbekenntnis und Kirchengemeinschaft. Das Modell des Konzils von Konstantinopel (381)*. Freiburg-Göttingen (1982).

Livingstone, Elizabeth A. (ed.), *Studia Patristica* vols. XI (Berlin [1972]), XXVI, XXXII (Leuven [1993 1997]) (several relevant contributions).

Lyman, J. Rebecca, *Christology and Cosmology: Models of Divine Activity in Origen, Eusebius, and Athanasius*. Oxford (1993).

Meijering, E.P., *Orthodoxy and Platonism in Athanasius: Synthesis or Antithesis?* 2nd edn, Leiden (1974).

Nordberg, H., *Athanasius and the Emperor*. Helsinki (1963).

Ortiz de Urbina, Ignazio, *Nizäa und Konstantinopel*. Mainz (1964).

Prestige, G.L., *God in Patristic Thought*. London (1952).

Quasten, J., *Patrology* vol. III. Utrecht-Antwerp (1963).

A.M. Ritter, *Das Konzil von Konstantinopel und sein Symbol*. Göttingen (1965).

—— 'Dogma und Lehre in der Alten Kirche – Kap. I–III', in Carl Andresen (ed.), *Handbuch der Dogmen und Theologiegeschichte Bd 1 Die Lehrentwicklung im Rahmen der Katholizität*, Zweiter Teil. Göttingen (1982), pp. 99–221.

—— *Kirche und Staat im Denken des frühern Christentums: Texte und Kommentare zum Thema Religion und Politik in der Antike*. Berne (2005).

Roldanus, J., *Le Christ et l'homme dans la théologie d'Athanase d'Alexandrie: Étude de la conjonction de sa conception de l'homme avec sa christologie*. 2nd edn. Leiden (1977).

—— 'Die Vita Antonii als Spiegel der theologie des Athanasius', *Theologie und Philosophie* 58 (1983): 194–216.

—— 'Origène, Antoine et Athanase leur interconnexion dans la *Vie* et les *Lettres*', in

Elizabeth A. Livingstone (ed.), *Studia Patristica*, vol. XXVI. Leuven (1993), pp. 389–414.

Rousseau, Philip, *Pachomius: The Making of a Community in Fourth-Century Egypt*. Berkeley, Calif. and London (1985).

Rubenson, Samuel, *The Letters of St. Antony. Origenist Theology, Monastic Tradition and the Making of a Saint*. Lund (1990).

Ruhbach, Gerhard, (ed.), *Die Kirche angesichts der Konstantinschen Wende*. Darmstadt (1976).

Setton, Kenneth Meyer, *Christian Attitude towards the Emperor in the Fourth Century*. New York (1941).

Sieben, H.J., *Die Konzilsidee der Alten Kirche*. Paderborn (1979).

Staats, Reinhart, *Das Glaubensbekenntnis von Nizäa-Konstantinopel. Historische und theologische Grundlagen*. Darmstadt (1996).

Stead, C.S., *Divine Substance*. Oxford (1977).

—— *Doctrine and Philosophy in Early Christianity: Arius: Athanasius, Augustine*. Aldershot and Burlington, Vermont, USA (2000).

Thümmel, Hans Georg, *Die Kirche des Ostens im 3. und 4. Jahrhundert*. Berlin (1988).

Vischer, L., *Basilius der Große*. Basel (1953).

Williams Rowan, (ed.), *The Making of Orthodoxy: Essays in Honour of Henry Chadwick*. Cambridge (1989).

Young, Francis, *From Nicaea to Chalcedon: A Guide to the Literature and its Background*. London (1983).

Index of notions, persons and places

Index of patristic references

Related titles from Routledge

Early Christianity
Mark Humphries

Examining sources and case studies, this accessible book explores early Christianity, how it was studied, how it is studied now, and how Judaeo-Christian values came to form the ideological bedrock of modern western culture.

Looking at the diverse source materials available, from the earliest New Testament texts and the complex treaties of third century authors such as Lactantius, to archaeology, epigraphy and papyrology, the book examines what is needed to study the subject, what materials are available, how useful they are, and how the study of the subject may be approached.
Case study chapters focus on important problems in the study of early Christianity including:

- the book of Acts as a text revelatory of the social dynamics of cities and as a text about the inherent tensions in Hellenistic Judaism

- Orthodoxy and Organization in early Christianity

- Early Christianity and the Roman Empire.

Also including a comprehensive guide for students that lists major collections of literary and non-iterary sources, major journals and series, and major text books, it is an excellent aid to the study of Christianity in history.

Hb: 0–415–20538–7
Pb: 0–41520539–5

Available at all good bookshops
For ordering and further information please visit:
www.routledge.com

Related titles from Routledge

Women and religion in the First Christian Centuries

Deborah F. Sawyer

Women and Religion in the First Christian Centuries focuses on religion during the period of Roman imperial rule and its significance in women's lives. It discusses the rich variety of religious expression, from pagan cults and classical mythology to ancient Judaism and early Christianity, and the wide array of religious functions fulfilled by women. The author analyses key examples from each context, creating a vivid image of this crucial period which laid the foundations of western civilization.

ISBN10: 0–415–10748–2 (hbk)
ISBN10: 0–415–10749–0 (pbk)

ISBN13: 978–0–415–10748–8 (hbk)
ISBN13: 978–0–415–10749–5 (pbk)

Available at all good bookshops
For ordering and further information please visit:
www.routledge.com

Related titles from Routledge

Evagrius Ponticus
A. M. Cassiday

Evagrius Ponticus (c. 345–99) was a seminal figure for Eastern monasticism and had a strong influence on Western monasticism as well. He left more writings than any other father from the Egyptian desert. However, many of his writings were lost after he was condemned as an Origenist in the sixth century. During the 20th century, numerous works were recovered (especially in ancient oriental translations from the original Greek) but very few of these works are available in English translation; many of them are not readily available at all.

This collection presents complete works drawn from the full range of his writings, many of which have not previously appeared in English, offering translations of some of Evagrius' letters, his notes on various books of the Bible, his treatises and his 'chapters' (a genre popularised by Evagrius that consists of condensed, interconnected sentences). All of the works included here are translated in full.

The translations aim to present the material accurately and accessibly. The volume is prefaced by a substantial introductory essay that presents Evagrius, his works and influence, and modern scholarship about him in a way that is of great use to students and also comprehensible to beginners.

Hb: 0–415–32446–7
Pb: 0–415–32447–5

Related titles from Routledge

Gregory of Nazianzus
Brian Daley

Gregory of Nazianzus, a complex and colourful figure in a crucial age (4th century AD), when it was permissible for the first time to be a public Christian intellectual, was well placed to become one of the outstanding defenders and formulators of Church doctrine.

A gifted and skilled rhetorician, poet, and orator, as well as a profound theologian, Gregory was ordained a bishop and served, for almost two years, as head of the orthodox Christian community in Constantinople, where he played a crucial role in formulating the classical doctrines of the Trinity and the person of Christ. Under fire from opponents in the Church, the enigmatic Gregory eventually retreated into a quiet life of study and simple asceticism in his native Cappadocia, concentrating there on bringing the broad canon of his own writings to their present form. The body of his works, including poetry, letters, sermons and lectures on religious themes, and written with the precision and elegance of classical Greek literature, was recognized in the Byzantine age as equal in quality to the achievements of the greatest Greek writers.

A collection of new translations of a selection of these works, with an extensive introduction to Gregory's life, thought, and writings, *Gregory of Nazianzus* presents to us a vivid portrait of a fascinating character, who deserves to be regarded as one of the Christian tradition's outstanding theologians, and as the first true Christian humanist.

Hb: 0–415–12180–9
Pb: 0–415–12181–7

Available at all good bookshops
For ordering and further information please visit:
www.routledge.com

Related titles from Routledge

Gregory the Great

John Moorhead

Gregory's life culminated in his holding the office of pope (590–604). He is generally regarded as one of the outstanding figures in the long line of popes, and by the late ninth century had come to be known as 'the Great'. Along with Ambrose, Jerome and Augustine, he played a critical role in the history of his time, while during the middle ages his intellectual influence was second only to that of Augustine.

This volume provides a biographical and intellectual context to Gregory the Great, and new translations of his most influential writings.

Hb: 0–415–23389–5
Pb: 0–415–23390–9

Available at all good bookshops
For ordering and further information please visit:

www.routledge.com